Teaching Human Beings
The Role of Language in Education

Clark McKowen

June 24, 2006
My best to my highschool friend and to Colleen.
Regards,
Clark

LAUREL MOUNTAIN PRESS
LIGONIER · PENNSYLVANIA

Copyright © 1999 by Clark McKowen

All rights reserved. No part of this book may be used or reproduced in any form whatsoever without written permission. For information, write Clark McKowen, 729 Laurel Drive, Ligonier, Pennsylvania 15658; (412) 238-4747; fax (412) 238-4410; e-mail: cmckowen@

(724) 238-4747 Fax: 238-4410
e-mail: cmckowen@charterpa.net
http://www.charterpa.net/cmckowen

Library of Congress Catalog Card Number: 98-91640

ISBN: 0-9665272-0-8

Printed in the United States of America

Credits

Page 57, by Adélia Prado, from *The Alphabet in the Park: Selected Poems of Adélia Prado*, translated by Ellen Watson © 1990 by Adélia Prado, Wesleyan University Press, by permission of University Press of New England.

Page 85, by Robert Frost, from *The Poetry of Robert Frost*, edited by Edward Connery Lathem © 1956 by Robert Frost, copyright 1928, © 1969 by Henry Holt and Company, Inc., © 1997 by Edward Connery Lathem. Reprinted by permission of Henry Holt and Company, Inc.

Page 111, by Juan Ramón Jiminéz, Madrid-España, 1973.

Page 113, by permission of Jelaluddin Rumi, originally published in *Open Secret* by Threshold Books, 139 Main Street, Brattleboro, Vermont, 05301.

Page 117, by T. S. Eliot, from *Collected Poems 1909–1962*, by T. S. Eliot, copyright 1963 by Harcourt Brace & Company, copyright © 1964, 1963 by T. S. Eliot, reprinted by permission of the publisher.

Page 147, by Archibald MacLeish, from *Collected Poems 1917–1982*. Copyright © 1985 by The Estate of Archibald MacLeish. Reprinted by permission of Houghton Mifflin Company. All rights reserved.

Page 151, by Maggie Anderson, from *Cold Comfort* © 1986. Reprinted by permission of the University of Pittsburgh Press.

Page 201, by Tomas Tranströmer, from "Guard Duty," translated by Robert Bly, from *Selected Poems 1954–1986*, by Tomas Tranströmer, edited by Robert Hass. Translation copyright © 1975 by Robert Bly. Reprinted by permission of The Ecco Press.

Page 215, by Robert Frost, from *The Poetry of Robert Frost*, edited by Edward Connery Lathem, © 1962 by Robert Frost, © 1969 by Henry Holt and Company, Inc., © 1988 by Alfred Edwards, © 1997 by Edward Connery Lathem. Reprinted by permission of Henry Holt and Company, Inc.

Page 278, Linda Pastan, from *Waiting for My Life*. Copyright © 1981 by Linda Pastan. Reprinted by permission of W. W. Norton & Company, Inc.

Page 283, by William Carlos Williams, from *Collected Poems: 1909–1939*, Volume I. Copyright © 1938 by New Directions Publishing Corp. Reprinted by permission of New Directions Publishing Corp.

Cover Photograph: *Parting of the Soul*, 1990. Robert Lauro. Painted iron and glass. Used by permission of the artist and Eleonore Austerer Gallery, San Francisco.

Contents

Foreword *vii*

Preface: It Ain't in No Book *ix*

1 Why Teach?
Vocatus *1*
Do You Know the Way? *10* • A Few Words from Charlie *11*
Bliss: Teaching as Art *13*

2 Why Learn?
A Piece of the Action *15*
A Profile of the Learner *21* • *Things We Forgot to Tell You* *22*

3 Superficial and Supralogical Thinking
Making the Sun Come Up *27*
Language and Creativity *28* • *Creation, Creatures, and Creativity* *29*
Coming To *32* • Reveille *35* • Let's Be Practical Here *36*
Poiēma: The Poem of Creation *37* • Doing Research *38*

4 English: What She Is and What She Ain't
A Big Bite of the Apple *39*
Minding Our Own Business *41* • Chasing Our Own Tails *43*
English for Everyone *44* • Readings on Education *52*

5 Why Teach the Native Tongue?
Mirror and Window *57*
A Spirit Quest *59* • In the Human Realm *61* • Just About Anything *61*
The Subject of Every Discipline *62* • Back to Basics *63* • The Feel of Language *64*
Language and Learning *64* • The How of It *66* • Getting Down to Business *66*
Language as Metaphor *68* • *Metaphor: Both Nose and Heart* *70*

iii

6 The Process
Safe Cracking 75
Teachers Should Be Unprepared 76 • Wise Sayings *83* • The Sound of Music *85*

7 A Hummy Sort of Day
The Music of the Spheres 89
Music for a Quiet Mind *90* • Alpha Rhythms and All That *92* • Harry Belafonte, Guy Clark, Louis Armstrong, Joni Mitchell, et Alia *94* • That Voice *96* The Sound Envelope *97* • Natural Music *98*

8 The Structure
Keeping the Party Going 99
Getting Started *99* • The Second Day *102* • Day Three, ad Infinitum *104* Units of Study *105* • *A Generative Unit* 106

9 The Manner
Rhythm and Blues 111
Lecturing Is Not Teaching 112 • The Name Game: Who Are *You? 113* Karl's Christmas Party *116* • Test Day *120* • Paying Attention: Surface Features *121* • The Brain *126*

10 Teaching Reading
Turning Prose into Poetry 129
Reading Programs *130* • Throw Out Reading Programs? *134* Reading and Therapy *135* • Teaching Literature *137* Little More Than Seasoning *138* • Getting What's There *139* The Best American Short Stories of 19___ *142* • The Safe and Settled *143* Why Teach Reading? *145*

11 Mandalas: Who *Are* You?
Thumbprints and Weather Reports 149
A Few Words from the Students *154* • The Art Gallery *155* • Verbal Mandalas *157* Student Writing *158* • Implications *159*

12 Teaching Writing
Spirit in Matter 161
That Impulse to Correct *163* • Editing *167* • What Makes Students Want to Write *170* • Honing: Correctness and Precision *173*

13 Reflective Writing
Living Is So Dear 177
Reflective Writing in Freshman English 178 • Responses to Reflections 183
A Reflection Sampler 184 • Syntheses: Pulling the Course Together 194
The Research Paper 195 • The Last Word on Teaching Writing 196
How to Write Swell 196 • Mentors, Books, and Workshops 197

14 Mutual Aid
The Gene Pool 199
A Mutual-Aid Investigation 200 • Competition 202 • A Leap of Faith 202

15 Fear as a Motivator
And No Birds Sing 205

16 Judging People
Turning Poetry into Prose 211
Expert Judgment 213 • Teaching Without Testing 216 • The Myth of Objective Testing 218 • Unobtrusive Measures 221 • The Heisenberg Effect 222

17 Minimalist Teaching
Trying Without Trying 225
Assigning Grades 230

18 Getting Help
Relinquishing Control 233
The One-Room-Schoolhouse Concept 236 • Teacher's Pets 237
Selecting Teaching Assistants 239 • Foreign Students as Teaching Assistants 239
Reading Daily Reflections 240 • Simplify, Simplify 242

19 Teaching Grammar
The Net of Enchantment 243
Literacy 246 • Appalachia and Times Square: Anyone's English as a Second Language 248 • School English 249 • The Structure of English 251
Why Not Take All of Them? 253

20 Eccentric
Islands and Causeways 255
My Hearing Handicap 257

21 Large, Compressed, and Combined Classes
Laboratory Schools 261
Class Size 261 • Compressed Classes 265 • Combined Classes 267
Laboratory Schools 269

22 *Objets Trouvés*
The Poetic Mode 271
Words and Things 272 • There's No Hurry 274 • I Came To 275
From Prosaic to Poetic 276 • Reflections 277

23 Teaching Poetry
The Sound of Water 279
Poetry as a Subject 282 • Ulteriority 285 • The Poem Itself 285
Is This a Poem? 286 • Foreground or Background 288 • Messing Around 289

24 The Idea of a College
Out Looking for Trouble 291
The Idea of a College 291

25 Earth Probe
Synthesis 295

Afterword: Teaching Human Beings
Serve Tea; Read the Leaves 305
A New Plan for Teaching Reading—Or What Have You 308 • Be a Mirror 309
Be a Window 310 • Learning Theory 310 • Doing Nothing 312
Koans for New and Renewing Teachers 313 • It Ain't in No Book 314

Suggested Reading 315
Index 317

Foreword

Having just finished reading *Teaching Human Beings*, I would have to say its ending with the words "It ain't in no book" is a lot less valid than when those words appear at the beginning, for "it"—or at least the part that can be expressed in words—*is* in *this* book. True, the art isn't ever going to be fully expressed in talk about it, but this book comes closer than any I have ever seen to encouraging the kind of teaching that actually demonstrates the art, particularly when it comes to expressing how the language of any subject can be investigated. The multiplicity of practical examples provides an exceptionally vivid picture of the process and makes its underpinning quite understandable.

If the engagement of spirit in matter is what genuine education is about, the focus on investigation and discovery through hands-on experiences and the exploration of ideas is right on target. And by encouraging teachers to step down from the authority platform, McKowen frees them to direct their respectful attention toward each individual student—and thus to create the truly student-centered classroom so often advocated, but so seldom accomplished. With emphasis on group work instead of lectures, the teacher as co-inquirer is less tempted to impatient interjections that rob students of that pleasure of recognition or discovery that is the only thing that can keep them interested and enthusiastic learners. One can get good evidence of the resulting excitement in one of the text's most valuable sections, the reflection sampler. Further, the teacher comments show how to communicate appreciative response, without feeding or flattering egos.

Classes in education characteristically advocate the need for a philosophy of curriculum, but McKowen gives example after example of how an organic philosophy is actually practiced. Furthermore, his own conversational, even slangy, descriptions are calculated to have far greater appeal to students than the deadening dullness of most—sadly, but ironically—education textbooks.

Having received my own bachelor's in education, I speak from experience! Not a single useful idea from any of my texts has stayed with me through the years—albeit the years are so many that it may not be entirely the texts' fault that they now seem so eminently forgettable. On the other hand, many of the ideas expounded here have stayed with me almost thirty years since my first contact with them through McKowen.

If enough readers are persuaded to give the process a try, perhaps the picture of education envisioned forty years into the future may not seem so unrecognizable nor unattainable after all. Wouldn't that be wonderful!?

Sister Vincent Walz, D.C., Ph.D.
University of Texas at El Paso

Preface

It Ain't in No Book

*Conventional wisdom
tells us the earth is round.*

It's the 1970s and I'm in the middle of an investigation on how the mind cannot observe two things side by side and not connect them—somehow. We didn't have *I Ching* handy, so I had suggested using our textbook. We would come up with an idea we wanted to explore, then randomly select a page and see what happened. I had said it would tell us exactly what we wanted to know. We were casting about for some way to select the page. A pair of dice would have done, but we hadn't any.

Meanwhile, Brian Walker is messing around in the back of the room, doing God knows what, but certainly out of it. This drives me nuts. I can't stand even one kid not totally involved. He doesn't *have* to be here. After all, it *is* a college. I keep on with the class, and Brian keeps on screwing around. *Inconsiderate creep! I thought he liked this class.* Brian does not look like a scholar. He's wearing a sweatband around his stringy, greasy hair, and his clothes are rumpled and a bit soiled. But I know he's one of the best students in the class, and I know he's seriously planning to be a doctor. This isn't a fantasy. He really could do it. Till now I had thought we were getting along pretty well. Maybe he thinks what we're doing is stupid. I hate that.

I'm beginning to boil and thinking up other choice names for him. He could at least give it a chance. I'm debating throwing him out of the room, yelling at him—something. But I go on with the class and briefly forget about Brian, when I see him making his way to the front of the room. He hands me a pair of dice he has whittled out of a piece of chalk.

Fast forward to 1992 or thereabouts. I have a hotshot teacher visiting my class, and things are messy as usual. I tell her to sit in on groups, talk with anyone she feels like, make herself at home. Ahmad Azizi is sitting in the back, not getting into the groups, just hanging. I notice this out of the corner of my eye. It doesn't bother me.

Afterward, in my office, the hotshot teacher critiques my class. Among several violations of teaching principles she has ferreted out, there is the matter of Ahmad: Yes; I had noticed him.

"How would you have handled that?" I ask.

"He should have been brought back into the class. You should have gotten him into a group or asked him why he wasn't participating. You should have helped him get involved."

"Yeah. But then, he might have been whittling some dice."

From 1957 on I continue to learn things about teaching that fly in the face of conventional wisdom. It ain't in no book. And that is the reason for this one. The Brian/Ahmad story is a lesson in butting out, in leaving creative people alone. But there are hundreds and hundreds of incidents like that. Together they form a pattern and reflect a philosophy. How should we teach? What is the best atmosphere for learning? What about discipline? What about class size, length? What about content? What is it all about in the first place? And what about all those human beings who pass through our classes? What do we want for them, each one so unique on the planet? The answers brought me to a place I never anticipated. The better the classes the less they looked like classes. What would people think? I chose the disreputable path—or rather, it chose me. It is a long way from the quiet groves of academe, but what a journey, what jewels along the way. Chalk drawings, talismans, a pair of dice. And wondrous creatures at every turn.

Clark McKowen

1

Why Teach?
Vocatus

What's for breakfast?
—Pooh

My friend and fellow English teacher at Diablo Valley College, Karl Staubach, used to say there is no word in Spanish that translates out as "teaching." There's *enseñar*, but that means "demonstrate" or "show." The person in charge may have the title of professor, or the students might address him or her as *maestro*, a person who is pretty good at whatever is being demonstrated. What the Spanish students do is *aprender*, "apprehend." The one demonstrates; the other apprehends. As Gary Zukov points out in *The Dancing Wu Li Masters*, English definitions of *master* include the element of control, but when he asked T'ai Chi Master Al Huang about the word, he said, "That is the word other people use to describe me." He did not think of himself in such terms; Al Huang was simply Al Huang. When pressed to explain further, he said, "A master is someone who started before you did." Bob Norton, another DVC English teacher, used to drive the faculty nuts with questions like, "What makes you think you're teaching?" Or he would say, "I haven't taught a thing all semester." Imagine the administration explaining *that* to the taxpayers. When colleagues talked about teaching methods, course content, testing, and so on, Bob would chuckle.

I remember standing before my first group of students—tie, jacket, and polished shoes—and wondering who I thought I was. How did walking through that door transform me into "teacher"? What did I think I was doing? I had never been asked these questions in college or graduate school.

It was assumed, by all of us I think, that teachers provided information not readily available and were good at explaining things. Without thinking much about it, I shared that view. I would teach what I had been taught. Someone out there knew what that should be, and it was in the textbooks. A good teacher imposed discipline, was well organized, stuck to the lesson plan, kept the room properly ventilated, didn't stand on the desk, erased the chalkboard for the next teacher, kept records of attendance, meticulously corrected assignments, and so on. In fact, textbooks for teachers that discussed these and myriad other elements making up the teacher's job were available. That's what teachers did. That was how a teacher was identified. Is it surprising, then, that few school people ever wondered what the point of it all was and why bother in the first place? Everyone was so distracted by the details that fundamental questions rarely surfaced. I had never heard anyone say, "You can't teach anyone anything." I would have found it ridiculous.

By the end of the first day, I knew I would never be comfortable as a repository of special information. I wasn't a library. Even in 1957 it was easy to see, given the fantastic amount of information available, no one knows much. Even within one's own field, however narrow, one's store of information is severely limited. Then, of course, someone is out there this very minute tinkering with the facts so that you can never be sure if a martini before dinner is good for you or bad. Besides, from my shelves of books and stacks of lecture notes, which information should I transfer to my students' notebooks? Without what data would they be reduced to impoverished lives? Does everyone really need to know this bit of history, this fact of chemistry? Why? Life is not a trivia test. There is no information that is universally essential and no teacher informed enough and wise enough to make that judgment.

I considered myself a pretty good explainer. In high school and in college, I had regularly helped my buddies understand an algebra process, write their essays, catch on to a rule of punctuation. I felt good when they succeeded. I knew, if I really applied myself, I could make anything clear to someone else. So at least I could honestly play that role. I didn't mind staying up until one or two in the morning figuring out a way to make a lesson lucid. I could teach the textbook and not have to bother my head deciding on content. My reward was pervasive ennui. Not only that, they weren't getting it. My classes were boring even to me, and, worse, there was hardly any retention. Terrific. Thirty or forty years of this?! It was no comfort to discover that my experience was the norm. Perhaps 10 percent of all that huffing and puffing is retained. We were all 90 percent ineffective. Imagine a dog trainer with that rate of success.

Some teachers thought that was OK. "If I can affect just one life, it's worth it." *What about the other twenty-nine kids—are they chopped liver? They must endure an hour while you talk to one student?* Others deliberately addressed the brightest and best and ignored the rest. But the kids at Stagg High School in Stockton, California, in those days were from well-off homes and had their eyes on Berkeley and Stanford. The whole school was the top 10 percent. But it was no easier stuffing things into their skulls than it had been with inner-city kids in Westinghouse Junior High in Pittsburgh, Pennsylvania. These were nice, polite kids. In their families, for whatever reasons, a B.A. was a valued asset; they didn't have to be convinced. Besides, I was greedy. Reaching two or three teacher's pets stunk. The bell-shaped curve was a nutty idea, too, with the mass of students rated "average" or "satisfactory"—in a word, mediocre. I wanted every single misfit right up there at the top. I wanted joy. Picture Isaac Stern: "Honey, I sawed out another so-so tune this evening"; or Robert Frost: "Elinore, think I can slip this slop past the critics?" Is teaching the profession of mediocrities? Are teachers petty civil servants, test proctors, record keepers, purveyors of information, custodians of the culture?

So, what to teach? Then, how to teach it? How do you get students motivated? But didn't these questions hinge on a prior question: Why teach in the first place? When I went to Diablo Valley College six years later, I had worked my way through these questions and had the schematic of a teaching philosophy in place. At DVC I found the whole staff engaged in this very dialogue. It was a young school dedicated to a fresh approach to teaching. It was a given that we must be well grounded in our subject, but our college had hired us because we might be good at teaching it. We did not turn over our classes to assistants while we did research and wrote for professional journals. We were *teachers*—not chemists, mathematicians, or literary critics. It was agreed that DVC was a student-centered school. But how was *student-centered* to be defined? And what constituted good teaching? Was there only one answer to that question?

We had debates, arguments, guest speakers, seminars, retreats, even occasionally an honest-to-God dialogue. It was great. One of the books we all read during that time was Nevitt Sanford's *The American College*. One chapter was devoted to how teachers perceived their role. A logician considered himself a member of an elite club. His job was to groom initiates for entrance to the fellowship and to weed out riffraff. Educated people were an elevated class that, through effort and special qualities of intellect, was removed from the common mass. A humanist was part of a priesthood who prepared the catechism for sacred works and administered the sacraments to the common folk. The stage actors' jobs were to put on a good show. Drill sergeants instilled discipline, respect for authority, habits of punctuality, hard work, and obedience. Prep-school types were coaches who got kids ready for the next prep school, which prepared them for the next, *ad infinitum.* An English teacher policed the language, ticketing degenerate usage—teacher as officer of the law. There were lots of *instructors.* Their job was to stick stuff in. Or try *unterrichten:* Karl Staubach added the blacksmiths, whose job was "hammering pig-headed clods into shape or shaping them up to fit a particular mold."

Elitist, priest, ham actor, martinet, coach, cop, custodian, authority, judge, fact peddler, blacksmith, magician—there was something disquieting about them all. I imagined myself as a student. In every instance, *other people* had something in mind for *me*. Not once was *I* consulted. We instinctively hurry away when someone comes toward us to do us good. How dare others presume to know what's good for me, as if I were an automaton to be programmed by agents of the collective culture. But if you are confined and cannot hurry away—if you are stuck in row seven, seat C—how can you defend yourself? Disengage your computer, that's how—go blank, glaze over, get bored. Autonomous organisms know instinctively when they are being invaded, and they always take evasive action. Anyone who thinks that he or she can motivate someone else hasn't a clue. Motivation comes from within. If someone is going to do your thinking for you, why should you? Hence, my students' passivity. Teachers were pushers, but the product wasn't selling.

Is there something worth doing, essential? What is the purpose of education? What is it for? Why does society send its kids to school? What is the hoped-for result? Forget society for a moment and think what the victim might want. What does each creature want for itself? Perhaps not consciously but with all its being, each organism has a built-in drive to fulfill itself. The genetic code seeks to flesh itself out in its own unique fashion. Each mind makes its own way, has its own compass: the pursuit of happiness—if by "happiness" one means the self-reliant ability to deal with one's own life. Don't we all want that, if not for others, at least for ourselves? A good way to create a society of neurotics would be to thwart that thrust, to try to redirect it, to try to stuff it into someone else's mold. By and large, that is what our schools do, one way or another.

That's not what the founders of our society envisioned. Our form of government was created for a society of self-governing individuals, free men and women who could direct their own affairs. Indeed, the education code of every state mandates the schooling of every citizen toward that end. For the masses to run their own affairs, they need to be thinking individuals, lest some King George decide things for them. They need to know how to steep tea in Boston Harbor. To ensure a free society, every citizen must be a watchdog for civil liberties. All that is philosophy, and the neo-Jeffersons and neo-Hamiltons are still going at it. *Your people, sir, are a great beast.* And a modern Jefferson might respond, "Yes, and I want that beast to shred any god who would impose his will on any single human being, however scruffy or vulgar." And so on. It *is* philosophy and rather far removed from the classroom. But on the side of Jefferson, every teacher must carve out a personal philosophy or let George do it.

That is the problem I encountered as I tried to find some base that would inform all my actions. Fundamentally, what you think you're doing will determine whether you will use fill-in workbooks, lecture, give kids coloring books, even keep the room tidied up. Keeping-within-the-lines is a political activity, an attitude toward self-determination. Self-direction or rule by others? The training of Allied soldiers and of those of the Third Reich demonstrates the difference. D-Day was chaos, but each Allied soldier knew his ultimate mission; so when the plan got totally screwed up, individuals proceeded on their own. They improvised. Their self-reliance is considered the reason for the ultimate success of the mission. By contrast, German soldiers were trained to respond unquestioningly upon command. If the command was not forthcoming, they sat on their hands.

Which way to go? Each teacher has to work that out. All the nuts and bolts of curriculum, method, and classroom management are the expression of a position. That *raison d'être* has to be durable enough for a lifetime; it has to be organic, not some patched-together camel. But without knowing in your bones what you are doing, nothing connects. Do you teach a bit of Robert Frost's biography when you read "Birches"? Why? How does "Birches" connect with algebra, or does it? Is Frost connected to linguistics? Punctuation? Mandalas? *What do you think you're doing?* Without an organic philosophy, the curriculum is a pile of materials that never get shaped into a house, a sculpture, a painting. Or worse, it becomes some ramshackle piecing together of all sorts of styles and materials. Teachers of math, accounting, electronics, and biology all have the same problem: What, in the deepest sense, do you think you're doing? You can train people to perform mathematical operations. Does that go deep enough? Or will your students become technicians in some vast blind bureaucracy? Without a center, no teacher can do much of a job.

Usually there is neither time nor incentive to seek that center. You can get a job in the colleges and universities of California with no course work in education whatsoever. Once you start in, it is all you can do to cope, much less ponder the point of it all. You are reduced to imitating the bankrupt teaching methods of your predecessors. Never mind that those practices don't cut it. For example, the lecture has proven to be one of the worst ways to teach. Guess what is the most common teaching method in colleges. Sometime or other, before plunging back in, it wouldn't hurt for a teacher to sit on the bank as long as it takes to figure things out.

Even if you think of human beings as blank slates or malleable clay, you have to find some way to get to the slate to scratch your will upon it, some way to penetrate the walls to get your hands on the clay. It turns out the clay has an impregnable will of its own. Any attempt to threaten, wheedle, trick, beg, or bribe these sturdy organisms will fail. But then, what about this body of knowledge called chemistry or biology? These kids have got to learn this stuff—and now. Next semester is built on this one. We've prepared this delicious meal. What's wrong with these kids? They won't eat. Who's in charge here? Whether you like it or not, it's the diner. To figure out what to teach and how to teach, there is no choice but to ascertain the appetite of the dinner guest. That can be done. It is simply a matter of taking cues from the organism and building your curriculum, step by step, according to its instructions.

In Taiwan, physics is *Wu Li*, patterns of organic energy. As Al Huang explained it to Gary Zukov and the physicists at an Esalen conference, "The Wu Li Master does not speak of gravity until the student stands in wonder at the flower petal falling to the ground. He does not speak of laws until the student, *of his own* [my italics], says, 'How strange! I drop two stones, one heavy and one light, and *both* of them reach the earth at the same moment!' He does not speak of mathematics until the student says, 'There must be some way to express this more simply.'" In this way, Zukov observes, the Wu Li master dances with his student. For teachers of any subject, whatever their philosophical bent, the message is clear: The learner leads. It is a biological necessity. To set a yummy table, you have to interface with the organism and get the order right. However cynical you may be of students' capacity to direct their own learning, you will "teach" more math by dancing *with* them than by talking *at* them. If you love mathematics, learn to follow.

That is the only efficient way to "teach." But the prior question remains: Why teach? For me, the common explanations didn't hold up: "It's a dirty job, but somebody has to do it," "I want to help people," and so on. Self-sacrifice wears thin over the decades, especially when the needy reject your care package. So what's in it for the teacher? In *Patton* the general says, "The scent of battle, God help me, I love it!" Why conduct an orchestra? Why daub a canvas, make a poem? Why eat popcorn? What soldier would want his or her life in the hands of a wishy-washy general? As depicted in the movie, Patton loved being in the thick of it. It wasn't the outcome but the process itself he loved. Of course you want to win, but if you don't love the process of getting the ball into the receiver's hands, you probably won't.

Why teach? Why get up in the morning? The search leads to the essential question: Why do anything? When asked the meaning of life, Alan Watts said, "I can tell you what it is not; it is not to get through it as quickly as possible." The purpose of a symphony isn't to get to the end of it. The paycheck at the end of the month or doing good for humanity are false answers. Kids don't eat their cereal because it's good for them or to make Mommy happy. They don't play on the slide for the exercise. We don't eat bananas for the potassium. And so it is with teaching.

I came to this realization by accident. The early days of teaching were dreary for me. I wanted to be a good teacher—as I conceived it—but it was turning out to be a dismal business. Noble calling, pats on the back, and respectability didn't cut it. When I went to graduate school, a practical friend asked, "Will you make more money, Clark?" Another said, "If you do what's right, maybe you'll get to be an administrator." I rarely considered such ends. I wanted to do a good job teaching, but I wasn't having a good time. It was not a spring meadow at dawn in Pennsylvania. It was not a roller-coaster ride. It was not being in love. But *sometimes* it was. When I forgot the lesson plan, when I accidentally got caught up in a fascinating discussion, when I found myself in a symphony of intellectual music, it *was* like love. During such moments, I didn't care whether school kept or not, and it was clear the students felt the same way. Strange as it might seem, we were thoroughly enjoying talking about language, a short story, what it means to be a human being.

> "When you wake up in the morning," says Piglet, "what's the first thing you say to yourself?"
> "What's for breakfast?" says Pooh. "What do *you* say, Piglet?"
> "I say, I wonder what's going to happen exciting *today*."
> Pooh nods thoughtfully. "It's the same thing."

Why do anything? Because doing anything is full of wonder. Why teach? Because it's wonderful, that's why, and if it isn't, then we have to stop everything and make it so. We must make it marvelous, full of marvels, or lose contact with our spirits. Life is not life without the spirit. A teacher has no choice; the process has to be a creative endeavor. We know we are in that mode when there is a tingling sensation along the spine, when there is no awareness of time passing, when there is no consciousness of self, when what you are doing feels effortless, when Yeats's dancer and dance are one:

> *O body swayed to music,*
> *O brightening glance,*
> *How can we know the dancer*
> *from the dance?*

I discovered, if one is disreputable and irreverent enough, that it is possible to identify the mechanisms that set the stage for such timeless moments. In fact, an entire course could be designed to invite the artistic mode—for that *is* what brings Michael Tilson Thomas back to the podium each time. If you have the guts for it, teaching can be like any other art. And any work that is allowed to be as fresh as the first morning *is* an artistic endeavor. I decided that was as far back as I could push the question. Right or wrong, it was something I could give myself to wholeheartedly. If wrong, at least it would be splendid while it lasted. I could feel good every day, and I could enjoy walking through that classroom door. If condemned to hell for my sins, then, with Twain, I thought, "Heaven for the climate, hell for the society."

Over many years the elements of the process revealed themselves, little by little and then in bunches. Once it was clear what I thought I was doing, it was utterly simple to work out the details. The maze of divergent, complicated, contradictory aspects of teaching coalesced into one beautifully clear "dew-pearled" morning, a scene of fantastic complexity, yet elegantly simple in its unity. The practical task was to cut away anything that cluttered the painting. How do you carve Chief Crazy Horse out of that block of marble? Cut away anything that doesn't look like Crazy Horse.

I was certain that this was work I could do the rest of my life. The next problem was, How can I get away with it? The carving might come close to looking like Crazy Horse, but it sure didn't look like any teaching I had ever witnessed. How to keep the master-at-arms off my neck while the students and I made beautiful music? I was not indifferent to societal pressures. I wasn't anxious to be booted out of the best game in town. So I went back to the original question: What are the terms of my contract? Can I make what I love doing fit the state and federal mandates?

From my perspective, it turned out that what was happening in my classes was exactly what I had been hired to facilitate: the emergence of an enlightened citizenry. The students were getting into the habit of using their minds, of enjoying using them, of initiating the process on their own, of doing it whenever they felt like it—not just in class but anywhere. Recognizing one's ability to fend for oneself is empowering. Isn't that exactly what the founders envisioned, a citizenry with deep respect and compassion for each other, who found pleasure in mutuality, but individuals with the self-esteem to tolerate no bully's heel on their necks? Doesn't that sound like self-governance? Isn't that the kind of environment we would all like to inhabit? Isn't that indeed where humanity needs to go? That suited me just fine, and I felt I could find the pedagogy to support it.

There is indeed tons of stuff: learning theory, human information processing, profiles of creative behavior, humanistic psychology, communication theory, neurolinguistic programming, and the turn-of-the-century prophetic observations of John Dewey—all point to the processes I had stumbled on experientially. The liberal arts are all about the human spirit and its expression and about the nature of other organisms as well. Biology, too, and even the physical sciences confirm nature's drive to fulfill itself. Even in quantum mechanics, it is clear that energy, even nothingness, has a mind of its own and will not be pushed around, no matter how much observers (teachers) might want to impose their will upon it. The word for physics, as noted earlier, in Taiwan is *Wu Li*, "patterns of organic energy." That is, matter is *organic, alive!* We become witnesses and participants simultaneously. The justification—translated into educators' jargon—is that this method gets the job done, from whatever angle viewed, better than any other and without the negative side effects. With such broad and deep reinforcement, fending off critics from whatever quarter was easy. With my back covered I could give myself to the process itself without distraction.

One piece of the puzzle remained. What about the students themselves, not *en masse* but each separate entity? Well and good that society gets its enlightened citizenry, splendid that I myself am now having a marvelous time, but what about Lisa Manuel, Adam Kwok, Gina Cecchettini, and the thousands of human spirits in my classes? For it became apparent early, regardless of what the institution wanted or I wanted, we could not achieve it if it was not what the "learner" wanted. What any organism wants, consciously or not, is to flesh out its unique genetic thrust. I had discovered that was what I wanted, and it seemed the best bet about other people, too. If my spirit was the most important thing in the world, it was the same for every other spirit. That meant education is not for the middle group or the top 5 percent. The entire course, every bit of it, is for the dozing kid in the back of the room. Until the class is so arranged that no one slips through the cracks, it needs more tinkering. In a room of seventy students, there are seventy-one individual courses being generated (mine being one of them). The art of the teacher is to cultivate seventy-one growing plants. A measure of success is not more uniformity but less, more divergence, more distinctive blooms.

So regardless of what cogency there may be in all that I had pieced together, foisting it on you or me would be criminal. We unique beings *ourselves* have to yearn for it. That is the first and final consideration. Society must value the individual so much that no one else's intentions can take precedence. That is the only idea of a democracy that can stand. It is what is meant by a student-centered curriculum.

Do You Know the Way?

Reading over this chapter, my colleague Karl Staubach wrote: "'Why Teach?' you ask. I recall a scene from *Our Totem Is the Raven*, the little movie we used to show our classes, which you also know":

> Using his newly carved Raven clan staff as a walking-stick for the first time, Grandfather stepped off the scenic tour bus with his hulking grandson David, who turned toward nearby Queets Cafe, the only refuge in sight as the bus disappeared in the tree-lined distance.
> "I'm hungry; when do we eat?"
> Grandfather was already headed into the ancestral rain forest across the road.
> "Later."
> David had trouble following Grandfather's trail, and had to hurry to keep pace. The woods seemed ever darker and deeper, and he called out ahead, "Do you even know where you're going?"
> "Of course," Grandfather's voice echoed through the woods. "Try not to fall behind."
> Soon Grandfather was out of sight again. David tried to catch up but stumbled and fell heavily, losing his bearings.
> "Wait, Grandfather, wait!"
> Grandfather reappeared almost at once.
> "Can we have something to eat now?" David seemed perplexed.
> "No food today, David: this is your Spirit-Quest; if you're thirsty, you drink from the stream."
> "You crazy old man! What are you doing to me?" David struggled to get up on his feet. "I'm going back!"
> Grandfather's eyes glittered, reflecting perhaps an eternal campfire. Perhaps an eternity of campfires, past and future.
> "Do you know the way?"

A Few Words from Charlie

In the spring of 1988 Charlie Dodt did some practice teaching with me. He was finishing some course work at California State University at Hayward and would be getting his credential in June. Mostly he took my courses like any other student, but he also got to teach a couple of sessions all by himself. Here is part of his synthesis:

Dear Clark,

There are a few basic principles about teaching that seemed clear to me almost from the first, and which have been embellished during these last few months. Be honest. Trust your students. Trust yourself. Don't try to do things out of *duty* or *responsibility* if they don't feel right. Try to cultivate and nourish, with praise and attention, all the things that students do *right:* their honesty, their spontaneity, their excitement at the possibility of new and unexplored worlds. Don't worry too much about the things that go wrong; they're mostly self-correcting. And respect your students, because that seems to be the best way of teaching *them* respect for each other and for all life.

These all seem so simple. Why can't we learn these ideas early and save ourselves years of sometimes grinding experience and the study of useless things? Why can't we keep them in mind to guide us through rough times? Maybe it's because, like Macon Leary in *The Accidental Tourist*, we want to institutionalize and systematize everything so that we'll be safe from change and perhaps impervious to pain as a result. A good, solid grading system could be a real bulwark against change. A familiar lesson plan is like a map through well-known territory; why go charging off into the wilds of spontaneity, where who knows *what* you'll run into? The system, the system. We don't want to beat it, we want to *join* it.

From October until December of last year, I learned what might be called Theory of Teaching. I learned all the important things to do: turning in grades on time, being in class on time so the District doesn't get sued if somebody steps on his shoelaces and breaks his neck, having a lesson plan every day and adhering to it, making sure to cover everything in the Course Outline (more threats of suits here if the material isn't covered as promised in the catalogue—somebody enterprising and not overly scrupulous could teach a course in Suing Your Way Through College), the Duty of serving on faculty committees, and so on. The teacher I had for this course was an administrator at Chabot Community College and quite sincere in everything he taught us. It's a point of view I probably wouldn't have gotten otherwise. But I was having a lot of second thoughts by the time I came to DVC in January. I was having a hard time recalling what it was that had made teaching seem like such a good idea.

It didn't take me long to remember. That freshman English class was a real turning point for me. I got my first experience in teaching and in reading student papers, but beyond that, I saw something of what it was like on the other side of the podium. I got to see what it is like for *you*. Here was a man who seemed to love what he was doing. Here was someone secure enough to ask questions that pull emotional, unpredictable responses out of most of the people in the class and to *accept* those answers, or gently suggest that we take another look at our responses. I saw someone who was not afraid to ask questions that have no clearly definable answers. I saw that teaching can be a lot of fun.

The seeds for what I have learned were there for me to examine the first few days, but it took much longer for me to assimilate and give words to what I saw. And all of the lessons I've learned were infinitely renewable. For instance, I know that what we are manifests itself in everything we do. Nevertheless I am amazed over and over by what appears in the mandalas I draw, and what my friends' mandalas reveal about them, and just how eyepoppingly *diverse* every class's mandalas are. The lesson is never redundant, as some might say, because every time I learn it, I see it to be true in a different way. If I set out to draw something that will show what I *want* to show, the "real" me finds a way of slipping through the cracks and undermining the image I want to project. If I stand back and try to draw aloofly, without emotional involvement, I get sucked right into the picture before I'm aware of it. And so on.

The most vivid moments this semester have come at the times when the class was most engaged. I remember the surges of energy and anger when we discussed infidelity and greed and capital punishment, and the wonderful rapt faces of an entire class with its eyes closed as we took the dream walk. I think of the grins on people's faces as they got up to walk around the room and find out everyone's names. I see slow-walkers moving through the trees of the campus like somnambulists from *The Cabinet of Dr. Caligari*, all of them paradoxically more alive than the "normally" walking people streaking past them.

I wanted to talk more about the highlights of those three classes—freshman English, literature, critical thinking—but I'm finding it hard to narrow it down; so many things worked so well. I loved the visit to the art gallery, that big group "painting" the class pieced together from their individual enlargements of bits of Demuth's *#5*. Richard Feynman, Woody Allen, singing "Momma Look a Booboo," an experience that will probably become a legend in local Vietnamese-American culture; the novels, the films, the *Best American Short Stories of 1987*.

I learned a lot about conducting class discussions, including the idea that students will come up with some amazing insights and connections entirely on their own. It's another variation on the theme of trust. It's surprisingly effective to use newer novels and stories rather than material that has been interpreted to death already; there is something very exciting about feeling a number of people make the same connection at the same time, a sense of discovery.

Charlie

Bliss: Teaching as Art

Well, Charlie, you're on your way. Let's put it this way: What happens *inside* a teacher during the fifty-minute hour should be what happens when a painter paints and when a composer composes. A math class, a philosophy class, a welding class is an artist's studio where an artist works in the presence of *and with* a roomful of fellow artists. Nothing can serve a discipline better than the release of artistic wonder among students of that subject.

This deep pleasure is a fundamental and powerful force that has kept me returning to the classroom for thirty years, doing the same old things—but seeing them as if for the first time and taking a whole bunch of students with me. That's what you saw going on, Charlie. It is a wonderful antidote for the mania for uniformity, predictability, and utility that is grinding its way through our schools. Let's make a case for joy, Charlie.

2

Why Learn?
A Piece of the Action

It's a thing that happens to you.
—The Velveteen Rabbit

Teaching is an artistic endeavor because we have no choice. When we take the low road, we get colitis or heartburn. Although we don't entice the artistic state of being for ulterior purposes, nonetheless an abiding outcome *is* health. In the midst of a peak experience, though, neither teacher nor student is thinking, "What good is this? Will I make any money?" I am told a similar altered state prevails at the height of lovemaking. You can justify your good time with supportive pedagogy, but the jewel is the moment itself manifesting.

Only art teaches. Everything else is torture.
—G. B. Shaw

Look at what happens, to use Lawrence Durrell's image, when we decorate the sackcloth and ignore the cloth of gold beneath: By late elementary school 20 percent of the kids dislike school. Those who say it's OK go on to describe it as boring, dull, or inadequate. Ungrateful wretches. It gets worse: Observers of conventional classrooms say the activities are boring and there is general program dullness. Other studies show students' evaluations of the whole affair—teachers, curricula, even feelings about themselves—become less favorable as they progress through the system. At Stagg High and at Diablo Valley College it was the same: faculty trying to teach, students trying to stop them. Some teachers described it as going into the trenches. The stupid clods couldn't even get the headings on their papers right. No matter what, papers still came in thirty ways from Sunday. Continual moaning and groaning in the teachers' lounge.

Passive, indifferent classes drive teachers nuts. But what is the source of this ennui? We don't have to search far. Consider Rosan Staubach's experience teaching elementary kids in Benicia, California. She had taken the kids on a field trip, all the way to the empty lot next to the parochial school. Each kid had a brown bag and was allowed to gather up ten things. Within minutes they had bagged their quota and insisted on more, so she upped it to fifteen. Thinking about the experience later she remarked to her husband, my colleague Karl, that she couldn't get over the sharp contrast between the apathy in class and the vitality, curiosity, and intensity out in the field. Why did they change so dramatically? "You know why," said Karl. "It's because a classroom is where everything isn't."

The kindergarten environment is sumptuous, lots of stuff, lots of primary colors. And cookies. Music, dancing, a little nap. But with each passing year, more and more stuff disappears. By college all that's left are chairs and an occasional antiquated audiovisual aid. When I gave college literature students crayons and colored paper to draw mandalas, some said they had not had a crayon in their hands since sixth or seventh grade. A classroom is where everything isn't. But evidence indicates that rats grow bigger brains in stimulating environments, and human beings thrive in an encouraging environment. A warm and friendly place may not solve your problems, but at least it won't exacerbate them. If you're genetically depressive you won't feel so bad that you are.

Why is it so hard to teach? No one likes to be taught, that's why. Everyone loves to learn. When we try to motivate kids with our ideas of what they ought to be learning, good heavens, we have a whole roomful of Mahatma Gandhis! We don't want to be "schooled." Each being has its own necessity and willingly opens its sensorium to nourishment. It's biological. Schoolmasters get it upside down when they attempt to instill discipline, motivation, and "good" behavior, from the outside. If we want to *educate*—that is, "lead forth"—we haven't any choice but to see what's going on in the individual. Even the organization of a dust mite is fantastic. How much more so is the organism called man? To teach well we need to *realize* (make real) our own beautiful selves and then take as much time as we need to *real*-ize each student. In that light, futile methods and ridiculous materials evaporate. Let's get *real*. When we see stupid or retarded kids or underachievers, we are looking through smudged lenses. *Real-eyes* even your own fingernail, and it will be a good day to teach. To realize a student, take a long, loving look:

> What is REAL? asked the Rabbit one day, when they were lying side by side. Does it mean having things that buzz inside you and a stick-out handle?
>
> Real isn't how you are made, said the Skin Horse. It's a thing that happens to you. When a child loves you for a long, long time, not just to play with, but REALLY loves you, then you become Real.
>
> Does it hurt? asked the Rabbit.
>
> Sometimes, said the Skin Horse, when you are Real you don't mind being hurt.
>
> Does it happen all at once, like being wound up, or bit by bit?
>
> It doesn't happen all at once. You become. It takes a long time. That's why it doesn't happen often to people who break easily, or have sharp edges, or have to be carefully kept. Generally, by the time you are Real, most of your hair has been loved off, and your eyes drop out and you get loose in the joints. But these things don't matter at all, because once you are Real you can't be ugly, except to people who don't understand.
>
> —Margery Williams, *The Velveteen Rabbit*

When a teacher loves you, not just to play with but really loves you, then you become real. Then the games stop.

Still, to get to the heart of the matter, we have to get beyond kids and stuff. What makes a kid take up some driftwood on the beach and labor the whole afternoon on a sculpture she knows she will leave there when everyone piles into the van and heads home? What's the motivation? What does it feel like? Here's an experiment readers can try out for themselves. I use it in classes and in seminars to illuminate the conditions of productive classes:

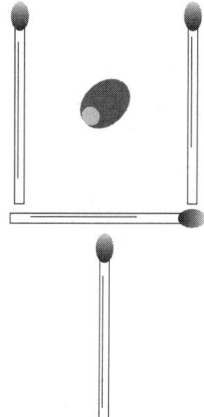

> Move two matches once only. The shape of the glass must be the same, but the olive must be outside it when you are finished.
>
> The answer is on page 19, more or less, along with an explanation of the significance of the experiment.
>
> (No fair peeking.)

If you want to *experience* what motivates a student to participate in class, solve the puzzle before reading further.

If you don't hang out in bars, this might be a new puzzle for you, and in solving it you will have seen the reason people learn. That is, first you have to accept the offer, be it driftwood, a math concept, or getting the olive out of the glass. Maybe at first you mess around, but then you get into it; and if the endeavor goes well, you *see* the solution in a flash. One moment you don't and suddenly you do. More specifically, you can feel the solution coming on before your know it consciously. You know you are getting it before you get it. It is that moment when it all comes together that is the payoff, that surge of realization, of illumination—if you will, an epiphany. This drive controls all human effort. On one level it's the drive to figure things out; on a deeper level it is the insistence of the spirit on illumination, enlightenment: in the solution of a barroom puzzle, in seeing energy up close (quantum mechanics), in making a painting or a poem—the instant when it all connects. A classroom is functioning properly when there is this buzz of energy and playful fooling around that leads to an unselfconscious engagement that leads to a mental, physical, and spiritual focus that leads to an uncontrollable drive to connection—the violinist and the music melded into one thing going on, humans in the midst of being. *That's motivation.*

The way people play the matchstick game represents their approaches to life in general. In any group there is virtually the full array: Those who don't try at all because they "know" they can't do it, because they had planned on something else, because they don't want to risk ego deflation, and so forth. Those who try a little and then give up. Those who want hints. Those who follow someone else's lead, the imitators. Those who want to be given the answer. And those who struggle with it and solve it.

Some students get the solution immediately. They see it by accident. There is a little bit of pleasure in that, but nothing to write home about. Some cheat. Some already know the solution, so there's no payoff, no learning. Too often such students can ace tests and get A's but learn the least; so their payoff is hollow. Some give up early and some don't even try. Some try for a long time but grow discouraged.

When most of the group have the solution, I ask if we should explain it to the rest. That leads to a discussion about the effect of giving learners answers. Some want us to tell them. Some would rather not, even if they never get it. So our philosophy is involved: what we think life is all about and how we choose to participate in it. Those who do struggle and solve the puzzle experience at the instant of discovery the thrill of living poetically. Though the puzzle may seem unimportant, its very triviality is a key to what education has to be. It has nothing to do with jobs or bread or the future. It is an intrinsic and intense pleasure in itself. The clarification of one's experience is not for ulterior motives like survival or power, though these are often by-products or perversions. We have a biological imperative to have a good time —or die.

But think of how most of us have been trained to teach: "Today, we're going to learn how to solve problems. In this little matchstick problem most people will have trouble because they get locked into only one way of seeing. They think they must move the matches completely. If they slide the horizontal match only halfway to the right, the upper left matchstick can then be moved over to the bottom right. See?" The students write dutifully in their notebooks and glance at the clock. It is the teacher's show from beginning to end. Everything is done *for* the student, no excitement whatever, no payoff. This is what passes for teaching throughout our schools. It is the cause of program dullness and student ennui. If learning doesn't embody the intensity of pleasure that can be felt on a smaller scale in a barroom puzzle, it is not true learning but mere accumulation of data. Learning is always that flash of discovery, the synapse in which two things fuse.

Whether you want to teach people to get good at solving problems or just know about the process but not actually go through it, do hands-on stuff *first*. If the learner has not chosen to become engaged, efforts to force-feed will fail. But our contractual obligation calls for something more fundamental than solving problems. Animated participation in one's own growth and change must become a habit. That wedding of spirit and matter at the flashpoint of discovery is what turns us into self-actualizing human beings who can run our own lives and mutually direct the business of our society. To honor our contract, *we teachers have to go with the internal motivation*. We have to rub some sticks together and get the fire going. I wonder what's going to happen exciting *today*. I wonder what I can *make* happen. Emotion is central to learning.

Emotion is central to learning. What makes a human being choose to "learn"? The kick is the discovery, the feeling of being fully alive. Students slump in their seats because they see no possibility of that sense of wonder occurring in this place. Or they think it's all over; kindergarten is a dim memory. School is a plodding process of accretion, not downhill skiing, not *seeing*. But school must be life to the hilt, not because it's more fun that way—though that is plenty good enough—but because the biology of learning requires feeling. Unselfconscious enthusiasm (*en-* + *theos:* possessed by a god, inspired, the spirit within) is part of the equation. "I turn on the music inside me and outside, and it just starts flowing. I'm just happening," says the artist. "Are you happy when you work?" "Oh, yes! Outside my studio there's a sign: Children at Play. That's me."

Motivation is not an adjunct to the curriculum, it is *the* curriculum. Everything else follows. The focus of teachers' conferences ought to be on how we learn and what makes us want to, not on how to teach. That's all backward. *Learning* is what schools are all about. Witnessing students in the process of learning is a great pleasure, like seeing a ballet or a Puccini opera. It is hard to imagine a teacher not loving it. It is even better to be a part of it. When a teacher joins in, then the classroom is complete. When the teacher fiddles with language (or physics, accounting, music) along with the students, the curriculum continually refreshes itself, each time being literally the first time. That is the ideal classroom, something in it for everyone. The teacher renews and refreshes along with the students. To find out why students learn, teachers need look no farther than their own selves. The rest of the job is to make sure the classroom is a learning lab every single time—for students *and* teacher.

When Wu Li Master Al Huang does physics, he is not explaining the world, as many people including some physicists believe, he is only dancing with it. As Huang described it to Gary Zukov, for the Wu Li master every lesson is the first lesson. "It does not mean that we forget what we already know. It means that what we are doing is always new, because we are always doing *it* for the first time." There is course content, but this way of interacting with it keeps it fresh and alive.

In a humanistic classroom the structure is organic, whole, and complete all the time. The world doesn't start all over for each new baby. Nor does the teacher begin at the beginning. "Let's figure out this matchstick puzzle." We plunge right in. We begin at the center. We do not lecture on the techniques of problem solving. We do it and *then* notice what we did to get there. The usual method is to break down the task or skill into a step-by-step process to be learned by rote. The effect is mind-numbing tedium. When that happens, students get the entirely wrong idea that learning is always preceded by months and years of benchwarming. If every "practice" is a musical experience, a complete experience, everyone leaves the session refreshed—no burnout. Watch a baby "practice" walking or talking, and you will see a model for a graduate class in physics. No burnout.

The big surprise isn't that students hate to be taught. It is that teachers hate to "teach." Even if we could get away with it, deep inside we despise being fact peddlers or drill sergeants. But we all love what happens to us while we are learning. The art of teaching is the art of learning in public.

A Profile of the Learner

All things are connected. One of my colleagues read through evaluations of his sociology class and discovered the students didn't like it. "I see a lot of you think this class is boring. Well, tough!" He figured it's *supposed* to be boring, and a mature, responsible student must cope, get the job done regardless. That is a common attitude, a smug indifference to the effect of teachers' behavior on their audience. Isn't it remarkable that a *sociologist* can have no interest in the *social* interaction of the lives he affects so intimately? Or the psychologists, from whom I learned so much about human behavior, conducting their classes as if they had never read humanistic psychology? You have to wonder.

The gulf between learner and teacher could be tolerated were it not for the negative side effects. I once asked a class of college sophomores how many of them loved themselves, or at least *liked* themselves. I was amazed that only three out of forty or so raised their hands. I thought maybe they were being modest, but class discussion and written reflections confirmed that they really did not feel very good about who they were. How could this happen?

Suppose you have teacher after teacher, year after year, saying, "Forget you!" Suppose the school finds more and more wrong with you and piles it all up in your cumulative file? Suppose they take your crayons away! Suppose you are *never* invited to the table, and you must sit in an unnatural, passive state, hour after hour, day after day, year after year. Would you like yourself? Well, tough! The effect of faculty indifference is metaphoric lobotomy, and there is no way it can be excused or justified. The systematic destruction of the human spirit is a crime against humanity. It also violates our contractual mandate. Remember, the bottom line is a self-governing populace in the pursuit of happiness.

How we feel about ourselves has a central influence in how we learn, the posture we take toward school. We have to feel good about ourselves; we have to have a sense of self-determination. Teachers who ignore the mental health of their students cannot succeed. Until the teacher has made contact with each student, and they with each other, the day's work hasn't really started. How many teachers' manuals point that out?

I was thinking about how important to the learning process it is to like oneself when I was asked to give a graduation address at DVC a few years back. I wanted the graduates to think about how lovable they really are, how lovable we all are. I wanted them to know how smart they are and see in the mirror something marvelous, something fantastic. Here is what I told them.

Things We Forgot to Tell You

My title is "Things We Forgot to Tell You." I'm going to give you three or four points. I considered connecting them all up for you at the end, but I decided against it because I know your mind will do that for you. That will be a little test of the idea that your mind is a connecting organ. It's true. Your mind loves to make connections. If it gets into a confusing situation, it's going to find some way to get rid of that confusion. It just loves to do that. So it's quite natural for you to solve problems. That's what I want to talk with you about tonight: How easy it is for your mind to organize things for you and to solve problems for you.

The first item has to do with how smart you are. I want to get it on the record that every human being in this audience is very smart. Not just our graduates tonight, but all of you, all of you are very, very smart.

The reason I'm able to say that is that I'm aware of the wonderful miracle of a computer you've got right inside your head. It's so big it has to be wadded up to fit in there. If you were to take that brain and spread it out and take out all the wrinkles, it would be the size of the top of a card table. That brain of yours is something new on the planet. In the time span it's been here, in the history of Earth, it's like the wink of an eye. A very short time. It's called the neocortex, the new brain, and it can do amazing, unbelievably complex things. Wonderful things.

Before you get out of Diablo Valley College, it is important that you realize just how well you use that computer, because it's going to keep you out of hot water the rest of your life.

You have always known how to use that computer. In fact, when you were born, you were using it expertly. You used it better then than perhaps you used it when you were in college.

Right at this moment you are using that brain to pull off some very neat tricks. You are using it right now to regulate your heart beat; you're using it to digest your dinner; you're using it to grow fingernails, daydream, listen to me, and work out all sorts of puzzles and problems simultaneously.

It is abundantly clear that even at your worst you use your brain in powerful and miraculous ways. It is possible for me, then, to say, compared to everything else we know about the planet, only the most cynical sourpuss could doubt that the kind of thing you are able to do is pure genius. You are all just wonderfully brilliant. It is important that you know that about yourselves. You do have to be aware of it.

I'm sure with a little prodding all of you could supply me with lots of complex programs you have stored on your own in your computer. So I'm going to give you just one example of something powerful and fantastic that you did before you even got into kindergarten. Do you know what that was? Here it is: When you were still a baby, in fact from the time you were born, you began to, and did, teach yourself a language.

A language is much more complicated than calculus or chemistry or anything else you will ever be asked to learn in your adult life. It is much more complicated, and the amazing thing is that you taught your language to yourself. You taught yourself. We have plenty of research to show that nobody else did that for you. In fact, if you were to analyze it thoughtfully, you would know that nobody is knowledgeable enough or has enough information to deliberately and consciously be able to stuff that program into a little kid's head. They just don't know enough about it.

So here you are, by the time you are two years old, fluent at this complex program called language. And by the time you're five, you are ready to go to kindergarten, and you're an expert.

How did you do that? Do you remember how you did that? Of course you don't. The point is that you don't have to know *consciously* how to do it. It's like learning to walk. No one knows how to teach it to you, but every little kid learns it. Child's play. Learning a language, learning how to walk, are child's play. Play. And the neocortex, that new brain of yours, that's your sandbox.

You did all the tricky stuff, all the complicated stuff, in your nonconscious mind. That's the part of your brain that doesn't speak a language. So, of course, it can't tell you how it operates. Nevertheless, it does just fine; it functions beautifully. And it can do that without your conscious knowledge. You don't have to know how it works, but you do have to trust that it *will* work for you.

It is busily and happily working out all sorts of complex problems all the time. It is doing it right now. But it is shy and childlike. And it will not tell your conscious mind its wonderful solutions if you mistreat it. If you mistreat it, it won't communicate.

This means, if you want to enjoy your job or your studies, if you want to tap into your powerful computer, *you have to live a life with a heart*. A life with a heart. This is a practical matter. Your computer is just hardware—well, wetware. It takes its instructions, not from your conscious mind, but from your heart (or your spirit, or your self, or your soul). If your spirit doesn't give its OK, your computer malfunctions. It won't know what to do, and whatever it does won't feel right.

As one of my students put it, there is a door between your conscious mind and the part you are not conscious of. If you try hard to think, the door remains shut. But if you love yourself, as a little kid loves himself or herself, then that door will open wide for you. If your self knows that it is lovable, then what you did effortlessly as a child you can still do.

Your brain will function well only when it is fired by your enthusiasm, your joy, your pleasure. *That means you have to find out how to be full of joy under all circumstances.* The secret is to know once and for all that you are lovable. I can guarantee you that you are. In all my years of teaching, I have never gotten to know a spirit that wasn't lovable and huggable. You cannot look into another creature's spirit and remain untouched. I know I am on safe ground here because I know that not one of you can look into your own deepest self and deny it.

And you also know that your deepest, truest self is sweet-tempered, spontaneous, generous, and loving. When you were a kid, *that* part of yourself directed all your activities. You know how terrific that combination of mind and spirit was. And you know that when you are at your top level of performance, you behave exactly like you did when you were a kid playing, playing at language, playing at walking, playing at taking over your computer.

What this means is that you have a lot more going for you than you may realize. If calculus or English or managing your life seems hard for you, it simply means you are probably trying to use your new brain in an unnatural way. If you use it the same way as you did when you were a little kid, you will solve problems effortlessly. *Effortlessly.*

On the other hand, if you have to make yourself do something, if you start feeling Grouchy or Grumpy or Sleepy or Dopey, it is a clear signal to stop and try another way.

The natural way is almost upside down from what we have been led to believe. We are taught to work hard at our studies or at solving problems, but that is not the way our brains work best. The brain works best when it is in a playful, loving, enjoying mood. We can use our conscious minds to set up problems, but we have to get playful if we want to solve them.

We have been taught that a person should be dutiful and responsible. The truth is that the great thinkers, the great artists, the great scientists of the world have treated their work as if it were play. They have been, you might say, irresponsible. That is not to say they haven't done things that turned out to be valuable to the human race. But while they were thinking, they could not also be dutiful and serious and responsible. So it is the opposite of what we are used to hearing. That is something you need to know about. While you are thinking, while you are trying to solve problems, you cannot be *working* at them. You can only be having a good time, like a kid in a sandbox.

Afterward, if you want to make those things become a reality, let yourself become absorbed, play at that part, too, and you will get much better results. If you want to discover, if you want to use your mind really well, you must be *playful*, *irresponsible*, and *joyous*.

If you can remember these things about yourself, you will be in great shape.

3

Superficial and Supralogical Thinking
Making the Sun Come Up

Because a fire was in my head.
—William Butler Yeats

Ordinarily, we get along with conscious, superficial thinking: "To get to the bus station, go to the third traffic light, turn left, and go one-half block. It's on the left." When we need to satisfy several variables in an architectural design or in a complex mathematical problem, such thinking can become extremely taxing. If we confine our thoughts to only the known, we are stuck with getting-to-the-bus-station kind of thinking: linear, conscious, sequential.

But another kind of thinking unique in human beings—as far as we know—is available to us. Remarkably, even though it is exclusively ours, it is generally neglected and ignored. Schoolmen and -women seem oblivious to this kind of thinking even though it is the heart of any school system—or ought to be. The mixture of spirit and flesh in a metaphor, once understood, is a model for this supralogical thinking, coupling the reservoir of nonconscious, right-hemispheric icons with conscious, logical processes. It does not make "sense" to see one thing in terms of another, yet this process is the basis of all culture: the bridging of distinctions, the developing of a single concept for a house—or the entire universe.

Examining each instance of the universe in a systematic, step-by-step manner, we could never comprehend anything so infinitely variable; we would soon break down under the weight. (Most schools seem designed to do just that, however, and continue dishing up basket after basket of plastic-coated facts, never mixing chemistry and poetry, algebra and oil painting.) We become human only by jumping to the conclusion of *language*. The benchmark of an educated person is having made that leap—and realizing it, realizing that only through symbolic, metaphoric thinking can we grapple with such complexity.

In ordinary conscious thinking, images and words are stripped of their ambiguity and are used to compare one thing with another in detail-for-detail parallels. In supralogical analogy, however, there is an instantaneous blurt of association, compressing the totality of a situation in one immediate flash of insight. "Aha!" The mind leaps over the intervening steps and details and arrives at a solution all at once. Point-for-point identification takes a long time for all the nuances to be seen—if ever—but metaphoric thinking travels at electronic speed, establishing thousands of connections in a flash. Becoming consciously aware of this process and mastering its use is the work of the maturing mind. Those who stop at logical thinking might as well retire at forty, but those who use their whole minds, right and left hemispheres together, travel a thrilling road into the years of light.

Language and Creativity

A workshop I conducted at Marillac College in St. Louis in 1971 had been planned for me by the head of the Humanities Department, Sister Vincent, and her associate, Sister Josephine. They asked if I would focus on creativity. I don't like that word much because lots of screwy stuff goes on under that name. "Creative writing" is one example. It's like versifying or generating metaphors mechanically, just the opposite of what education is all about. Creative behavior is not some diversion or pastime engaged in after work. But I realized the workshop would be a chance to demonstrate the centrality of creation in ordinary life. So I gladly accepted the job.

We did some hands-on experiments and exploration—activities my college students did all the time. The teachers all made mandalas, for example, and went on a slow walk and made a gallery show of *objets trouvés*. But after everyone had had some experience of the process, I did talk about the subject of our workshop directly.

Creation, Creatures, and Creativity

Why come together and talk about creativity? For a long time in my own teaching, I didn't realize my job had anything to do with that word. I never cared much for the self-consciousness I observed in the few creative writing classes I had taught. The atmosphere dripped with ego. Everyone seemed to be acting out a role. Feelings were fragile. So I steered clear of that sort of emphasis. What interested me was authenticity, autonomy, spontaneity—for reasons I will get to shortly. But at first I didn't realize that that was the kind of behavior I enjoyed being around. I started out, like most responsible teachers, armed with a well-thought-out lesson plan, my blueprint for meeting my goals. I had a map, and I intended to get to the places marked on it. And in a manner of speaking, what I wanted to happen did happen. The trouble was that it wasn't much fun. I knew intuitively, on the edges of consciousness, what life ought to feel like. I always knew that—you do, too—and I always knew when it felt just right. But that wasn't happening in my classes. Instead, some prepackaged set of actions took place, right on cue.

My students weren't enjoying our classes, either, not really. I don't think most of them were conscious of their boredom—or at least the source of it. Most of them no doubt thought school was supposed to be tedious. But being very creative, they would tell me how bad off things were by neglecting their assignments, by inattention, by apathy and all those fine indicators of misspent activities. Does any of this sound familiar?

But every once in a while, something unexpected would happen and it would be thrilling and educational. We would *dis*cover something, *un*cover something. We would suddenly get a glimpse of reality we hadn't been able to see before. Accidents would take place. We might be discussing *frames of reference*, and someone would say "frames of preference." Then someone would say, "We have trouble shifting frames of reference because they're really frames of preference." Suddenly a new insight emerged. At first these accidents just happened, and at first I was afraid of them. I thought my lesson plan was being ruined. *I've got to cover the lesson*. Matters of that sort. Meantime, there would be a glitch, and everyone would be very responsive for a few minutes or maybe half an hour. We would penetrate into an area that was really important to us; it brought us closer to an authenticity that we couldn't get at by other means. You can't just say, "Let's be authentic today. Let's get real." At first these incidents would crop up unexpectedly. I didn't know how to set them up. I began to value them—they were so iconic—but I had no conscious idea of what made them happen. So I just had to wait. But it wasn't long until the mechanism came into focus. It turned out we were dealing with a phenomenon others have called "creativity."

What made us want to shift into that mode of thought? What caused us to turn toward the "accidents" even against our better judgment and stay with the tangent even though we were being naughty and not doing what we were supposed to do, not sticking to the lesson? One way to say it is that it was our natural need to be alive, to feel alive. It sounds simpleminded to say that life needs life to be life. And yet that seems the best way to put it. Life recognizes itself and demands its necessary nutrients and will not put up with its opposite. When a living creature finds itself stifled, it has built-in protection from that terrible quiescence. Never be upset with boredom: It tells us where we shouldn't be. Apathy, headaches, upset stomachs are designed to turn us in a more living direction, toward a oneness with the processes of life. To be creative is to be at one with the flow of creation. It isn't something added on to life; it is the very heart of life. And it is the common element of all living things.

Being Authentic

In retrospect, it is clear that in those moments of discovery we were, for those brief creative moments, authentic. During those moments we were unself-conscious. We were so absorbed that we forgot our personas, our masks, and we interacted with each other directly, not through our egos but as authentic beings. In the midst of play, life tricked us into coming off it, and it felt fine. Our minds were functioning extremely well, our nerve endings were fine tuned. We were so interested in whatever had caught our attention—we had found a way to *be* interested—that we didn't have to put up defenses, all the artificial paraphernalia we think protect us. So I began to realize we have two dramatically different ways of being, the one prosaic, the other poetic. When we are in our poetic, our creative, mode, we experience the facts of life intensely. And that mode is healthful and desirable.

Another reason to participate in such behavior is the delight in being among people behaving authentically. You get to talk with them directly, not through their masks. It is a warm and satisfying experience. In these moments we were most alive, most vital, most participatory. What's more, the entire class would be galvanized. The atmosphere was so contagious no one could remain passive. Over time, it has become apparent that the conditions for genuine and affective education are precisely those for genuine living. And stepping further back, we see the conditions for education are exactly those for all things, for atoms and planets as well as for warm-blooded and cold-blooded creatures, for rocks and trees, for stars and galaxies, the very same necessities.

Those familiar with *Oedipus Rex* may wonder why the play has such power. The reason is that the characters speak directly, without censorship of ego. The pure self is the foreground. The actors wear masks, but the effect is to strip the character of ego. What we get is authentic dialogue without distractions. That is exactly what happened to my students and to me during our creative moments. Authentic dialogue *is* creation, ideas being generated on the spot. When that is going on, we are in the midst of life. Taken in its broadest context, dialogue is a tension between poles that sets up the possibility of synapse, the melding of idea pools. The whole drive of a "lesson plan" clearly ought to be toward such pure dialogue.

The possibility of such fusion is one reason I enjoy working with people interested in creative behavior—which, as I have said, is simply life going about its business. For, as I have found out from years of working with students, all human beings, all of us, unmasked, are poets, the creative force shaping our own evolving lives. But most of us never realize it. We mistakenly experience life as though it were prose when in fact it's poetry. Through the interaction of our minds and spirits with our surroundings, we put the life back into life. We restore its surprise, delight, and wonder.

Naturally, when I meet people who are somehow liberated into being alive, I find them so delightful and so refreshing that I can't help but gravitate toward them and want to be around them. That's probably why most of us like teaching, though most may not realize the reason: Young people are much more prone to living poetically. Pure and simple, people behaving creatively are refreshing. And as far as curriculum is concerned, it isn't making things, it isn't products (essays, planter boxes, fourteen calculus problems solved). No, it is the process itself. We are engaged in releasing the active spirit, the generative spirit that resides in us all. Making contact with that life force is exciting, and realizing one's own spirit is exciting. Whether we know it or not, that's why most of us teach.

It isn't so much making or doing, then, as it is *being*, being alive, being aware, being spontaneous, being intimate. It is being autonomous; it is being authentic. When people are like that, they are not going to have to be so busy. Surprisingly, the more creative we are, the fewer distractions we need. You will find fewer people taking watercolor classes, probably. You will find fewer people making knickknacks for roadside stands. Only those to whom it is a meaningful activity and not a *pastime* (isn't that an ugly word, "pastime"?) will be engaged in such pursuits. This is not to say there will be less art. On the contrary, we will have authentic art and it will be more and more attractive. The by-product of being alive is physical, material stuff that is unique and beautiful, beautiful in the sense that it speaks to me intimately and directly. When I cleanse myself, gird myself for action, when the artist has done that, too, then the opportunity for this polarity to function is tremendously increased. Our work is cut out for us: Set the stage.

So being creative is not so much doing something to life as allowing life to do something to me, allowing it to speak through me, sitting quietly, being quiet, so that it fills me. My spirit and life can commingle and generate whatever they will together. And I, as a creative participant, work carefully and quietly to permit, not interfere with, this natural process. When we get down to it, creativity is nothing more than humans *being*, life processing without interference or hindrance.

Coming To

Time and again I have seen students surprised by their own thoughts. "I can't believe I said that!" I love those moments, moments when the mind wakes up to itself and what it's doing. It saddens me when I see people who think all they can do is plod along mechanically from dawn to dusk; it is such a denial of what's there. The behavior we explored in the creativity workshop at Marillac College is not, as I have said, a province of special people but of all creatures. I looked up the Indo-European root of *create* not long ago. It means "to grow or cause to grow." So we teachers don't really have a choice. To grow is to create. We are all the creators, authors, sculptors of our own organisms, both physically and mentally, or better, we are mind-body, one thing growing.

It is also clear that the mind is the sculptor's workshop, and the language chip is a crucial element of the studio. When we use the mind out-of-awareness, sometimes we can get in a pretty good day's work. We can get ideas—which may become something physical but not necessarily—without consciously knowing how we did that. Lots of wonderful artists "just do it." They don't dwell on how they pull it off. Some of my colleagues think that's close enough. Those who enjoy using their minds, who get a kick out of their discoveries, lead amazing lives. I must admit I would feel pretty good about an institution whose graduates were prone to enjoying themselves at that level. They are usually in a good mood and are pleasant to be around. They are always into something, and their conversation goes beyond mutual funds and backbiting. They usually have an engaging insight to lay on the table. Yes, they are refreshing. Let's not knock anyone that alive. And I think any institution is obliged to shoot for at least that for all its students. It's easy enough to accomplish.

The mind is capable of much more, however, and I think it is shortsighted to settle for the middle ground. Many human creatures are indeed satisfied with being able to run their own lives and with having enough experience of using their minds to deal with whatever problems they may encounter. Each of us is unique, and we should not be coerced into traveling farther than we are ready or willing to go. Nonetheless, we must not lose sight of the possibilities. The opportunity must be there in all classrooms, just in case.

That is why all classes must be conducted poetically. The only way we understand anything anyway is metaphorically, so whatever their level of awareness students will grow optimally in a poetic atmosphere. If a student can say, "I'm not creative," you will know something got screwed up down the line. Like my students who suddenly realize how bright their ideas can be, we all would benefit from coming face to face with our unique qualities. As I have said before, we cannot meet a soul or spirit without being amazed. Every student needs to take a good look in the mirror—beyond pimples, eccentricities, and quirks, to the unmasked self—not the stage performance the ego puts on. The possibility of that encounter needs to be there in every class, every day.

Realizing life every minute of an ordinary day may not be possible, but that does not mean we shouldn't give the saints and poets in our classes a crack at it. Who are these saints and poets? Anyone with a *pure* connection to the cosmos. Guess who has such a pure connection? Everyone. Of course, this purity is usually camouflaged so that most of us are confused about what we are really like. But not *really*. Somewhere inside there is a pure spirit (poet, saint), and we all know it. We just don't want to admit it. We get a big kick out of the stage play. *Well, look at me, behaving so rottenly. What a mean fellow I am. I'm so evil I'm just hopeless.* Meanwhile, another part of the being is looking on and saying, *Swell performance. Fine job acting it out. You should be in the movies. Won't it be a relief when you take off the greasepaint and get back to being your own sweet self?* That sweet self, of course, is the benign, scintillating universe.

As poets of this universe, we realize—make real—the world we look upon. William Carlos Williams referred to it as getting "an intense vision of the facts." If I see this pencil as only a pencil and do not see it in the context of the universe, do not see it in the context of paper, desk, floor, Earth, stars, galaxies, and beyond eternity, I haven't really seen it at all. When we switch over into our poetic mode, we do see with such intensity.

Everyone is a saint and a poet with cataracts and nasal congestion. We need to blow our noses and do some I surgery. Every class has to be a "creativity" workshop, for only when the self is allowed to come out of hiding does the being function optimally. The unexamined life is the unpoetic life, and we all know Socrates' views on that. In other words, each of us is the creator, the sculptor, of the perceived universe. So let's take a good look, for heaven's sake. We could get it all screwed up. Chardin said it's either that or perish. Fundamentally, it is our function to see, to perceive, to create meaning. When we get up in the morning, the question every day is always the same: What would this world in conjunction with me like to become? (And keep in mind, "The world is warmed by the questions we ask of it.") I can remember years ago a student, Mike Harrison, writing about a perception he had of going to the beach:

> The sun was shining, the tide was out. The place was truly waiting for us. It knew we were coming and had a fabulous show ready. I could hardly wait to get down to the bottom of the hill and look around in the water. The life of the sea always fascinates me. There are strange and beautiful things there just waiting to be understood and have some recognition in our world. Well, I don't pass them by; I stop and say hello every time I'm down there.

I also like what Gary Mello, another student, said:

> Everything around me is screaming at me to be recognized and given meaning and to be freed from nonbeing. Everything is reaching out to me, straining and stretching and pleading. I gain a completely new and real importance. I think for the first time I have really become the center of my own universe.

The human beings in our classrooms are "strange and beautiful things" waiting to be recognized, too. Any teacher who turns the beam of attention on a roomful of students will be shocked at the gemstones waiting there to be recognized. But if one jams the airwaves with intention, with one's own designs, then it will be hard to hear or see what's being transmitted. So we do have to clear out the static, but that isn't hard at all, once we understand the principle.

When people say they are not creative, they are simply saying, "I don't recognize myself as the author of my own life. I see some other person, some other condition, as being responsible." When I feel that way I abdicate my authority, my role as author, my right to shape the experiences that come into me, that are open to me. So I sit, dumb and apathetic, and wonder why everything is so boring, when right before me in this very room is the bejeweled universe. A miracle is nothing more than some part of the physical or imagined universe perceived, grasped.

Reveille

One of my favorite cartoons depicts a little man looking rather dissatisfied. He takes out a horn and blows it. "Toot." The sun fills the next panel. In the next panel, the man smiles. We could say that being aware of our creative nature is learning how to make the sun come up, learning how to create a new sun every day. Though I know not everyone will travel this far on life's journey, I would say that no education is complete short of that destination. Although not all of us will reach that level of awareness, education does require that we all at least know of the possibility. Our classes must never foster the idea that the sun comes up every day. When we do we treat life as a cliché, and then experience becomes a drug instead of unmolded clay. Students need lots of experience in unclichéing their worlds. "A man should stir himself with poetry," says Gary Snyder, "stand firm in ritual / complete himself in music."

So it is a matter of getting in tune with, in *touch* with, our nerve endings, which paradoxically is getting in touch with our selves, the nonconscious wellsprings of well-being. Paradoxically again, tuning up our sensorium for more direct experience involves lots of wordplay, fooling around with words, so that we can get glimpses beyond them. Whitman said, "The substantial words are in the ground and sea. They are in the air, they are in you." True, but we are led back to that threshold *via* his words, his metaphors. And we must not linger there. We must take the next step, as in this incident recorded in Paul Weinphal's *Zen Diary:*

> Walking back, I again have the experience of identification with the world. However, this time the identification is with a bamboo tree. Standing before it, I first have a brotherly feeling for it. Then I feel that it and I are one. I merge with it. It becomes conscious.

The artistic life, the only life worth living, is allowing a bamboo tree to become conscious, allowing a math concept to come alive. Ordinary life is extraordinary. The participant-observer melds with "the first object it looks upon" so that that object gains its being through the consciousness that observer is custodian of. A teacher whose consciousness melds with a student's releases that student's consciousness by recognizing it. "Ah!" says that student. "So that's me!" All it takes is the teacher's attention: "At times you were even more attentive than my dog," wrote Richard Ferreira in his final synthesis. That's the idea. Who gains from this process of witnessing, teacher or students? I think you would have to say, "There is no difference between them. The universe gains. The cosmos has gained consciousness."

That's when the "rich, manifold life" comes to the surface, "close to the eyes." It's the world Thoreau's cleansed senses discovered out at Walden Pond:

> *The morning wind forever blows,*
> *the poem of creation is*
> *uninterrupted; but few are*
> *the ears to hear it.*

We teachers are not really sight and hearing impaired. We just need to calm down and sit still long enough to allow these senses to function magically. When my students and I close our eyes and stop talking, everyone marvels at how bounteous the sound envelope is, the poem of creation.

As I have noted earlier, the person who learns to be "creative" in the sense I have been describing will have no need of busy-ness but will become still, letting go so that things can come in. The bird is allowed to light on the open palm.

Let's Be Practical Here

When I talk about this process, I like to point out its "practical" aspects. For me, the recognized (re-cognized) spirit is quite enough. But when spirit enters *physical* matter, as it does in metaphor, we get architecture, automobiles, luscious fruits and vegetables, melodies, songs, computers. Those who have found their centers become remarkably good at meeting difficulties, knowing what to do in the physical sense, figuring things out. Rather than fearing the unknown, such beings accept their authority and will be good problem solvers. When we are not encumbered with artificiality and clichés, we can see where the problem lies and can work on it directly. So the poetic mode is more practical in the worldly sense than being "practical" could ever be. We creatures are not merely "practical"; we all know we are much more than that. However spirit is defined, however ephemeral it may seem, we do function *spiritually*—as spirits—in this universe. Somehow, we are consciousness and light, and we bring that tone with us in our goings and comings. Teachers and students have the option of awareness. I cannot imagine anyone so degenerate as to deny that we do. There is everything to gain in fostering our artistry and everything to lose in denying it.

Poiēma: The Poem of Creation

As a postscript to this section, let's hear from my teaching assistant Valerie Turner. This is one of her daily reflections, written in January 1987.

It's Not Just Greek to Me

The excitement of what I want to write today may not be adequately expressed in the words I choose; so I'll just tell you right off the bat, I have tingles down my spine! And the meaning behind what I have to say may remain vague, so let's just leave it as rosebuds take their own sweet time to bloom—we watch and interpret the changes as best we can.

I was working on my Sunday-school lesson today when I was struck by one phrase, or more precisely one word. Ephesians 2:10 says, "For we are his *workmanship.* The footnote interpreted this as "the believer is God's handiwork, and is, therefore, the product of God's creative and saving activity." *Workmanship* was given as the translation for the Greek word *poiēma*.

I looked at the word and immediately thought *poem.* I called my friend from the seminary and asked if he had the time to give me a lesson in Greek. We looked through his Greek translation for Ephesians and sure enough there was the word *poiēma*. The commentaries we consulted said that we derived our English word *poem* from the Greek *poiēo* and its derivative *poiēma*.

That made me wonder where we got the idea that a poem was simply lines of verse. I checked out the dictionary. Definitions 1, 2, and 3 were pure literary translations. Definition 4—"a beautiful object or experience" Etymology < Gk. Poiēma, lit., *anything made.*

We then checked the Bible Concordance for other places *poiēma* shows up. In Romans 1:10, the universe is described as God's creative poem, and believers are presented as God's redemptive poem. In each instance the poem is to point beyond itself to the Master Poet whose eternal power, deity, and grace are displayed through His craftsmanship. The life of His people is God's crowning work of Art. "Once he has experienced the grace of God, the believer finds that he devotes himself to good actions because they express the *essence* of his very nature." Sounds like poetry in motion to me!

The word *poiēo* means "doers of the word—an act to express one's inner thoughts and emotions." That fits the definition of a mandala.

How does this tie in to class? I'm sure you see the connection. When I wrote in my journal before that people and the universe are poems, I was writing somewhat abstractly, or metaphorically—but here it is in gospel print. I'm not sure how you meant it when you said everyone and everything can be a poem. Did you mean anything can be the inspiration for a poem? Or were you referring to the deeper essence of what we are?

I realize we are still using metaphors here for a truth that can't be fully expressed in words. But it does give me joy to think of myself as God's poem and of poetry as a spiritual experience. We talked before about the significance of the word—*logos*—as the beginning of creation, so it's only appropriate that a poem be the culmination of the creative power of God.

Clark, you're preaching to these kids whether you know it or not! They are poems and at their deepest and outermost levels they are holy manifestations of God's artwork.

The research I did also made me more excited about writing poetry. What I write can be filled with a spirit and a life of its own. Through words I can breathe life into images or pictures that were formerly held motionless in my head. Maybe there's something to that saying that poets and artists are touched with a divine spark?

Doing Research

Valerie's reflection turned out to be a short research paper, and that reminds me of an ongoing debate among English teachers: Should the research paper be taught at all, and if so, how? I think what happened with Valerie is how. When we care deeply about something, it's rather natural to do research. I have seen it happen again and again in my classes and elsewhere. We are back to motivation. I have seen people who were anything but academic do remarkable research—because they were absorbed. They even go for the niceties and subtleties, as Valerie did checking out *poem*. To be sure, standard footnoting and so forth are not cultivated, but if you check over Valerie's reflection, she does give enough information that her references can be examined. At any rate a good style manual is not so arcane that ordinary people can't master it, if need be.

4

English: What She Is and What She Ain't
A Big Bite of the Apple

A word is dead when it is said, some say.
I say it just begins to live that day.
—Emily Dickenson

Browsing my shelves of books about English and about language, I am still astonished at that mine of rubies, emeralds, diamonds, silver, and gold. To have stumbled on such a mother lode—and get paid for it! Amazing stuff, all pointing to the ghost in the machine, the human spirit expressing itself. Every day my students and I would get out our picks and shovels and see what we could unearth. Were we trying to get rich? What is it about an emerald that enriches us, its market value or its beauty? When we fully realized, fully *experienced*, the relationship between a word and what happens in the mind in relation to it, we got chills up our spines. But we couldn't market that sensation. It didn't have a dollar value. Yet it was no less beautiful than a gem held to the light and clearly seen.

I am sure it is the same in the discipline of English as it is in the discipline of physics. When people asked what theory in quantum mechanics he was trying to prove, Richard Feynman said he wasn't trying to prove anything; he was just trying to get a good look, to see what was there. What motivated him was the pleasure in finding things out. Every once in a while, in our explorations in English, we would *see* something. We would be enjoying drawing or writing or listening and suddenly we would go into a deeper level. The separation between conscious and nonconscious would dissolve. We would be all-at-once, *in* the moment, clairvoyant. We were doing it through the investigation of language; it could just as well have been through history or through music. And language being *the* medium in which all else in a culture is embedded, we often overlapped, as when we traced the history of *thimble, personality, budget, pecuniary, scion,* or a name like *Moore* or *Cecchettini* or *McKowen.*

There wasn't any marketplace value we could put on what we were doing, at least not directly. We were simply taking a good look, and every once in a while we fell into beauty. But that is hard to get across to a school board or the legislature. There are indeed marketplace offshoots of examining how we think and the role of language in thinking, but it is a mistake to focus on them. In most cases, linguistic fluency does indeed follow, and understanding the nuances of language is a key to academic development, but the essence of a liberal education is the courtship of beauty, and that is beyond price. So what we were up to in our English classes was what all disciplines were up to —or ought to have been. Let's put it this way: Beauty is a clear look at one's own soul.

Helen Keller's first realization of language comes to mind. Annie Sullivan had been struggling to show that *d-o-l-l* stood for both Helen's ceramic doll and her rag doll. And she could not get her to distinguish between *m-u-g* and *w-a-t-e-r.* Most readers know the story. After Helen had smashed the ceramic doll in the frustration of not "getting it," Annie had taken her outside and down the path to the pump house. There, Annie held her hand under a stream of gushing water and spelled into the other hand *w-a-t-e-r,* at first slowly, then rapidly.

> I stood still, my whole attention fixed upon the motions of her fingers.
> Suddenly I felt a misty consciousness as of something forgotten—a thrill of returning thought; and somehow the mystery of language was revealed to me.
> I knew that "w-a-t-e-r" meant the wonderful cool something that was flowing over my hand. That living word awakened my soul.
> —Helen Keller, *The Story of My Life*

Education is all about this sort of experience. In our English classes we might be examining the structure of a sentence or the language of a Picasso drawing or the words that made a story melodious. But getting a glimpse of the mystery *beyond* language was always our quest, as I am sure it must be in all other disciplines as well, "a misty consciousness of something forgotten." All the conscious activity is merely to lay the groundwork for that mystical experience. Working in the garden, every once in a while over our shoulder we glimpse the universe unfolding—or a butterfly. We spend our years in school to realize it is a human being's role to witness and merge with this flowering.

Like Helen Keller we are trying to remember something, something we forgot. When we do, "it becomes almost physical," as one student wrote, "(but then we can't ever separate mental and physical), but anyway my body reacts. Tension builds sort of. Some of the things I've written stagger me with their implications." We have reports from Marcel Proust, too, and G. K. Chesterton's "forgotten blaze"—that "burst of astonishment at our own existence." The object of an artistic and spiritual life (in a word, *education*) is indeed to dig for that submerged sunrise of wonder.

For me this fusion of physical and spiritual is a definition of education. It is the essence of teaching and learning. Anything that goes on in an English class is fundamentally for that emergence of wonder. Meanwhile, schoolmen and -women, at least in the public institutions, have to sell their programs to taxpayers and over the years have fallen into the trap of selling education as a commodity, something quantifiable. "Gimme a pound of beauty. Plastic's OK." The United States and society in general are more and more a market economy. It is almost embarrassing even to hint at wonder, joy, beauty, and mystery. The accountants want to see numbers, not spiritual angels dancing on metaphoric pins.

So every once in a while, one of my practical colleagues would decide that the English Department was out to lunch and would write an article in our staff journal about how poorly our students write or read or talk. No one ever complained about kids not getting pleasure from stories, poems, or novels; not appreciating multifaceted metaphor; and so on. Invariably, it was unedited writing or brazen use of their own dialects: in other words, window dressing, never the beauty of the moment, never the joy of discovery, that concerned my colleagues. Just for fun, I decided to send a little something to the *Forum* to suggest the sorts of things we actually do in English classes. Here is how that went.

> ### Minding Our Own Business
>
> Daryl in the chem lab sure knows a lot about my business. He'll have to get in line. Everybody—backhoe operators, chemistry teachers, my big brother—knows a lot about my business. They are always telling me how to teach English, what kids ought to know, how they ought to talk, what bad "grammar" they got. I would be more responsive if they would let me return the favor. I have some neat ideas about how to teach typing, how to sop up blood

in operating rooms, and certainly how my brother ought to train his German shorthairs. Getting back to my own business, here is what an English teacher thinks it's all about.

What language—in our case, English—is is the avenue of the human spirit for its outerance into the physical world. What students of English do is explore myriad aspects of this miracle, not to alter their table manners but to bear witness, to kindle a lifelong fascination with this uniquely human phenomenon. English is a humane study, one of the humanities, intimately related to the entire culture of the English-speaking world, and indeed is its mirror and vice-versa. Spirit embedded in matter. Language is nature thinking about itself.

English is a journey out of India through Germany into the lands of the Jutes, Angles, Saxons, and back again and on to China, South Africa, and Australia.

English is a daisy, the day's eye, the eye of the day: Metaphor. An attempt, collectively, of human beings to express their experience of the universe.

It is, "For all the history of grief, an empty doorway and a maple leaf":* Poetry.

It is the spirit and meaning of events. "Once upon a time, long, long ago": Literature.

It is rhythm and music, air shaped by intention. Individually unique and commonly shared.

Dialects, pronunciations, paralanguage, structures, vocabulary.

It is semantics, linguistics, the vehicle through which we explore history, political science, physics, mathematics, and tomatoes.

It is much, much more and it is beautiful.

It is not penmanship. It is not "expository prose."

When I came to DVC in 1963, the English Department was in the midst of defining its discipline and itself. No other English program I know of has achieved such depth and breadth. Our discoveries flew in the face of tradition and convention. So there were battles. Could we teach freshman English in the context of culture, as language, as a humane study? How did it all fit together, was there a central focus out of which it all grew?

Since there was no model, we had to learn our content and our method as we went along and somehow keep it all consistent with how people learn, how

---

*From "Ars Poetica" by Archibald MacLeish.

we grow and change. Our struggles made us different, forced us all to articulate our views. It was continuous in-service.

We have learned and are still learning, but one thing we know: We are not TAs for political science teachers. Or physics teachers or business teachers. We know something about how people develop in their use of language. We could advise other teachers on how to avoid interfering with this process. If they want their students to write, we could show how to encourage that.

But we will not do their work for them. We have our own business to attend to. In so brief a time, we can only scratch the surface. And our students may never, ever again have such an opportunity for exploring and investigating their own language.

Teachers of other disciplines who are willing to learn something new could enroll in one of our freshman English classes and thereby, perhaps, help dispel the pervasive ignorance in the academic world of its most fundamental discipline. They might even pick some silver apples of the moon or golden apples of the sun.*

So how do you like *them* apples, Daryl?

Chasing Our Own Tails

I wanted to give our staff a feel for what really goes on in an English class, what sorts of things we give our attention to, and I wanted them to realize correctness and precision in writing and speaking were no more our bailiwick than theirs, from secretaries to math teachers to the college president. English is a distinct discipline with subject matter such as I touched on in my article.

(I also wanted to hint at an *attitude* toward teaching. As I have said throughout this book, correcting people is wrong. It is an insult to the human spirit and presupposes a hierarchy of authority I cannot abide. But if we *wanted* to teach a skill, as I have pointed out, we would not do it by finding fault. We are most efficient when we find and point out appropriate behavior. Instead of seeking out the negative, we look for the positive. At the very least there will be fewer neuroses.)

But it isn't the fault of Daryl or my brother or the PTA that they have these limited ideas about our field. After all, where did they get those views but from all those years in English classes? English teachers themselves

---

*As William Butler Yeats might have been inclined to phrase it.

drilled diction, marked up compositions, put the humanities on the back burner. There were precious few John Wheatcrofts out there lingering over a Keats poem or a Millie Martin relishing a gorgeous periodic sentence. So of course those determining where the tax dollar goes think we ought to get tougher on the cretins slipping into upper-level classes.

Any change in how schools and the public regard the field of English studies would have to begin in English classes. As I began focusing on the heart of the discipline—and indeed the *heart* of education is what this book is all about—I realized that most of us English teachers were flying by the seat of our pants. My colleagues—and I must admit, I myself—simply had not thought it through, or at least not deeply. It is indeed a complex matter. Even if English teachers gave three cheers for all the things I touched on in my article, there is still the problem of how to stuff it all in without chaos. There has to be a center. It can't be a little of this, a little of that.

Meanwhile, I was noticing what was actually passing for English studies among my colleagues. What a mess! There didn't seem to be any cohesion. We all had our own ideas. So, in 1963 I got that off my chest in an article I sent to the *English Journal*. Here it is.

> *English for Everyone*
>
> I never did nothing like this before, but I made a little jack out of this root beer and hamburger joint I got, and being as I'm twiddling my thumbs around the pool all winter anyway, I figured even if all this writing don't pay off I can take it off my income tax, so what the heck.
>
> By the time I graduated State U, I figure I seen about every kind of English teacher in the business, what with all those courses I kept taking so as to get into freshman English and out of high school English. I'm what you might call an Expert on the English-teacher business. But what got me thinking about them (English teachers) was my wife, Kate; see, once we got the root beer wrung out of the greens, she started fancying up and wanted some classy magazines to leave around on the inlaid walnut end tables. Well, one was open on a story called What Is English? by some guy what's been working at it up in Harvard for twelve years and don't know yet. Well, that made me feel pretty comfortable, because to tell you the truth I been kind of uneasy about that myself. I seen right away I wasn't going to do better than this expert. But, like I said, I watched plenty of them come and go, and got pretty good at figuring them, knowing what they thought it was, even if they didn't know what they thought it was, if you get what I mean.
>
> Almost all of them figured it would make me *better* some way, even though they never asked me if I wanted to be, which I have to say I didn't particularly.

I was raking it in pretty good even in high school and have since found being better always hits me in the pocketbook. But I was always willing to let them have a go at it. When you aren't feeling any pain, it's easy to be tolerant.

They had it pretty clear that it was reading books, but it was always entertaining to figure out *why* each one thought this was so. Some had a sort of antique-shop approach. If it had enough mold on it, it was a good book. It had stood the test of time, they said. They would give your choice the smell test. If the nostrils quivered and the old girls begun to pant, you were in; if the nose went too far up, you had had it.

They told us all about these old writing people living very low on the hog, being ignored by everybody, sitting around waiting to stand the test of time, which is why they died broke, I guess, because I estimate it takes about a hundred years. I was getting some kicks out of *Arrowsmith*, *The Human Comedy*, and *Jeeves*, but I naturally gave them up when I found out some of them weren't even fifty years old. I gave up newspapers and magazines, too, of course. They must of known what they were talking about, because I have not felt any loss. Lately I filled up Kate's inlaid walnut bookcase to the satisfaction of her couth friends by saying to the bookseller, "Leave me have anything over one hundred years old." (These teachers also favor antique English, which they use themselves, and I have tried it but have not found it very useful in closing a deal.)

The way this antique method was supposed to work was you say to somebody, "Dickens." He comes back, "Tale of Two Cities." You counter with, "Great Expectations." Whoever gives up first is losers. Or you can play it with quotations or characters. This is termed Knowing Your Cultural Heritage. There are not too many people in my line who are familiar with the rules, so I have got rusty over the years. Six years ago this old gal comes in for a ham submarine and I got as far as "Old Curiosity Shop" and had to throw in the sponge. But that was not a fair contest. Her language gave her away as one of the greatest antique methoders in the racket.

One sporty old girl, Millie, sort of looked at herself as a haberdasher. (I guess, looking back at it, that was what most of them had in mind some way or another.) She was great at fitting us out in literary duds and language finery. When we got to her she could see good enough that we were most of us decked out pretty shabby. If you came out of her shop so anybody could still recognize who you were or where you came from you could see she was sad about it. She dressed up two guys from my neighborhood so good that people kept mixing them up. They both went up to State to teach eventually. I understand some wiseacre in the department for some reason or other calls them Rosencrantz and Guildenstern.

You can't tell a book by its cover, but what about its dust jacket? I have to admit old Millie had a pretty good thing going. See, the "in" group had all the goodies. How to get them? Well, you had to learn how to imitate them, of course. Good old Millie had been in, knew all their secrets *and* the password and was ready to help everybody else get in, too. This took a lot of cocktail drinking and a back-breaking dose of small talk, but Millie took it all without complaining—which shows you what a generous sort she was. (But I couldn't help thinking if everybody could pass, how could the ins tell who was out?) What you did was like find out what book the ins were talking about and what they were saying about it. (Millie cut us in on all that.) Then you find one tidbit, a sexy one if possible, that you drop into the yakking while raising one eyebrow and trading an empty for a full. Hell, there's nothing to it once you get the hang of it. I even passed the system on to Kate who is now getting along swell with her snooty friends because of it. Me, I'm always sticking out the wrong finger. But I'll be glad to pass on Millie's system to anyone who has some use for it.

Then there was Ruthie who took her English like the Puritans took their religion—come to think of it, English *was* a religion. Shakespeare the Father, Wordsworth the Son, Chaucer the Holy Ghost. I don't believe any of these fellows ever went to the toilet, they were that pure and fine. Ruthie stashed a few icons of these saints around the room: kinda got you in the proper frame of mind to receive the word. Why, holding a copy of the *Lyrical Ballads* was the next best thing to going to church. And Ruthie wouldn't put up with any foolishness from other teachers either: One newcomer (didn't last long) read *Twisted Tales from Shakespeare* to his class after they read *Macbeth*. You should have seen Ruthie light into him! Scurrilous, said she. Sacrilegious, say I. Of course, our writing and speech had to be sanctified, too. See, Ruthie knew that there is a pure form of English somewhere, handed down from God like the Holy Grail or the Ten Commandments. Well, if God's taking that much interest in how we speak English, busy as He must be policing all of the other languages of the world, why, it'd be downright ungrateful not to speak it the way he does. Ruthie went up on the mountain and got the word like a prophet and passed it on to us. You couldn't ask for a better soul. As you can see, I've done considerable backsliding, languagewise, but they got you going and coming anyway, so it might as well be for bad grammar as for stealing or beating your wife. And I really don't think I could of made any money Ruthie's way. It just didn't seem to go with superburgers.

There was a whole bunch that considered the types I just told you about as spouting a lot of foolishness. These were the drill masters: hard, tough, nononsense cookies. I'd rather get a traffic ticket than have one of them on my back. We did everything by the number. We'd get into freshman English, by God, or there'd be hell to pay. Boy! First you got the sentence down pat—every word of it. And buddy, you'd better know the part of speech of every word. And then the paragraph (usually we didn't get that far). Write a paragraph using contrast, comparison, argument, definition. Underline THE topic sentence.

Oh, it was slick. But the peak, the absolute tops, was THE 500-WORD THEME. Thesis sentence, transitional device, three paragraphs each with transitional device and topic sentence (the body), THE conclusion. When you're up against it like that and the heat's on, naturally you try to cheat a little—which, with my born gift for the capitalistic system, I was pretty good at—so I figured I'd just find a few of these 500-word themes and copy them—to make the gals and guys happy. I never could find a 500-word theme in any books I hunted through. None in Thoreau or Jefferson or Franklin or Mill or Dale Carnegie or Norman Vincent Peale. Well, I had to hand it to them, figuring out a thing like that. Nobody that I could find ever wrote a 500-word theme—at least for publication. You have to admire someone who knows writers and writing good enough to find just the one thing the kids couldn't find samples of to steal from. Now, those were teachers!

And they weren't in a rut on writing either. Why, they could make work out of anything. They were geniuses when it came to poetry. We classified and sorted every poem we got our hands on. We put little marks above every syllable (some of them make awful pretty designs, especially if you used different colored ink), counted the feet, which anybody can see is important when there's more than two of them, and found all sorts of figures of speech. I can tell you, I really developed a healthy respect for a poem. When there's that much work in something it *has* to be good. Besides, you have to protect your investment. We learned to step lightly around anything where every line began with a capital but didn't end with a period. And I guess that's what they were after. You wouldn't want just anybody slopping around something as serious as all that.

What great military minds those English teachers would of been. They had system. They had fire. They had grit. They could deploy their regiments, prepare battle plans, bowl the enemy (the entrance tests—or the student, whichever seemed to need it) over with ruthless force. You have no idea how useful their kind of training is in preparing a person for battling the bankers for a 4 1/2 percent loan. For Christmas, I send K rations to some of my favorites. Before, I was kind of easy going; they made a man out of me—for which Uncle Sam and me are both better, me for the increased jack, him for the taxes.

There are lots of other types, some jumping back and forth among the ones I already told about. There really isn't any two of them that much alike. That's the wonder of it. It was good, you know what I mean? Just like life—unpredictable variety. You think you've seen everything and up pops a new type. It takes footwork to keep up. That's what I liked about it; it fitted right in with the side-stepping and out-guessing I was doing already in the business game.

One semester, I had a guy who was pretty good to us. I think they call him a clean-desk man. In his class you knew what to expect pretty quick. That's comforting. You came in, got the workbook, did the exercise, had a monitor correct it, and another one put your grade in the book. Then you read four pages in *Kidnapped*, answered the questions on the board, and that grade was recorded as per the above. Every three weeks you turned in a book report, and the monitor gave you credit and put it in the wastebasket. Old clean-desk sat in the back of the room getting teaching materials from a stack of *National Geographics* and *Lifes*. He got sick ten days a year—some sort of lung disease, I guess, because sometimes when I had to go to the trout streams to restore my own health, I'd see him going through the mountains very fast in his MG with the top down, one of them French tams on his head, breathing lots of that pure air. It was sad. But he wasn't one of these complainers. He went right on gathering educational materials right through the summer—when he should of been resting—in Acapulco, New Orleans, Hawaii, and Las Vegas. I'm glad to tell you he has had some good luck, though. The way he ran his class got so well known that he won the best-teacher award for the county. He went into administration, where his clean-desk techniques won him wide acclaim; he is now superintendent of schools.

Miss Maud taught us how to talk on the phone, how to write a friendly letter, how to conduct a business meeting, how to apply for a job, how to talk on a date—lots of practical stuff like that. But she wasn't very well thought of. I don't see why. I think at the bottom of it she was working for the same sort of goals as the haberdasher type was. Maybe the duds weren't as fancy, but she got you clothed and comfortable, and she *was* helping you get on in the world, just like the others. And probably you can use her stuff for a lot more mileage than the cocktail or tea variety.

The butterfly approach was one of my favorites. Part of the fun was seeing what kind of getup Miss Ina would have on: Oriental sheath with a six-inch side-slit for haiku, bulky sweater, leotards, and flats for reading Ginsberg, and so on. Up close the make-up was kinda flaky, but from a distance it blended together like a van Gogh. I often thought how profitable it would be for my carhops to study her for a while.

In the butterfly method, the technique was to nibble at Frost, dip into Freud, hint at Henry Miller, Caldwell, and *Hecate County*. Then flit to being creative with FREE verse and short stories. We spent some time dallying with Wordsworth's unbrotherly relations with his sister and that French business, Byron and Augusta, Shakespeare's young male friend. I believe we also did something with the *Decameron* and something called fabliaux from Chaucer. If the object was to get you to remember those guys, it worked, because I still do. Miss Ina had quite a book that told the secret lives of the great writers— which was far superior to *True Romance* and *Confidential* because it required so much more research. Yep, she knew just what it took to hold your interest. I must say it was entertaining. I believe you were supposed to get appreciation from the course. I certainly did; it was classy. Her chief words were *exciting*, *dilettante*, *fun*, *risque*, and *bizarre*.

One good thing about English was that any number could play. See, it was so important that they often had to bring in teachers from other fields like history, art, P.E., language, and woodshop. It was a treat to get one of these, because they were very versatile at tying in their specialities. One year we studied for vocabulary terms like *tone*, *abstract*, *perspective*, *vanishing point*, *focus*, *surrealist*, *impressionist*; read biographies of Matisse, Brueghel, Picasso; wrote essays on "Mixing Watercolors" and "How to Decorate a Room for Twenty Dollars." Another time we read books like *Build Your Own Six-Room House for Fun and Profit*; wrote essays on "How to Build a Dove Cote from Peach Lugs," "An End Table with a Difference," and "The Six Most Important Tools for a Beginning Woodshop and Why"; and listened to lectures on how to use a miter box. Vocabulary: *dowel*, *six-penny*, *tourniquet* (just in case), *tongue and groove*, *joist*. If you got a speech teacher, you got very good at three-minute speeches; the drama guy would oblige with an eight-week unit on the history of the theater; the Latin teacher did a lot of stuff with roots and prefixes and suffixes. I think you're probably getting the idea pretty good. You could get a liberal education without even stepping out of the English classroom. At the time, I thought it must of been accidental, but now I realize that somebody up high must've planned it that way. You couldn't get so much variety just by chance.

What with all that background and all and the great training it gave me in figuring out people (which is a *must* in business), you'd think I ought to of been more than satisfied. And for the most part I was. Mostly you figured things out pretty quick, knew which side the bun was buttered on and all, and could settle down and be comfortable. Things were figured out for you, and you knew the teacher knew what was good for you, and everything fitted into place. But there was one guy I'm afraid I can't compliment. I just showed you what English is all about, and there wouldn't be any doubt at all (that's the way I like things) but this guy kind of messed things up on me.

First off, he didn't *look* like an English teacher, and he didn't talk like one. You know how they clip their words off like they spent a long time in England or something and how they say things like, "I should be pleased if you would . . ." or "It is I" or "With whom do you wish to speak?" You know, very elegant and careful. Well, he looked and dressed like just any other American, and he talked just like any other American. That's unsettling. But the real trouble was he didn't have any idea what English was about or what it was for. He'd ask the dumbest questions. He started out asking, "Well, what are you all doing here? What's an English class for? You already can read the sports page and the funnies; isn't that good enough? What do you expect me to do? Why should the taxpayers spend money on this nonsense? Why read if you can get just as much fun out of playing tennis?" Well, naturally, with all my background I tried to help the poor devil out, but when I tried to explain English to him he'd keep interrupting with dumb questions like "Why? So what? Who cares?" He was the thickest cluck I ever run into. And inconsistent—he'd watch television and turn right around and go to a French movie—but I doubt he ever got anything out of them, probably kept saying, "Now, why did he do that?"

Then you'd write something nice for him out of the encyclopedia and what would he do? He'd say, "So what? What's this got to do with you? What's it have to do with an English class? Who cares? Do you?" I got the idea that he thought there was too much writing in the world already, and if you didn't have something you really wanted to get off your chest, you shouldn't bother. You'd give him a paper: "What do you want me to do with it?" And he wouldn't tell you ANYTHING. He'd play tapes and show movies (big violation of rules right there) and then he wouldn't tell you what you were supposed to see in them. Instead, he'd say, "What did you get out of it? What good does it do to know that?" Then, he'd expect you to tie everything together. He'd play some *Mark Twain Tonight* and Bob Newhart and ask if there was any relationship or if they were related to a *Peanuts* cartoon or *Mad* magazine, for God's sake. Then, if you'd baby him and *find* some relationships (which did surprise the heck out of me, actually), he'd turn around and say, "What good does it do you to know that?" Just to show you how weak and poor he was, he wouldn't even diagram. "What would I want to do that for?" he asked. Once he showed a film on language and the guy in it said, "We study language to find out what human beings are like." Then this nut turns right around and asks us, "Well, now, how in the world could that be true?" What did he show the film for, if he didn't believe it himself? And what good does it do you to know what human beings are like? Where's the money in that?

Oh, it was bad, I can tell you. You could never get comfortable. Everything came unstuck. Pretty soon you got so you were asking questions yourself, no kidding. You couldn't be satisfied anymore. It was a damned *disease*. And *he* gave it to us. What happens to all your comfort and ease that you worked so hard for? It's gone, that's what, and unless you're very lucky, you're ruined for life. It puts an awful load on a person, what with no help and having to figure things out and all that. I mean, teachers are supposed to *tell* you stuff, aren't they? Can you imagine what would happen if *all* English teachers got infected by a guy like that?

I guess that's why they got rid of him. I don't like to see anybody out of work, but there are limits, and you do have to think of the welfare of the kids. Besides, where would this great country be today if everybody was so ignorant he had to go around asking Why? all the time? I can certainly see why English teachers would want him stopped. I mean, you wouldn't want the kids asking *why* study English? There was enough of that already among the clods that couldn't adjust to the haberdashers and antique-shop proprietors and so forth. But it was to the credit of those real English teachers that the clods were flunked out fast. Anyone in business knows you've got to agree with the boss. There's no room for doubters. It's an act of faith.

I wouldn't want to act smart about it, but I do want to help that Harvard guy out who doesn't know what English is. There's nothing to it. English is what the teacher wants it to be. It's manners, for the telephone or the cocktail party; it's a way to fool the enemy—clothes to put over your naked self so you can get in and get what you want from the swells; it's a pastime; it's a hobby; it's knowing the right things to revere—books, authors, the right names or words to drop; it's a game to play, like crossword puzzles or bridge; it's following the fads; it's one-up-manship. These things make you better. If they don't, they're supposed to, and that's what counts.

But you might get in some class and a guy stands up there and starts asking foolish questions like, "What's communication for? What does the study of language tell you about what it is to be a human being? What's language for? Why do writers write anyway?" Well, you'll know they're at it again, and the best thing to do is transfer out and get a real English class where things are orderly and the teacher has her feet on the ground. If you move fast, you may get out before *you* start asking questions. No telling where that might lead.

Well, I didn't make this 500 words and didn't underline the main head and topic sentences and what not, but maybe the English teachers will overlook it being as I'm doing this for them as a favor.

Readings on Education

For several semesters at our college, I gave in-service workshops for our staff. I "taught" the same way I conducted my English classes. Everything we did was exploratory, investigative, and reflective. Teachers turned out to be just as responsive as students. Why not? The surface features of human beings are infinitely variable, but the wellspring is the same. That means we can—we must—be ourselves, but we have a common ground of being, too. It was touching to see how hungry everyone was for something more of the depths and heights. We had some good talks.

One semester the workshop was called "Readings on Education." There were seven or eight teachers from various disciplines. We generated the course as we went along, and everyone wrote reflections and a synthesis at the end, just as in my regular classes. We also read six or seven books by teachers or about teaching, among then, *To Teach, To Love* by Jesse Stewart, *The Way It Spozed to Be* by James Herndon, *Teacher* by Sylvia Ashton-Warner, *The Water Is Wide* by Pat Conroy, *Journey to Ixtlan* by Carlos Castaneda, and *Zen Diary* by Paul Wienpahl. I found these teachers just as enthusiastic (I love the etymology of that word!) as the students. Something Sylvia Ashton-Warner wrote may explain why. We had many "moments" in our workshops. Those moments, I think, are what teaching—life—is all about. Ashton-Warner wrote:

> At each of those times I saw the meaning of life and knew that I saw it. . . . Every time I reached those heights, I said, "All my life before and my life after is justified by the wonder of this moment." I am inspired to go on because I have seen the meaning myself.

The message of those workshops was obvious: Teachers, like all creatures, want to experience their moments intensely. I am sure if all those teachers I wrote about in "English for Everyone" got down to it, they would be just as passionate for lives filled with moments.

Even though I despair at those empty moments in typical classrooms, I do know all beings, students and teachers alike, would give anything for intense living. It is as necessary to the spirit as water to the body. In a few hours of dialogue, teachers in those workshops figured things out that had been subliminal concerns all their careers. It isn't all that complicated. All we did was wipe away some of the dust and get a clear look. Here are a few paragraphs from the synthesis of one of the participants in the "Readings on Education" workshop.

At first I couldn't get this synthesis to come out right. It wasn't comfortable. So I tried it again and liked it better this time. So that's what you're stuck with:

It seems the closer we get to something (the atom, the grammar of a language, the origin of mankind, and so forth) the fewer the truths we can say about it. The paraphernalia we constructed to make it all work seem ludicrous and emerge as supports for the scientist's doubts rather than efficient mechanisms for productive interaction with the target environment.

It's the same with teaching. I was taught how to make lesson plans, how to construct reliable and valid tests, how to treat students, how to get the message across. We graduates of the early fifties knew a lot—most of which I do not now know. But instead of feeling rotten about it, I feel great. In place of knowledge I've developed improved perception. I see more at a glance than analysis ever yielded.

This seminar has brought me, it seems, to the threshold of a third departure in my teaching behavior. It is not just the seminar, of course; it includes conferences I've attended, a new course in reading and study skills I'm trying, workshops and consultants we've had here at DVC, my own experiments with second-semester freshman English and, more probable, the natural development, mental/physical, of the organization of cells called me.

Thinking about this seminar and writing reflections about my teaching have brought it all to a head. For me, nothing works better than pondering on a regular basis aspects of teaching that bug me. It gives me a strong base from which I can be very sloppy. That is, with a center I can be loose. When I don't have one, sloppiness is unbearable.

Our dialogues were as helpful as the books we read. In fact, we could have had those discussions without the books at all—except that having read them made us fellow adventurers. All of us had been somewhere together and had come back to talk about it in our own way. That last sentence clears up another puzzle for me. I wanted to discuss methods and philosophy, but hardly anyone else seemed focused there. Now it's simple. If we had all been across Africa together, we would *not* have expected each other to focus on any one thing. Instead, each would have his/her own tale to tell, and we would all enjoy hearing each other's take on our adventure. So in our classes and in in-service workshops, once we've been through something together, we will not expect sameness but will figure on lots of variety. In fact, it is impossible for any two travelers to take the same trip.

My own bias centered on the underlying mechanisms of each learning situation, and it does seem to me, as diverse as the books we read were, they all did point toward one destination. Herndon was the extreme participant observer. He had the guts to allow students to generate their authentic interests. He *was* teaching, though. The environment he created was itself a teaching method. The environment was the method. Herndon got that right. You can't do much with an uncommitted mind. He rejected good-for-you education. I do too. "But, gee, I'd never have learned drama if they hadn't forced me!" In that case, I'd rather you hadn't.

In Wienpahl's case, there he is laboriously studying philosophy, learning the subtle differences, sweating over Kant and Locke. I would have said he was wasting his time. But look what happened. No, he did not get a philosophy of life from barking up the wrong tree, but he did get something he hadn't counted on: the ability to stay with something. Without that he would not have been able to cope with his first real teacher, the Zen master. From a distance it looks like the arrow was headed straight for the bull's eye all along. My basic teaching principle is that if I should ever get a Wienpahl in one of my classes and he wants to spend twenty years doing something I consider stupid, I will let him. He may well get something he hadn't counted on—which is what he was really looking for in the first place. "My habits protect my life," said Mark Twain. "They would probably kill you."

But what if a *teacher* wants to put a Paul Wienpahl through such drudgery? Maybe even that is OK. If a student has the option of taking or not taking that teacher's class, things will probably be all right. You won't find people who have free access to authentic growth choosing tedium.

When to behave like don Juan or the roshi? At some times and with some people. I think we will know when it's appropriate—if we have learned to listen and observe. Someone like Herndon *could* take action. Self-actualizing people enjoy making decisions, even for other people, but their joy is the actualizing process itself. They love being in the midst of that growth and *will get out of the way* whenever they can.

Pat Conroy was so full of himself I would not worry about all of the mistakes he made. His thrust was pure enough that his presence among the kids was growth enhancing and not counterproductive. He was a somewhat unconscious model. But his vivacity was perceived and emulated by the kids. Kids have to witness *somewhere* someone who has not given up; indeed someone who prevails—not necessarily in the material sense, but spiritually, never *feeling* defeated. Or if defeated, able to rise up again and laugh and go on—till death comes.

If these writers demonstrate anything, it is their distinctly different personalities and styles of teaching. There is no one way to do it. The more actualized teachers are, the less their work is going to resemble anyone else's. All of these teachers created their own universes. This authority over their own lives is illuminating; it goes beyond any calculus problem a class might be doing. The medium in which the problem is being worked on is what students really absorb. The principles of calculus may fade, but that environment will have a lasting influence.

This workshop is all about cleaning up my act. The clearer and more centered my behavior is, the easier it will be for students to get the idea of how they can be. A methods class isn't about how to do things; it's about how to be.

5

Why Teach the Native Tongue?
Mirror and Window

Before Names

*I don't care about the word, that's commonplace.
What I want is the grand chaos that spins out syntax,
the obscure birthplace of "of," "otherwise,"
"nevertheless," and "how," all those inscrutable
crutches I walk on.
Who understands language understands God,
Whose Son is the Word. It kills you to understand.
Words only hide something deeper, deaf and dumb,
something invented to be silenced.
In moments of grace, rare as they are,
you'll be able to snatch it out: a live fish
in your bare hand.
Pure terror.*

—Adélia Prado

If we want human beings and not automatons teaching our English classes, the environment of each classroom will have to be unique. There is no way to make classes and teachers interchangeable. We all do our best work, students and teachers alike, in authentic environs. Most of the teachers I satirized in "English for Everyone" were well meaning. It was the unfocused English classes that bothered me. Most English teachers are doing the best they can. That is probably why students are willing to put up with so much nonsense and are so compassionate toward ineffectual activities. By encouraging teachers to be themselves in the classroom, though, institutions can get better teaching from these human beings. That would free them to level with the students and not profess things they are unsure of or simply do not know. That would be a leg up. "I don't know" has a nice ring to it. We should practice saying it.

So personalities or styles aren't the problem. It is something deeper, like Noam Chomksy's idea of deep grammar. Chomsky's theory is that each human being is born with a biological pistol, cocked and waiting to be triggered by a language environment. Every biologically normal infant will assimilate whatever language envelope—Spanish, Japanese, Hopi—it finds itself within. If there are several, it will acquire them all with equal ease, like learning both WordPerfect *and* Word or using a PC *and* a Mac. Likewise, we should not be surprised at the variety of programs "spoken" in English classes. But what is the "deep grammar" of all of them? That is what we need to find out. We need to know where we are coming from.

Most of the ideas in this book apply to teaching in general, regardless of the field or discipline. All education takes its cues from the deep grammar of learning. In that sense, we are all doing the same thing, and in that sense our classes will all be the same. Kids in France learn French the same way Navajos learn their tongue. Likewise, the deep grammar of learning operates in the study of mathematics as well as in the study of history or the humanities or the native tongue. But at the next level each discipline needs to find its own basis, its own commonality. What are we trying to do when we study mathematics—in *all* mathematics classes? Once we can answer that, there is room for all sorts of variations on *one* theme. We need that awareness in the study of English, too. Why do we require native speakers, people who are already fluent, to study their own language throughout their schooling? What is it all about? What is the common ground?

"English for Everyone" showed lots of ways not to teach English, but it didn't really say why we should bother at all. So the following year I wrote "Why Teach the Native Tongue?" for the *Journal of Secondary Education*, suggesting a basis for all English classes. We all acquire language out of awareness. It is so natural we don't even notice that we did that. Little kids get a big kick out of blowing bubbles, gurgling, imitating significant speech sounds. They just do it; it is not something they think about consciously. Within two years' time they crack the code and continue for a while longer shaping up their language facility and having a good time at it. By ninth grade, however, this fascination levels off, and by twelfth grade for most people language has become invisible. Like touch typing or driving a car, it is something we do but not something we are conscious of. If it gets the job done, why would we also think about it?

The answer is if we don't think about it, we can never take charge of our own lives. Our minds will be bound, even imprisoned, by the very faculty that should have liberated us. College students use their minds to perform all sorts of mental feats, but most hardly ever notice the mechanism. Few have even a clue about how the mind works, what makes it work. The ghost in the machine is invisible. That wouldn't be a problem except that the spirit—the self, the soul—is what it's all about. Or maybe who we are is *not* what it's all about, but we can't even discover *that* without examining language—the lens through which we catch a glimpse, now and then, of our selves. How can we pursue happiness if we haven't examined "we" or "happiness" or "pursuit"? And how about the way those words fit together? In some linguistic worlds the idea might not even be possible. There are cultures in which pursuing happiness is unthinkable, unthinkable because there is no structure in which to consider it. These are linguistic matters, having to do with syntax, semantics, metaphor. Our ideas about ourselves are stored in linguistic structures. These may or may not be giving us an accurate impression of what's what. So our only recourse, short of taking everything for granted, is to mess around with the mechanism and get some feel for how it works—or doesn't work. For most people, language itself is unthinkable, like the fish that never discovers water. My eye can see everything else, but it cannot see itself. So how do I see my eye? By reflection, indirectly. Catching a glimpse is a tricky business, but somebody's gotta do it.

A Spirit Quest

Why study our native tongue? To get a look at our selves, a spirit quest? For we do use language to witness the world. It does appear that "the world" and the "self" are really just one thing going on, so the whole business is narcissistic. Nobody knows for sure, but whatever we are up to, language is at the center. We do our research through language, in language, as language. (Logic: *logos*, a word, speech, thought.) Reasoning, *thinking*, is a linguistic activity (linguistic: *lingua*, the tongue).

> *In the beginning was the Word, and the Word*
> *was with God, and the Word was God.*
> *He was in the beginning with God;*
> *all things were made through him*
> *and without him was not anything made that was made.*
> *In him was life, and the life was the light of men.*
> *The light shines in the darkness,*
> *and the darkness has not overcome it. . . .*
> *The true light that enlightens every man was coming into the world.*
> *He was in the world, and the world was made through him,*
> *Yet the world knew him not. . . .*
> *And the Word became flesh and dwelt among us,*
> *full of grace and truth;*
> *we have beheld his glory.*
>
> —from the Revised Standard
> Version of the *Bible*

In its poetic ambiguity this passage can be all about Father, Son, and Holy Ghost, but it can also be taken as a blueprint of what happened when human beings acquired language. Just about every culture in the world puts the Word at the center of everything. Glance at it one way and the passage is humanity's relationship to God. But simultaneously it is about the effect of language on flesh, of spirit (*spiritus*, breath, the soul, life) on matter, and the fusion of sense and non . . . sense, thingness and no-thingness. There is no way to escape it. Language and the deepest and highest reaches of life are intimately related, one thing going on. Taken metaphorically, Father, Son, and Holy Ghost can be a way of describing the relationship between the Word—language—and the creatures with which it is joined.

Sometimes a Zen master will say to a novice, "Haven't you forgotten something?" It's not an unzipped fly or a burner left on under a teakettle. What we forget, unless we make it our business to remind (re-mind) ourselves, is the Word, what it means to use language. Clearly, this constant refreshing of linguistic awareness is more akin to playing music or dancing than to table manners or the getting of coin. The world was made through the Word, and the world forgot. That's Chesterton's forgotten blaze, the astonishment at our own existence.

So we study our own tongue to stay in touch with the wonder of our own lives. If we do not, we lead mean lives. We become obsessed with dispensables. When I was a high school English Department chairman, I remember spending a half hour discussing our writing program with our new principal, only to discover, to my amazement, he thought we were talking about penmanship. The window dressing is *not* what the study of the native language is all about. My classes might indeed get up a pretty good investigation of calligraphy; that's another way to talk about the beauty of the Word. But I would not want the study of English ever to settle for the surface features only. Our quest is what they point to.

In the Human Realm

This perspective puts exploring our own language squarely in the humanities. Its purpose is spiritual, of the spirit, humane, not utilitarian. Surely that is one thing all English teachers could indeed recognize and endorse. If we could get that far, I would not worry about any topic an English class might dream up. Spelling, punctuation, usage, business letters, and technical writing—all would be fine areas of investigation. Explore spelling as a humane topic, and you will soon be back at the wonder of language, its permutations and its variations. Take up words-on-paper as a subject, and you will soon be looking at morphemic systems, syllabic systems, print that snakes left to right and then right to left, or up and down, front to back, back to front, and so on. You are right back to the wonder of it all, the surprise of it, the miracle. Come to think of it, penmanship could be a wonderful study. Imagine framing one page from each student's folder and making a gallery exhibition.

Classes could indeed explore what's "proper," why it's proper, and if it's proper, but getting students to talk like other people isn't the point. When a class explores "correct" English, everyone has to think about *how language works*, *what it's for*, and *why we bother in the first place*. In a large group, plenty of conventional wisdom, lots of unexamined assumptions, and off-the-cuff ideas will abound, but there will also be profound and penetrating insights. Mix and stir well, allow to steep, and you have a lovely exposition on the use of language. *That's* the point. Everyone begins to get a tingling awareness of what it is to be a user of language.

Just About Anything

Just about anything that pops up in an English class has this potential. If someone says we study our own language in order to be better at communicating, well then, let's see where that idea leads. Is communicating really what we're trying to do when we use language? Or are there lots of reasons? Or is there some other deeper reason? Maybe it's all self-centered, centered on our own selves, and we communicate in order to gather data for an exploration of our own selves. And so on. We never have to settle for superficial answers. Maybe we do indeed end up "better" at reading or writing or public speaking. What keeps up our interest, however, is not utilitarian; it's the sheer pleasure of finding things out. It's Aha! Oh! and Ha!

That's how it could go. It isn't what we talk about; it's how and why we do it in the first place. It's getting down to basics. And the Word became flesh and dwelt among us, full of grace and truth: We have beheld his glory.

Whenever we take a good look, we always end up examining the *language* in which the ideas are embedded. No matter if it's reading a poem, writing a love letter, or kibitzing in large or small groups, some sort of *languaging* is going on. To get into the game we always end up asking about the meaning of the *language* in which the game is programmed. Do we live in a linguistic world? Is language a looking glass or a window on some nonlanguage this-ness? Do words embody spirit? Is it the words of a poem or the spirit or the experience of the artist we seek to merge with—or something else? What is spirit; is it fabricated? Is it one-with, the-same-as, separable-from, language? What's mind? What's brain? What's going on here? *That*, all that, is the discipline of English.

The Subject of Every Discipline

It's the same with other disciplines. In "Teaching into the Future," an address he gave in San Francisco in 1981, Neil Postman said it isn't really "history" students study; they study the *language* in which history is discussed. The discipline of "history" is a point of view about how the world works, what it is "like." In a word, *metaphor*. So if I want to get the feel of "history," it won't be dates and events that will absorb my reflections but the metaphors through which people talk about the ever-changing "past." Think of what a class could do with this statement from the movie *The Go-Between:* "The past is a foreign country; they do things differently there." Studying history is an interfacing of language systems, the students' and the teacher's. Students talk with a native speaker of history and can be said to be fluent when they can dispense with an interpreter. That is, they have caught on to the way historians talk. "History" is a body of linguistic structures, and an alert student gets good at it by asking questions about the language.

Postman went on to say that knowledge is a form of literature. So to study "mathematics" we would benefit by treating the topic as we would a short story. That is, geometry is a "story" expressed in a *manner* of speaking. "There is a rhetoric of knowledge, a characteristic way in which arguments, proofs, speculations, experiments, polemics, even humor, are expressed. One might even say that speaking or writing a subject is a performing art." Learning a subject is a hands-on process, and you have to knead the clay yourself.

The academic world, then, is a world of talk, and *talking about talk* is what goes on in schools. Could any argument for the direct examination of the native tongue be more compelling? But we don't become aware users by being stuffed with lessons. We must all become "linguists"; we have to get good at tinkering with a "story" and getting at its metaphor and then merging with it so that we become native speakers. Throughout the school years, we go to English classes to continue our investigations. Twelfth grade and graduate seminars need be no less wonder-full than kindergarten. Just as we don't get tired of beautiful music, we need never tire of experiencing our language in all its poetic beauty.

Back to Basics

Of course, students love this stuff. We are all fascinated with what it is to be a living creature on a spinning planet in endless oceans of space. Deeper down, we examine language to get a glimpse of our selves. Whatever the subject, we are always holding up a mirror to see what's going on. Sometimes we catch ourselves singing. Sometimes we are marveling at shapes and sizes, multiples and infinite reductions. In our sunlit new brain, in the violet silent deeps, we experience being: inert matter acting up. The discipline of English is much more than "Trivial Pursuits."

When we look at Frost's "To Earthward" or Ohm's Law or Pachelbel's *Canon in D Major*, we are getting someone else's "take." Why do that? To *re . . . mind* ourselves of, to *re . . . cognize*, to *re . . . new*, our vivacity. Why cultivate a vivid life? Because life longs for itself, as Gibran put it? London's call of the wild? "I feel so alive when I feel so alive." What are the basics of English studies? Waking up, coming to, loosening our tongue, using language more actively, with more awareness, having access to the pleasures and nuances. Through reflection, we activate a conduit between our tongue and our mind, between an utterance and its spirit. Or you could call it the right and left hemispheres shaking hands.

64   Chapter 5

The Feel of Language

The emphasis is on the *feel* of language. Storing these ideas as *information* is not why we study our own tongue throughout our schooling—throughout our lives. The moment of recognition (cognition: to know, from *cognatus*, to be born) is what education is about. If there isn't an electric sizzle of *re . . . cognition*, of *dis . . . covery* (un . . . covering), we fall asleep. Teachers cannot simply shovel this stuff into people's heads (instruct!) and think the job is complete. Information is only a beginning. The fun starts when we mess around with a theorem and suddenly glimpse the dazzling mind minding. We go for the gold, whatever the discipline. English is not a service course; it is not Ann Landers or Miss Manners or Carl Rogers. It is not Shakespeare, Robert Bly, or Herman Melville. It is not *The Gold Cell, Paradise Lost,* or *Catch 22*. It is what happens when a reader's spirit connects with the spirit stored in those linguistic vessels.

> *There was a child went forth every day,*
> *And the first object he look'd upon, that object he became,*
> *And that object became part of him for the day or a certain part of the day,*
> *Or for many years or stretching cycles of years.*
>
> —Walt Whitman

That is the discipline of English.

We set up our classes so that English is experienced and not merely heard of. What's what is illusive. We get intimations, "heart heard of, ghost guessed," as Gerard Manley Hopkins phrased it. When we tinker with linguistic structures, we are teasing the universe into revealing itself to itself, something wraithlike, of the depths—but right out on the surface, too. When it goes well we live and realize our lives at the same time.

Language and Learning

In *University of Tomorrowland* Jerry Farber imagines "Teaching Johnny to Walk": If learning to walk were taught in schools, we would probably have Walking Readiness classes, aptitude tests about walking, History of Walking, and the ever-popular Remedial Walking. There would be discipline problems. (Talking, of course, would be postponed, first things first. We would have teenagers in diapers practicing vowel sounds on their way to their therapy classes.) Some would be at grade level, and some would always think of themselves as poor walkers.

But we don't learn that way. We simply plunge in. Kids teach themselves walking, talking, and bladder control. That's their job. It's organic. They take to it enthusiastically and put in long hours. In a nourishing environment they learn as fast as their biology allows. Courses in walking, talking, or going to the toilet would interfere. We learn by doing.

There is a natural biology of thinking, too. The mind is a shiny new car, and we want to get our hands on the controls. That is, we *want* to examine, play with, and explore language, for language is the car keys. How can English teachers cultivate this ache to master language? Not by instruction, certainly. English teachers do need some awareness of how language works and of how human beings take control of the machine. But there are the even more basic questions of why we learn and of how. Learning is not lineal. There is a sense in which linguistic fluency is progressive and cumulative, but the day-to-day stuff goes on by leaps and starts. How surges of insight come about is what methods classes ought to explore. What are the mechanisms of catching on; what is the behavior that leads to insight? How we tick is the proper study of human beings, after all.

Students don't have to know what teachers know, but at some point they do need to know how to turn on the machine deliberately. They do need to know how to have ideas on purpose. After all, that is what being educated means. The real subject of all schooling is mastery of mental processes. For human beings, language is the path. The more we polish our lenses, the more we see on the printed landscape. In our culture we "read" all sorts of visual stimuli—movies, computer screens, road signs, snails, and hair styles—as well as print, and we use the same skills.

No two of us, of course, are at the same level of sophistication. So prescribing *Julius Caesar* for tenth graders or subatomic physics for grad students makes no sense. For some it could easily be reversed. (Physicist Richard Feynman got interested in the humanities in his midthirties.) But if a class does happen to be reading *Julius Caesar* together, then there has to be room for everyone to participate *somehow*. In a nurturing school that is no problem. In a one-room schoolhouse, learning is always individualized; everyone is valuable to the total mix. The unity lies in everyone progressing toward the released intellect—through the perceptive use of language. Every classroom has to be a one-room schoolhouse.

Language is an eye, but the lens must be adjusted for each viewer. Instead of having his student Samuel Scudder see through the teacher's lens, Louis

Agassiz obliged him to activate his own lens. He gave him a fish to look at and required him to stick with it for three days. Scudder remembered those three days as his best entomological lesson. It is the same with print. Students who learn to look at a paragraph through their own eyepieces will not hold Newton, Freud, or Frost sacred but will consider them fellow explorers with welcome viewpoints.

The How of It

We don't learn to see with our own eyes by being instructed. We catch on by being involved in situations in which autonomous viewing is likely. It all depends on how the investigation is set up. A teacher could say, "I want you to see how Picasso drew this sketch of Stravinsky. I want you to copy his drawing. Pay attention to the curves, what he has left out. Notice what he exaggerates." And so on. If the students accept this instruction, they will see what the teacher sees and no more. But look what happens if the teacher says, "Turn this drawing upside down and try copying it. Watch how your mind and hand work as you go along. Notice what you are feeling. We'll get together later and compare notes." There will be a spirited discussion afterward. If the drawings are displayed, everyone will be absorbed and will study each other's drawings in detail. Not only that, but the discussion will turn up most of the ideas the teacher would have wanted to discuss and there will be lots of surprises as well. Students may even discover, as Samuel Scudder did, that a pencil is one of the best eyes. In this way the students turn the activity into their own lesson, not the teacher's.

Getting Down to Business

Without a thoroughly thought-out philosophy, a common base, the discipline of English will continue hurrying and scurrying in all directions. What are we trying to do? Every gathering of English teachers needs to address that question until it gets cleared up. Every course in the teaching of English needs to explore it. Of course, down the hall, schools of education need to be investigating what teaching is all about, what facilitates learning and what interferes. All prospective English teachers need to face those questions, too. Nor can language, what it is and how it works, be ignored. Of course, if these areas of investigation are prescriptive and not investigative, if no reflection is invited, not much will happen. Those involved in preparing teachers should practice what they preach. Most courses in schools of education are conducted as though the teachers had not read research they ask their students to memorize. But these classes could be models of effective teaching. These education courses should be the best examples of what they profess. It is hard to teach effectively if one has never witnessed it. Experiencing the possibilities would be a leg up.

How could such a departure from the status quo be brought about? The National Council of Teachers of English, the Conference on College Composition and Communication, the Modern Language Association, and schools of education could restructure the way they do business. But it always comes back to individual teachers. That means taking risks, for most will not have had any experience of effective teaching. People like my student-teacher Charlie Dodt and my teaching assistants Rae Cecchettini and Valerie Turner got a taste of what it could be like and went on to flesh out their understanding on their own. I followed their course work through graduate school to see how they would prepare for teaching. They themselves saw to it that a good understanding of language and linguistics were part of their background. But they also studied how teaching was being done in all their courses and considered, in the light of student-centered teaching, how it might have been done. When I talk with them now, they brim with enthusiasm. They know what works, and they know how to tinker with activities or assignments that don't. I don't anticipate their burning out.

But Charlie's, Rae's, and Valerie's is not the common experience. Nor can we expect that the NTCE, CCCC, or MLA will drop everything and center on these issues. So, it does come back to individual teachers, all alone, risking their necks to try out methods they can only guess might work. There is one bit of comfort, though. We know students learn more and better in an experimental environment. Almost anything one tries will have better results than just plodding along in the same old way. Usually, there are enough unanticipated connections to keep a teacher's mind active. Add some reflective thinking and keep on questioning; even if you never figure it all out completely, the journey will be full of marvels. Students will be grateful and supportive, of course, and there won't be complaints. Taking chances isn't really dangerous. The worst thing will be the envy of teachers whose students hate coming to class.

Why teach English? It should be something like Nanao Sakaki's reason for writing poetry:

Why Do You Write Poems?

Because my stomach is empty,
Because my throat is itching,
Because my bellybutton's laughing,
*Because my heart is love burning.**

How can anything less be satisfying? If we are not on fire, what have we to offer our students? Education is all about love burning in the physics lab, in the stock exchange, in McDonalds. We need to think about that.

Language as Metaphor

When we examine how ideas come into being and how our conceiving of the universe affects the way we walk around in it, we bump smack into metaphor. If you take a simple definition of metaphor—an implied comparison—well, there it is: A language is indeed an implied comparison. It is tricky, though, to think about. From one perspective, a language is a complete network of interconnected ideas—or *concepts*, vessels of meaning—somehow thought up about . . . um . . . what's-out-there. But, gosh, by the time an instant of what's-out-there gets messed with by the mind, what ends up in our heads certainly isn't the same thing anymore, now, is it? So we look at this fabrication we busily dreamed up and call it the world. Whew! When we think, we think about what's in our heads, not about what's-out-there. "No, no. I'm thinking about a flower." Right, "a flower," words.

It's difficult to get beyond words, perhaps impossible. When we use language to think about language, it's like trying to catch our own shadow. So someone might say, "Why bother? It's really hopeless. We can never pin it down. And even if we could, what difference would it make? I use language. I'm getting along OK. Let's get on with things." It's true. We can never capture the miracle and power of language *in* language. But that is the whole point, for understanding is never *in* language. Human beings cannot be said to be educated until they understand that language is a means of catching on—not conceptually but in a nonlinguistic awareness. We acquire that awareness, paradoxically, by using language to tease it out of hiding. We carry around capsules of meaning within a larger capsule when we think we crack open these capsules and release their vitality. So it isn't the word but what is in the

---

*From *Break the Mirror* (San Francisco: North Point Press, 1987; Nobleboro, Maine: Blackberry Books, 1997).

word that we want to get at. An impermeable egg of stored meaning is a lumpy thing to have bumping about in our minds.

But now the word *meaning* has popped up. Well, where did *that* come from? All of a sudden, there is *meaning* where there was none before. Clearly, meaning isn't out there. It is something creatures do *inside*, in their computers. We say "meaning" is what we do to what's-out-there, but that isn't exactly right, either. It is more accurate to say it is what happens when a creature invents and packages a relationship *inside*. A relationship between what? Between two other packages it already created. None of these packages contains a smidgen of what's-out-there. Every single icon (word, picture) is something made up *about* what's-out-there. All the mental activity is a re-arranging and melding of icons. Once this process gets going, there's no stopping it; by the time a human creature is two years old, it has created a whole language system, loaded with meaning. But the meaning resides in the computer program, dormant till revitalized, not "out there" . . . I think.

Human beings can use all this power without realizing they are doing it. Indeed, most of us don't think about how it all works. We have this powerful tool that we use all the time, but we haven't the foggiest idea of what's up. So we can't use it on purpose. If it develops an engine knock, we don't even know to switch to a higher octane or where to go to get it fixed. So guess what: Schooling is about getting to know the machine. If we want to catch on to how the machine works and maybe get a little more skillful at using it, we are stuck with investigating language. And we can't just be jawed at. We have to open the metaphor and drink. We have to investigate how metaphor works, because it *is* language. Whether they know it or not, all teachers have Exploration of Metaphor in their job descriptions. That's what their disciplines are all about. They would find their work much easier if they realized what they are sharing with students is an examination of *the language of their subject*.

As was the case for most English majors in the 1950s, the role of language in education was not part of my schooling. In undergraduate school I took a course in philology, which dealt mostly with the structure of sentences and touched on etymology. I don't recall the word *metaphor* being mentioned. Things aren't much different today. So I always do a little consciousness raising every chance I get. Even if some teachers are aware of the role of metaphor in inventing meaning, it is always fun to think about how our minds work. There is bound to be some new perspective. Bringing our truths alive is what the study of one's native tongue is all about anyway. So part of the weekend workshop I did with the teaching nuns at Marillac College was devoted to metaphor. After we had done some hands-on activities, I talked about the implications for teachers.

Chapter 5

Metaphor: Both Nose and Heart

I used to think metaphors were something used in poems and that only poets would have anything to do with them. They were some sort of window dressing to make the world look nicer. It didn't occur to me at the time how far reaching the process actually is. Making metaphors seemed like a mechanical process. Anyone who knew the principle could toss them off. "I am a typewriter." "John is a pencil." It's the sort of thing clever verse writers do. Usually, the results are not particularly meaningful. But the process is much more: Metaphor impregnates matter with spirit, it *inspires*. As the poet Onitsura wrote 250 years ago,

> *Getting to know plum blossoms,*
> *one's own nose*
> *and heart*

At first metaphor seemed to me to be a specialized field, and it seemed the sort of thing that could be done impersonally—by anyone. When we begin to examine language and how it works, though, we soon see that creating linguistic structures is a metaphoric processing, and the first time we catch on to how to use a fabricated tool (a word) to get a grasp of a very slippery reality, we have made a tremendous advance in our thinking. It isn't long until these associations form webs and we have a metaphoric network, a complete system called *language*. It is a fabulous, fantastic achievement. When we are in the midst of the acquisition of language, we are taking part in an unbelievably complex process.

The process is always binary. It always goes forward in pairs, one next to one. If we lay one instance next to another, we may not be able to give the connection meaning. But if we then lay a similar instance next to that bundle, and so on, eventually we have enough experience with them to give them a title, say, *mother*. That is what little kids do. Once they catch on to the game, they go wildly about their world using the process on everything:

> Daddy's outside shaving the windows.
>
> Where's the confederate sugar?
>
> Would you like a grilled cheese sandwich? Yes, and then let's have a boy cheese sandwich—for Daddy.
>
> For heaven's snakes.
>
> I like those little red olives with the green around.
>
> My daddy got a lavender retriever yesterday.

Little children have a lively sense of language processes. In two years they "get it." It is fairly well known they do this on their own, with scarcely any help from adults. We wouldn't know where to start. Fortunately, there is a genetic thrust and a "language acquisition program" in every new human. That is, there is a *potential* for language in each of us. If the environment is sufficiently stocked with linguistic material, we download the available language program. Metaphoric process is a biological necessity. And *all language is metaphor*. It is the handle we have on our worlds. It is the means whereby each of us creates a reality. Children get to know another organism through touch and contact, but they can only hang on to that mass of data through some sort of compression into an icon, a symbol that stands for that whole gestalt, some handle like *mommy* or *mother*.

The miracle begins when we take the icon, *mommy*, out of physical contact with the organism, sit down quietly, and do something *inside our heads*. We are able to sit in our room and contemplate the being we imagine is in the kitchen. That, of course, would be impossible without some sort of icon to hang on to. In other words, this is a displacement process. That is the key to metaphor: one thing seen as though it were the other. There is no physical connection in any way. It is something my spirit does to two things it created, two compressions already invented. This is an amazing thing. Abstracting out some aspect from the undifferentiated blur, finding some other aspect, and fusing these forever in association is the act of creating. To be metaphoric, to create analogies, is the very nature of the living process. An organism itself is a feat of association. In the mind, things that never existed together in the continuum of the universe are suddenly fused in a warm synaptic flash. It's the same in the physical universe. These warm spots, these metaphors, are the *matter* of the universe. Space, emptiness, is the major characteristic of everything. Even in the atom there is infinitely more space than matter. The matter of the universe gets together, as Frost has said, in a few terribly isolated points and sizzles.

We are stuck with metaphor no matter what. There is no other way. If I touch an object, that seems just about as direct a contact with the physical universe as can be. But look more closely: Immediately an electrochemical impulse shoots to my brain. The "contact" is not even direct by the time it gets to the nerve endings. The touch is an *idea* right out there at the skin—before it even starts its journey to the brain. Right inside the epidermis the impulse is encoded, translated into a metaphor, and that metaphor goes zipping off. What reaches my brain is a tremendously reduced selection from the infinite information available at the point of contact. Even so, what remains is still so full of data that it must be compressed into an electronic symbol. And even that symbol must be reviewed by the mind and compared in the resident symbol system before meaning can be assigned. An implied comparison!

Of course, that's hard to accept. I touch my cheek and say, "It's warm, it's soft, it's me." But those words are ideas *about* what happened. The only "out there" there is is "in here." There *may* be something out there, but there is no way for me to get at it. I can only surmise. Or when I view something, I will be told that that certainly is not metaphoric. But we know that viewing, to begin with, is actually the *elimination* of data. The eye doesn't let much in. My eye brushes away most of what's "there." If it didn't, there would be only an undifferentiated blur. Physiologically, the eye is designed to receive only certain kinds of information and only a limited amount of that. And even in the eyeball itself, there is an immediate translation into an electrochemical code. The tree I see is real, I say. But what I am looking at is a reality *picture*, inside my head. And if you do some thought experiments, you will discover that you can think about that tree without actually running the video. You can manipulate the idea of the idea, as in math calculations. Usually, when we think, we do lightning-fast calculations without unzipping each icon of meaning.

From one perspective, all this may seem rather depressing. Our sensorium is extremely limited, yet that's all we have to work with. We can never "know" anything. We can only know *about*. But from another angle, what we pull off is utterly fantastic. With little tidbits of incomplete and inaccurate information, we have accomplished wonders. When we realize what goes on when we create a metaphor, the whole thing gets turned inside out. You could say that the metaphoric process is nature looking at itself. And we creatures are doing that. Keats found the process exhilarating:

> Now it appears to me that almost any Man may like the spider spin from his own inwards his own airy Citadel—the points of leaves and twigs on which the spider begins her work are few, and she fills the air with a beautiful circuiting. Man must be content with a few points to tip with the fine Web of his Soul, and weave a tapestry empyrean [*empyrios*, in fire].

Each person creates such a tapestry. As you can see, this is a lively process. But if I get accustomed to it, and if I permit it to become commonplace in my mind, I no longer feel myself sharing in this activity. I feel as though it is happening *to* me and as though I am not *making* it happen. The fresh human being knows better. For kids, it's child's play. If I don't keep metaphoric play alive in me, I feel let down, bored.

But you will have to admit, most adults have been allowed to forget how we make metaphors and that we make them. We forget making them is fundamental to awareness. We forget they are the world and that each one of us makes that world. No wonder so many people feel apathetic and dull. We are designed to bear witness, to take down a musical instrument every morning and tune in. What would this unmolded day in conjunction with my metaphoric potter's wheel like to become? For our mental health we need to recognize what we are doing. We will feel much better.

This process of shaping reality is similar to what goes on in dialogue. Dialogue is duality. Without it nothing happens. What happens in the atom is dialogue; it is what happens between print and reader, between plant and sun. Dialogue is what causes matter to sizzle. It is what permits spirit to enter matter. That flashpoint occurs when desire and its fulfillment make contact. It is the point where spirit makes contact with matter. It happens every time someone creates a metaphor, when we *see*. Every time. Obviously, as we grew older, most of us forgot how metaphoric we really are. We forgot that by our very nature, by the very nature of the universe, we are *poetic. It* is poetic. We thought we were merely clerks and recorders, when all the time we have been poets. It's our job. We have to do it. In fact, like it or not, we live metaphorically. When we deny or ignore our nature, we get a sense of defeat and unimportance.

As poet Edward Lueders says, unless one thing is seen suddenly against another, nothing really happens:*

YOUR POEM, MAN . . .

unless there's one thing seen
suddenly against another — a parsnip
sprouting for a President, or
hailstones melting in an ashtray —
nothing really happens. It takes
surprise and wild connections,
doesn't it? A walrus chewing
on a ballpoint pen. Two blue tail-
lights on Tyrannosaurus Rex. Green
cheese teeth. Maybe what we wanted
least. Or most. Some unexpected
pleats. Words that never knew

---

*Copyright by Edward Lueders, 1987. Reprinted by permission.

*each other till right now. Plug us
into the wrong socket and see
what blows — or what lights up.
Try*
      untried
           circuitry,
new
    fuses.
*Tell it like it never really was,
man,
and maybe we can see it
like it is.*

    Every analogy is false, of course, because it takes two things that are not connected in nature and slaps them together. Through this fiction, through invalid connections, we get glimpses beyond them of a marvelous mystery of which we are a part. Our role is to connect spirit and flesh. When we do this we are anything but dejected. We are creators, a nice job description indeed.

    Clearly, the command of metaphor is not a frivolous pastime. It is not so that we can be interior decorators, or to produce glitzy physical and verbal shapes. The job isn't to make things. It is to realize the universe, to realize the world we live in, to make it real, to allow it to be alive before our eyes.

6

The Process
Safe Cracking

The grave's a fine and private place,
But none I think do there embrace.
—Andrew Marvell

In all my years as a student, I can remember only one class in which something *happened*. It was only a little blip on the monitor, but I never forgot it. For all I know it may be the trigger that set off the messes I got myself into routinely throughout my brilliant career, the fluttering butterfly wings in China that precipitate a typhoon in Hawaii. All John Wheatcroft did that day in 1956 was come into our lit class at Bucknell University and illuminate a twelve-line poem by Ben Jonson. Instead of explaining or explicating, he simply took his own sweet time looking at it. He let us dis . . . cover what was there. He did it by not being in a hurry: a clear reading out loud of the poem, a good look, and another reading out loud at the end. Instead of covering the assignment, we uncovered it. I almost knew "On My First Daughter" by heart (isn't that really the only way to "know" anything: by heart?) by the time I left the classroom. I don't want to make too much of this, but I left that day feeling enriched, as if I had been to a concert. My god! That *never ever* happened in any other classes.

But it should. There is every reason to expect a history class to lead to such vivacity, too. The process isn't mysterious, once one realizes that all classrooms are artists' studios and that students are practicing their art, whatever the title of the course. The process itself must be an intense pleasure.

Education is the emancipation of the human spirit into matter. If the teacher and students experience surprise, delight, or discovery enough times together, it becomes a habit we deliberately set in motion in everything we do.

Some elements of this process were explained in an article I published in the *Junior College Journal* ten years after John Wheatcroft's excursion into Jonson's poem. Here is an updated version.

Teachers Should Be Unprepared

A counselor I once knew told me she had an idea in the middle of her sophomore year in college. She hadn't known she could do that. Her mind was never quite the same after that. I have seen students marvel at their own writings: "I can't believe I *did* that!" Once I saw a kid look up from his work and exclaim, "I'm a genius! I'm a genius!" No doubt he had suddenly realized what an amazing thing his mind was. Is this ME!? Yes, and it is sad that "down we forget as up we grow," as e. e. cummings might put it. It is critically important that human beings know they can think, that they can have ideas. If teachers value this sort of thing—and who would not?—then they will have to vomit up most of what they have been taught is good teaching.

Here are some principles of the new methodology:

- Come to class unprepared.
- Be unsettling, disturbing.
- Be messy; misplace your lesson plan. Wing it.
- Get lost regularly. See if you can find your way.
- Lose your dignity. Give up respectability. Be a little disreputable.
- Go off half-cocked. Applaud students who do.
- Dare to give up your authority—really, not just pretend.
- Learn to play in the classroom. Bring your favorite toys.
- Waste time.

The classroom is a delivery room for ideas, and knowing about thinking is not the same as experiencing it. So classes have to be set up so that lightning flashes prevail. Each session must be a new adventure. Peaceful as the conventional classroom may appear, I never saw an idea born there. Schools seem designed to put the mind to sleep, not inflame it.

For a classroom to become an idea laboratory, there have to be genuine unknowns. Nothing will happen if there is no risk. The teacher has to be in danger along with the students. *This might not pan out.* Typical methods try for just the opposite. The trained teacher studies the target material inside and out and anticipates loopholes—the lawyer preparing a brief. Then leading questions are prepared to reveal the "key" elements of *the* lesson. This is the guess-what-I'm-thinking game. Of course, every student can sense the artificiality. The teacher then casts about until somebody guesses what is predigested in the teacher's head. It's all worked out in advance. Answers or asides that might lead to some tangential insight don't even register. When you know what you want to hear, it is hard to hear something different or new. Some mind reader guesses *the* answer and gets a pat on the head and the next step in teacher-pleasing commences.

But what happens when a teacher is really unprepared, unprepared, that is, as far as *this* particular discussion, story, poem, or calculus concept is concerned? What if the teacher is no better prepared than the students? Then they must really go on the adventure together. "Well," they say to each other, "what do we have here? Let's see." And turning the target material over in their minds, they teach each other. Now genuine discovery is possible, and the classroom comes alive. If the teacher has anything to offer, it is a mind operating out loud on the problem and the ability to do this in public: to discover *with* someone else so that that someone begins to catch on. Mind, body, and spirit connect in a flash of awareness on the spot, for the teacher sometimes, for the student(s) sometimes, for everyone simultaneously sometimes.

The prepared lesson is sterile because any ideas that might have been born took place somewhere else and only the corpse is dragged in. No wonder students get classtrophobia (my grandson Andy's coinage). Rarely do they witness the delivery of a real idea and the excitement that goes with it. The well-regulated classroom is anathema to thought. Nonetheless, students are expected to go forth and think, never having witnessed the process. Ideation is cliff-hanging, but a lesson with a preconceived end is getting equipment ready for mountain climbing and then taking the chairlift. It is hard to blame chairlift teachers, though. Where would they have trained for mountain climbing?

The reason artists, scientists, any creative geniuses persist is the bang they get out of it. We all love it—or did; we were all kids once. Our students, too. It is not an aversion to thinking that teachers witness but an aversion to the ersatz, emotionless litany so prevalent in conventional classrooms. There is no thrill unless there is chance, and there is no chance in the prepared, planned lesson. Students need to see and experience, not the result of thought, but thought in action.

This does not mean teachers have to arrest their own mental development.

Outside of class we continue furnishing our minds. That is our homework, our lifework. But class goes best when the particular event is new for the teacher, too, not that one hasn't done lots of algebra problems, but that the particulars of *this* one are unique. The short story might be one the teacher has never seen before. Or, if it is a familiar poem, it has to be made *unfamiliar* somehow so that there is something for the teacher, too. The teachers' advantage—their reason for being there—is, one hopes, that they have been on intellectual adventures before. They are used to the equipment, the stance, the appropriate handholds, when to camp, when to press on. But they have never been on *this* particular mountain before. The sooner the other climbers can go it alone, the better.

External structure is the nemesis of thought. The more structured the course, the less likelihood of ideas being born. An idea is a structuring of data, a coalescence. If you want students to think, you must let them make the connections and create the structures, because that is what thinking is. Kids have to have something rough and incomplete to work on. Life is a mess; the mind is designed to straighten it out. Give students a pile of stuff. Let *them* make something out of it, out of it and everything else. Let it be *their* achievement. The disarray is not some addled permissiveness or sloppy teaching but a central and necessary response to the main concern of education. Nevertheless, a genuine intellectual adventure is always accompanied by at least as much technical "training" and information as is found in courses that strive only for such inferior accomplishments. Thinking requires the clearest verbalization and the most accurate information one can muster. They are adjuncts to the process.

These classes aren't nearly as chaotic as it might appear to a casual observer. Lots of noise, students scattered all over, a lot of different things going on. But there is always a focus. Everyone knows it's an "English" class they all come to every day. It is clear there is a "teacher." There are "students." Defining these elements is part of the dialogue. Our work is to make sense of these things and, if possible, to pull it all together into some sort of synthesis. We don't know what's going to happen. We are exploring, investigating, taking a look around.

But you can't go to class and say "Think" any more than you can say "Be happy" or "Calm down." So how *do* we think, and how do we get students to do it? I turn over an interesting bauble I found lying on the path. At first I don't know if it's going to *mean* anything or not. I don't even care. I'm just taking a look. From past experience, though, I know this is how things get started. I usually end up making connections, lots of little ones, sometimes big ones. But

I also know, if my stomach is in knots, if a prescriptive teacher has put the fear of God in me, my mind shuts down. So I have to get playful. I do have to have that tingle of excitement of a well-matched Ping-Pong game. The object of this game is to achieve insight, awareness, clarity, especially to invite the state of being in which we are "all there," focused, centered—object and observer, one thing going on. We forget we are in chemistry lab, we forget we are playing the piano. Time is suspended. We are there unselfconsciously doing it. That is the thinking mode.

Of course, we can't be working on a sculpture and at the same time be thinking about our dignity, or a lesson plan, or respectability. Thinking is not a mannerly process. It is the spontaneous utterance—a joke, an expletive, punning around—that turns up unexpected juxtapositions, wild connections. And these wonderful moments are certainly worth the loss of a little dignity. Nothing much happens if we go about it systematically and logically. The history of science, invention, and the arts is full of stories of accidents that lead to discovery.

When I was learning how this process might be set up in the classroom, I remember working with some students on the difference between writing and speech. The tendency would be to come in and lecture, to tell the students what I knew on the subject. And I did have plenty of information. But I realized it was all secondhand, even the parts I had thought up myself. Presenting the results of thinking is dishing up clichés. If the ideas were not fresh for me, what excitement would there be for the students? I wanted students to *experience* this difference, not just hear about it. It is the experience that brings them back to the table. We needed fresh insight.

I remember telling the students (I was substituting for a colleague that day) what we were to discuss. I suggested that we fool around with the topic and see if we could come up with anything worth saying. I wrote the word "writing" on the board. "Writing. Hmm. *Writing*. Wonder what it feels like. OK, I'm what you see on the board there. How do I feel? What am I?"

"You're chalk."

"Chalk, what is that?"

"Fossils."

"Fossils? *Fossils*. What's left over after the flesh and blood are gone. After the life is gone."

"Where's the life? Where *was* it?"

"In the writer. The writer had it."

"But it's gone now."

"I feel weak. I'm emaciated. I'm nothing but a skeleton; I want my flesh back."

At about this point, we went into overdrive. The rest was effortless. I could feel an insight emerging, and I think the students could, too. There was a sense of anticipation. All we had to do was let it flow and get out of the way.

"How do I get it back? From the writer?"

"No."

"Where?"

"From the reader."

Ah.

We left the metaphor at that point and began talking directly about the topic. We had found a wedge between our apathy and the assignment. It became clear that the written word is emaciated without a vital reader reviving it.

And so it goes with clichés, too. A more universal, spine-tingling insight is that all settled ideas, however profound, have to be invested with new life every time we take them out of the box: a violin concerto, a law of physics, every single classroom. Ah! That was what was wrong with most classes. They were carving cadavers. So some fooling around in someone else's class led to a specific insight about the written word that expanded into a pedagogic principle. Not a bad day's work.

The "chalk" investigation demonstrates most of the principles I have been trying to describe here. Students weren't even raising their hands. Things were being blurted out. "Chalk" was only one of a bunch of ideas and had been tossed in just for the hell of it, but it turned out to be a productive metaphor. You never know what's going to turn up. And once the game got going in earnest, I disappeared as the authority figure. I was trying just as hard as anyone else to see this thing in a new way. I ceased being conscious of my role as "teacher" and was saying whatever came into my head. I was not very dignified. It was clear that none of us knew whether anything would come of this fooling around. And things were chaotic for a while. In this case we were lucky. We were able to bring our play back into a rational framework. Often we can't, but over the years it has become clear that the more we trust the process, the more it is likely to work. We do have to be willing to waste time, though. Watching the clock or trying to "cover" the lesson will interfere.

To round out the "chalk" story, I must confess, being young and foolish at the time, I thought, "Boy! This is a hot lesson! I'm going to teach it in my next class!" You know what happened. You also know why. I had presented the cadaver. I hardly ever make that mistake anymore. It has become clear that we have to forget what we "know" when we enter an idea laboratory. You can't look at the topic directly but only out of the corner of the eye. It is as if the nonconscious mind is playing hide and seek. So you fiddle around over here and be ready to tag the great insight when it comes sneaking by over there.

Here is another example of how a lesson can go in an unintended direction and come out far more elegant than you planned. About the time of the "chalk" incident, our department prescribed a unit on monosigns and plurisigns—stripped-down versus fleshed-out messages. Geez! For an example of a monosign, the required text supplied from an electrical handbook: "When a fuse has blown, it is not sufficient merely to replace it with a new one."

I thought I would just write that sentence on the board, get someone to give me the only possible meaning it could have, and get on to my pal Dylan Thomas for plurisigns. But the kids took the fuse sentence as a plurisign! We never did get to Thomas. Isn't that amazing! It turned out that the atmosphere in *our* class had the effect of pulling almost everything out of its monosignificance. I hadn't fully real-eyesed that before. What happened was that the very first student crumpled my plan: "Well, for example, if you don't get at the reason for a nervous breakdown, you'll be going back to the san again and again." It turned out we had, to my mind, a first-class poem of the William Carlos Williams genre. (All of a sudden, we're doing "creative writing." That could never have happened if I had been following a course outline. Poetry comes the second semester!)

Poem

When a fuse
Has blown,
It is not sufficient
Merely
To replace
It
With a new
One.

One thing led to another—isn't that always the way? The class figured out *for itself* that anything can be a plurisign to the viewer, though it might not be intended as one by the originator. "Then how do you know which way to take it?" So that led to talking about form, setting, structure. Someone announced that talking in monosigns puts the mind in neutral. It was a neat idea to think about. The conversation was animated; there was a sense of discovery, ideation, insight. And that makes all the difference. That difference is the whole point. These were not new ideas to the world, but these were new ways of seeing, and that was exhilarating. Our own connecting organs were putting things together and making something out of them.

When you don't have an agenda clouding your vision, you are more apt to notice things. Once, in a discussion, someone burst out, "Hey! All language is biased!"

"That's ridiculous!" someone blurted.

"Why?" I asked.

"Because, if that's true, I'd have to rethink everything I ever learned."

"Could you say that again?"

"I'd have to rethink everything I ever learned."

"Maybe just once more—slowly?"

"I'd have to rethink everything I ever learned."

"Beautiful."

So the *way* things are set up is what it's all about. It's hard to explain to people, though. Once we did some sidewalk drawings with colored chalk, like they do in front of cathedrals in Europe. (It wears off, so no damage is done.) It was one of the best things my students ever did. During the process they were really artists. So, of course, the dean calls me in because he has had a complaint from a physics teacher who says we're defacing school property. Never mind that the total effect was stunningly gorgeous. So the dean says, yes, he understands that the kids are getting educational value, but if we want to do it again, we should get some butcher paper, and that way we won't mess up school property. Oy! The perfect way to drive a stake through our hearts.

And so it goes. The closer my idea labs get to what I think education is all about, the less they look like conventional classes. But when I participate in these marvelous events, I don't have much time to consider what others might think. It's none of my business anyway.

Learning to teach this way certainly pulled me out of the dark night of the soul. What a grindingly tedious penance conventional teaching is. Over the years it remains a deep pleasure to read students' reflections on the events of our classes. They are full of spontaneous metaphor, surprising insights, and intellectual power.

"This class has changed me from a pure scientific person," said David Scott, "into an artistic, poetic, intuitive scientific person."

"Many of my former English classes," wrote Steve Gayman, "tried to tune up my motor by washing, waxing, and buffing."

Wrote John Garden, "This class has blown my nose."

As I look back over John's words almost thirty years later, a shiver still goes up my back. "The tinned reality of the conventional class," as Chip Smith described it, doesn't stand a chance.

Wise Sayings

I used to love it when we would be messing around with an idea and an aphorism or turn of phrase would pop out of someone spontaneously. Or I would be reading a reflection and, bingo, there would be a neat simile nicely encapsulating the concept. Some were as crisp or profound or witty as any Pope or Twain or Nash. Over the years there must have been thousands. I copied down a few, but most flew by like flashes of light, illuminating our thoughts in passing. These poetic insights, these metaphoric nuggets, must surely have been the right hemisphere handing over directly the essence of our efforts.

My early left-brained classes and assignments rarely yielded such jewels. There simply isn't room for such accidents of thought and speech. No wonder most classes are so dull. All the beauty of poetic thought is wrung out and only the dregs remain. When we are in the midst of thought, such outbreaks emerge. That's one way to know minds are engaged. You could probably analyze tapes of class sessions and get some sort of metaphor factor: How many unpremeditated outbursts of brilliance per session? How many on day 1; how many on day 150? How does that compare with a control group? You could do the same with students' writings. How many poetic insights spill out on the page, as much a surprise to the writer as the audience? If Calvinists want an accounting, if they want to assess performance, why not look at the poetic content of work generated over a semester?

Most of those wonderful observations entertained or educated us and went their way. I did jot down some from time to time, but there were so many we all took them as a matter of course. Compared with conventional school experience, though, they were miraculous. You had to wonder how the hell it could happen. What in this structure permitted spontaneous insight to take the physical form of a metaphor or linguistic paradox or ironic insight? For such word play is at the heart of discovery, invention, scientific breakthrough. And it is, if justification were needed, practical and productive. This sort of thinking solves problems: whether to get a divorce, what work one should devote oneself to, how this conundrum in chemistry can be understood. It is all called creative thought. But it is not some frivolous adjunct of academic study. It is the heart of it. It is what education is all about.

Following are a few gems I did save one semester. Most of them are poetic in the sense that they compress complexity of thought into a word picture or a pun. I would love to see a math class that generated such thinking. As I ponder it, it is obvious that that is what $a^2 + b^2 = c^2$ really is. Some Pythagoras, hot on relationships among sides of a right triangle, must have seen it and then compressed it all into that simple, clean, well-lighted poem.

Learning a foreign language is like meeting a new person.

Insult *is* injury.

Critical thinking: The art of ignorance.

If you're not smiling, you're not thinking.

Critical thinking: Intuitive logic.

Nature is sexy. That's why it's called the big bang theory of the universe.

Judgment may be the only barrier to enlightenment.

Mandalas are mind maps.

Reality is a security blanket. No. It's an insecurity blanket.

Critical thinking: Living an amazing life.

Critical thinkers are good procrastinators.

To see the beautiful, just dig to the inside.

Only artists think critically.

. . . the endless possibilities of pure thought.

A koan a day keeps senility away.

Asking questions: Making love to the universe.

ASAP: As Slow As Possible.

Critical thinkers are slow learners.

Educated people treat their perceptions as koans.

There is no such thing as constructive criticism.

Nothing's wrong.

Critical thinking: Safe cracking.

I'm all for living a wonderful and amazing life.

With koans we just wake everything up.

Intuition is the nose of the mind.

Questions are instruments of perception.

All viewpoints are prejudiced.

Mother Teresa traded frivolous fun for joy.

Who *I* am is not an opinion.

Spare the child. Put away the rod.

Everything has more to it when you think about it.

Superficiality is torture.

Schooling is fixing things that aren't broke.

Not everything that's good for you is necessarily right for you.

Poetry is the eye of the heart.

. . . the marvelous human being we were all meant to be.

Life is too short to take seriously.

Critical thinking: being able to listen without purpose.

What's true is beyond belief.

Language is a verbal mandala.

Each organism is like a box. Something different is drawn from it by each perceiver.

Critical thinking: Enlightened spontaneity.

There is no such thing as a disembodied idea.

Critical thinking is learning how to remove the masks and unclear pictures and seeing something as it really is: beautiful.

Critical thinking is a slow walk around one's brain.

Logic is warmed-over yesterday.

The universe is not an opinion.

Common sense is another name for dead metaphors.

The purpose of education is to make my mind user-friendly.

The purpose of critical thinking is to rewrite the dictionary.

. . . to think about what we are thinking about.

Let's put it this way: Toto, I don't think we're in Kansas anymore.

Critical thinking supposes some kind of background of wisdom.

The Sound of Music

A Minor Bird

I have wished a bird would fly away,
And not sing by my house all day;

Have clapped my hands at him from the door
When it seemed as if I could bear no more.

The fault must partly have been me.
The bird was not to blame for his key.

And of course there must be something wrong
In wanting to silence any song.

—Robert Frost

Idea labs are noisy, no doubt about it. Group discussions can get loud, especially when everyone wants to talk at once. Add passion, and there is even shouting. All in all, though, it's a beautiful noise, music. But the liberal arts classrooms at our college were not designed for choir practice, so sometimes the classes next door, who talked one at a time, could hear us. I always try to get along with the neighbors, and most of the teachers were tolerant, even indulgent, of our unconventional sessions. But now and then, Ruth or Gus or Rose would look in and ask us to tone it down a little. They were nice about it, and we would try.

But one semester John Wilson from the History Department was teaching next door. He believed in hard work. He did not hold with the idea that life is too important to take seriously. It came to pass that I was teaching seventy students Harry Belafonte's "Momma, Look a Boo Boo" and getting up an orchestral accompaniment. The paper-crumpling section was tuning up, the key-ring group were rattling away, the foot-stompers were working on their rhythm, and we were into the third rehearsal. Everyone was getting caught up in it, Asians, Iranians, shy kids, everyone singing full blast. A joyful noise. It was a perfect example of what school should *feel* like. You can get that same feeling looking at a leaf or realizing a poem or having an idea. I wanted the students to make that connection, and it was working.

I'm in there singing away with everyone else—some of us might have been dancing—when the door bursts open and in storms John Wilson. It's 1991, and John is all dolled up as usual in tie, jacket, creased pants—the whole professional uniform that went down the tubes a couple of decades earlier. Very dignified! Everything comes to a screeching halt. The kids must have thought he was a dean or something. Grumble, rankle, arf, arf, and so on. He reads me out right in front of the students. Very self-righteous. "My students are taking a TEST!" *Well, there's your trouble*, I think. I tell him I'm sorry to have disturbed him, and so on, and indeed I am. I'm glad we were having such a good class, but I am sorry it disturbed the neighbors. Of course, that's the end of orchestra practice for that day. We're out of the mood.

But the event did afford us the chance to discuss what classes ought to sound like and feel like and whether a silent class is a good class. So in the end it all worked out OK. One of the bonuses for me was Scott Phillips's reflection. Here it is:

3/14/91 . . .

Today an angry instructor came into my English class. He didn't seem to want to not be angry. He just wanted to be angry with my happy English teacher. Well, my teacher was happy, but soon after the angry instructor said a few words (I assume angry and mean) my teacher became serious and set aside his smile to deal with the not so happy person. It was quite a tragedy all its own but unfortunately it caused a chain reaction. The entire English class became quite serious, too. Originally, the class were enjoying themselves, as students usually don't get to.

I couldn't quite understand why someone could be so angry on such a nice morning, not to mention sharing the anger with everyone else, dampening their morning as well. Maybe he was just jealous that our English class were enjoying themselves while he and probably his class weren't. Maybe his class doesn't like him, which is quite understandable considering his low tolerance level. And maybe he doesn't like his class either; he doesn't seem to like ours or our teacher. I'll bet he doesn't really like anything.

Maybe he should take our English course; certainly he could learn a lot about thinking clearly and learning to enjoy yourself. Then perhaps he could liven up his class a bit by teaching the students what they want to know rather than bore them with garbage. You know people learn better when they like learning. I like learning in my English class, so I learn more. On the other hand, my boring classes teach me only discipline and memorization, not thinking. My math class is like a sleeping pill, and my computer class seems like torture training. It's hard to learn in those classes.

A while back I wrote a reflection based on a koan I made up that said, "Too many people see school as a proving ground rather than a training ground." I feel some instructors and students spend their energy trying to convince others that they are knowledgeable rather than concentrating on knowing. Admitting ignorance is apparently very hard for a lot of people. The truth is that we all know very, very little. Everybody ought to know that. My well-schooled uncle admitted having a degree shouldn't be enough of a reason to grant someone power. (He has a Ph.D. in biophysics and is currently a leader in test-tube-baby development.) My roommate (degreed as well) explained the terms B.S., M.S., and Ph.D. to me:

> B.S. stands for Bull Shit.
>
> M.S. stands for More Shit.
>
> Ph.D. stands for Piled Higher and Deeper.

Maybe the angry instructor had the same experience in his education, so he thinks that's how he should teach it. And maybe his education wasn't complete. They probably just taught him discipline and memorization instead of beautiful ideas. I think I'm really lucky to have my English teacher instead of a grumpy professor. My English teacher is happy and makes me happy. He also has taught me to be happy outside of the course. I will have the golden egg he handed me even after the course ends. It looks as though I needed to see the angry instructor next to my happy teacher to see the contrast. What a bummer our class is almost finished. I wonder what will happen as time passes.

Postscript. Karl Staubach told me another John Wilson incident: The liberal arts rooms never had enough chairs, so teachers would gather up what they needed wherever they could. If they remembered, they would put them back, but sometimes they forgot. No big deal. If you need chairs, you go find them. But no. John Wilson stomps into Karl's class and right in front of the class accuses him of stealing chairs out of his room. (That particular day, Karl hadn't.) So the next time Karl comes to class, there are hardly *any* chairs in *Karl's* room. He starts down the corridor looking in classrooms for chairs, but they also have hardly any chairs. When he gets to Wilson's room, there they all are, piled to the ceiling. Karl's students apparently decided to make sure he had enough.

7

A Hummy Sort of Day
The Music of the Spheres

The man that hath no music in himself,
Nor is not moved with concord of sweet sounds,
Is fit for treasons, stratagems, and spoils;
The motions of his spirit are dull as night . . .
—William Shakespeare

The centrality of music in human life is so self-evident it shouldn't be necessary to say that a learning environment without it is "dull as night." The mind itself is a musical instrument and every morning one must take it off the shelf and do a few riffs. In fact, if we forget, we will be out of harmony all day. It is not an option. Every classroom has to be a music class and every institution a school of music. Can you imagine talking like that to a bunch of schoolmen and -women? Wouldn't there be much scratching of heads? We may be the only society in the world that tries to school its children with the music turned off.

But the biology of living things is indeed rhythmic and orchestrated. From the Taiwanese perspective, even rocks and subatomic particles are patterns of organic energy. The revolving planets, the universe itself, are variations of an electronic theme. Within each human being, too, is a melodic vibration attuned to the stars. We hear it with our inner ear; we feel it in our bones. It is this inner music that needs to be playing in the classroom. Students in architecture classes will indeed learn more efficiently if certain kinds of music are actually being played, but the unheard melodies are sweeter, as

Keats observed. Teachers need to make sure this inner music is involved in everything that goes on, guiding the hand of the sculptor, the mind of the economist. If you try to convince students that computer science is merely mechanical, they will tune out. No one likes drudgery; everyone loves making music.

> When I'm writing and the words just seem to be flowing out of me, then there is a good melodious rhythm inside of me. When I reach a block, the music is turned off and the song is awkward.
> —Judy Young, student

Another way of putting it is that learning is optimal when body, mind, and spirit are in accord. Lesson plans call it motivation. Institutions give the emotive component a nod, but most teachers treat enthusiasm as a dispensable nicety. My own experience is that virtually all pedagogy *but* the musically functioning mind could be dispensed with. If the whole learner is involved—if the student hears a band playing—it will be tough stopping that person. Music was always in my classes one way or another, but I became consciously aware of its impact on learning when I was putting together a college skills class. I got a clue when I read about some rapid-learning programs that used quiet music in the background. In *Superlearning* Sheila Ostrander and Lynn Schroeder describe setting up a learning environment in which the largo movements of classical symphonies are played in the background. I tried it out in my skills classes and got serendipitous results, too.

Music for a Quiet Mind

Students appeared in my skills classes with various problems and needs. The idea of the course was to show how to get higher grades without working so hard or wasting time. But it soon emerged that the major barrier to learning was anxiety. All the other problems they had identified were the result of self-doubt and fear. Reading problems, confusion, conflicts with teachers, workload, expectations, daydreaming, procrastination—all were the result of inner conflict. Their minds were on all sorts of things, except the task at hand. If they could calm down and pull themselves together, if the reasoning and intuitive parts of their minds were in harmony and not at cross-purposes, and if the whole being were involved in the job that needed to be done, it would be easy as pie.

So part of the skills course involved my showing students how to get into an optimal state of mind for learning. Beating their heads against the wall simply did not work. The conscious and nonconscious hemispheres had to be in agreement that the job was indeed something *both* wanted to do, and these two needed a chance to communicate with each other. To open the corpus callosum, I had them close their eyes, sit comfortably, and do a short relaxation exercise. I offered them three or four choices. One session it was counting their breaths. Another time it was imagining a rainbow of colors and experiencing them one by one from red to violet. Or it might have been paying attention to their bodies from toes to tops of their heads. In the background would be a slow movement from Bach, Corelli, Handel, Vivaldi, or some other instrumental music with the pace of a quiet heart beat, one beat per second.

I would lead the students through these exercises and would close my eyes and go through them myself. I knew whatever relaxation techniques I taught them would have to be short. They thought they didn't have enough time as it was. I made sure these exercises didn't take more than ten minutes.

So we're sitting in a classroom, eyes closed, lights out usually, with soft music playing: "Listen to the music. Get comfortable. Now without actually moving anything physically, move your attention down to your toes. Pay attention until you can actually feel all your toes. I'm doing that and I can now feel my toes, so I'm going to the soles of both feet. Now I'm going to the tops of the feet. Now the heels. Now the ankles. Now my feet are tuned up, so I'm going on up through the body. You can check back, if you need to, and make sure everything stays tingly."

And so on throughout the body. When we finished, we were calm and refreshed, as if we had had a nice nap, but not lazy, just quiet. Whatever we were to do that session went more smoothly, especially anything that required sustained attention. My own voice was quieter and my speech pattern less hurried. What I had to say was less effortful, the Mr. Rogers of DVC. It was downright pleasant. Well, well! I had intended these exercises for home use, but when I saw the effect they had on our class atmosphere and on me, I explored how to make them a regular part of the class. I decided to start each session that way. The students would be getting practice, but also the class itself would become the kind of environment they needed to simulate during their study time. And I would be doing a better job, too.

So now as the students came in, the music would be playing. Once everyone had arrived, we would begin with a relaxation exercise. The mad buzz that accompanies hurrying and scurrying through a school day simply stopped—as if a switch had been thrown. We were all more centered, just the condition the mind needs. We had pretty much dispelled distractions and could focus on what we were doing. In addition, when the students were in groups or when they were working on something or other, I would put on the music. Students valued the fertile environment and borrowed tapes and got lists of good composers: music for their own study sessions. Some brought music from their own collections—unsolicited feedback that showed students were getting the idea that they could indeed alter their learning environment.

One thing leads to another. Why should this good stuff be limited to the skills classes? All students should know about setting up a good study environment. So in my freshman English classes and in my literature and critical thinking classes, I showed the students how to switch gears for optimal thinking. It didn't stop there, and we began to start all classes that way. Music would be playing when students arrived; when we were ready to work together, we closed our eyes and did a relaxation exercise. Once everyone was used to the ritual, it didn't take ten minutes. We could shift into the state of mind we wanted within a minute or two. In fact, during class, when we needed a touch-up, I would say, "Everybody shut your eyes. Take a breath. Hold it. Exhale. Take another. Hold it. Once more. Hold it. Let it out." Then we would go back to work.

Initially, I felt self-conscious asking students to do these exercises. It must look, I thought, like some sort of sixties flower child, funky, touchy-feely junk, but everyone took it in stride and saw nothing strange about it. For one thing they liked the results. Possibly by the time I started using music and relaxation routinely, society itself was more familiar with mind-body research, so students didn't need to be persuaded. I had expected some resistance, but it never came, nor did anyone come to lead me to my padded cell.

Alpha Rhythms and All That

No one knows for sure why relaxing with classical music in the background makes it easier to learn, but there are several plausible guesses. It could be simple biology; maybe music really does soothe the savage breast. When the heart slows to about sixty beats a minute, brain waves slow to six or seven cycles a second. With slow, stately music playing, the body actually adjusts itself to the alpha-rhythm rate, and in that state conscious and nonconscious parts of the brain have free access to each other. The mind kicks into gear, and the thinker has full use of the powerful right-brained supercomputer.

Most of us have all sorts of thoughts skittering about in our minds all the time, so it's hard to focus on one thing. Counting breaths, experiencing the colors of the rainbow, noticing the body step by step—each shuts down all that random thought. The brain breathes a sigh of relief, *Finally, a chance to concentrate.* The busy, busy, busy left hemisphere calms down and is free, for once, to pay attention to the messages the powerful right hemisphere has been saving up. We are brilliant, but we need access to this intelligence. Music sets the pace, and a relaxation exercise turns off the boom box: body calm, mind fully awake.

Research is far from complete, but experiments at the University of California at Irvine found people who listened to ten minutes of Mozart just before an IQ test scored higher than control groups. (Not that IQ tests measure anything important; the point here is that there was a physical difference immediately after a Mozart session. *Something* was going on.) The effect didn't last, but Mozart certainly is a way to get one *started*, a way to wake up the mind to its possibilities. As for his own work, Mozart wrote:*

> When I am completely myself, entirely alone, and *of good cheer* [my italics] . . . my ideas flow best and most abundantly. *Whence* and *how* they come, I know not; nor can I force them. Those ideas that please me I retain in memory, and am accustomed, as I have been told, to hum them to myself. If I continue in this way, it soon occurs to me how I may turn this or that morsel to account, so as to make a good dish of it, that is to say, agreeably to the rules of counterpoint, to the peculiarities of the various instruments, etc. All this fires my soul, and provided I am not disturbed, my subject enlarges itself, becomes methodized and defined, and the whole, though it be long, stands almost complete and finished in my mind, so that I can survey it, like a fine picture or a beautiful statue, at a glance. Nor do I hear in my imagination the parts successively, but I hear them, as it were, all at once.

These various rituals are aimed at an altered state of mind. The soul (self, mind, spirit) has to be *fired;* that's a fundamental law of learning. Everything begins there. In his science fiction novel *The Mind Parasites,* Colin Wilson describes our ordinary way of thinking as a feeble beam of attention. We use our minds like powerful searchlights without a reflector. When it is turned on, the light rushes off in all directions. If you put a reflector behind it, the beam stabs forward, the light waves all going the same way and ten times more powerfully. Occasionally, the right switch is accidentally thrown, and the thinker enters this mode of thinking. Most "serious" thinking is of this sort. It has access to our power source but only indirectly, and most of us don't really understand the mechanisms that trigger this resource. Music and relaxation get us there directly and *on purpose.* But Wilson points out that the

---

*From the notes to the Philips CD "Mozart for Your Mind."

reflected light waves are out of step. If you pass the light—which I would say is coming from the right hemisphere—through a ruby laser, the waves now "march in step" and their power is suddenly exponential. In this altered state the right hemisphere operates directly, *without translation* by the conscious logic system. It is similar to a dream state. We forget time and place and for a while dwell in the intense pleasure of the moment. The great achievements of human thought take place during these laser-like concentrations of the mind.

There are operatives other than music and relaxation, however; one is playfulness, a common element in creative thinking. The thinker (you) messes around at first, without taking things too seriously. After a while you begin to "get" ideas, usually in images, ridiculous analogies, or metaphors. Where do they come from? One guess is that the conscious mind during playtime begins setting up the problem or question. The topic doesn't even have to be well formed. Because the mind is at ease, the circuits between the two hemispheres open; the right hemisphere processes the data with lightning speed and sends its solution back in the form of a metaphor. The nonconscious part of the mind is not linguistic and not sequential. It stuffs complete ideas into a single word or picture. The conscious mind then translates the message into a language system. But the solution was actually found earlier in the right hemisphere, and sometimes we skip the translation and experience the solution directly, as in a dream; we simply *see*. Like music and relaxation routines, play is a way of calming the conscious mind, setting the body at ease, and sloughing off distractions, allowing the mind to focus. Regardless of why, play is a part of efficient thinking, and I made sure it was a part of all my classes. I knew squinting effortfully makes things hard to see.

I often wondered what an evaluator visiting one of these classes might think: Students sitting around with their eyes closed, *breathing*. Music. All sorts of messing around. Joking, punning, having a good time. What a mess! What a lovely mess!

Harry Belafonte, Guy Clark, Louis Armstrong, Joni Mitchell, et Alia

The "music of the spheres" is more than a figure of speech. It used to amuse me when my rational friends would get all steamed lobbying for logical, deductive thought, their own demeanor nullifying their arguments. Emotion is essential to the thinking process. We have to use it productively, that's all. We have wetware, not hardware, in our heads, after all. We can't even get out of bed without *feeling* like it. We hope for a little action. Daniel Goleman's *emotional intelligence* is a good description of what is going on. My own emphasis would be *intelligent emotion*. That is, we are essentially feeling creatures—with intelligence attached. Everyone wants to have a good time. In other words, we all need to feel alive. We use our intelligence to hone life. We call that a good life. Who would dispute it?

We could talk about *emotional intelligence* or *intelligent emotion* in class, but I wanted us to have a common experience of it. We needed to make music. Then, when we were discussing thinking or writing or reading, we would have something concrete to refer to. That's why I "taught" the students Harry Belafonte's "Momma, Look a Boo Boo." We used up a whole session on it. The first run-through would be blah—no feeling at all. But with improvised musical instruments and with my insistence on more gusto, we began belting it out. By the fourth run-through there wasn't one self-conscious singer in the room. It was grand. Now we had a shared experience of being totally *there* in the moment and one with it. We had experienced together what it felt like to be so involved as to forget oneself. And now we could explore whether that degree of involvement was necessary in writing, in reading, in tying one's shoes. Does a full life require such intensity?

I tried to work in "Momma, Look a Boo Boo" every semester. Sometimes we took the show on the road, down through the quad, to the delight of students and staff lounging about with their coffee and sandwiches. Of course, once the bars were down, students started bringing in all sorts of music. I can remember a clarinetist, a drummer, several vocalists, a harmonizing quartet of hulking football players, and lots of tapes. Bill MacMurchy, one of my older teaching assistants, in full kilted regalia, once led seventy or eighty of us around campus, bagpipes blasting out an infectious Highlands march. Most of the students had been accustomed to separating their musical lives from schooling. We were putting the pieces back together.

Other times we would hike up the hillside at nearby Paso Nogales Park and assemble at the top where we could look out over rippling dry grasses toward Mt. Diablo with Concord, Pleasant Hill, and Walnut Creek below, and Martinez with its Shell Oil refinery and Carquinez Straits and the mothball fleet off to the left. We had various "lessons" up there, but one was Zorba the Greek. I wanted a physical experience of the idea that the *process* of life supersedes any destination. We formed a circle, and I recounted the episode in the story in which Zorba's young English boss is wiped out by the disastrous collapse of a trestle for hauling timbers for his mine. Reduced to the clothes on his back, he turns to Zorba and says, "Teach me to dance."

"Did you say *dance?* Come on, my boy!"

I put on the music from the sound track, and with arms on each other's shoulders, we began the Greek dance, at first slowly and then faster and faster as the music picked up speed. I still get chills picturing seventy assorted college students dancing together in a large circle to an ever faster Greek melody on top of a windy hill in Contra Costa County, California.

John Updike wrote that he liked going to church because it was the only place he got to sing. Listening or watching can be deeply moving, but it is not the same as dancing or singing or saying a poem out loud, or generating permutations and combinations in a math class oneself. There is a song about self-acceptance by country singer Guy Clark I thought my skills students ought to hear. It's about learning to let go, not caring what you look like, but getting so caught up in what you are doing that you forget to look over your shoulder. It has to come from the heart, the song goes, if you want it to work. Students need to realize that not holding back makes studies come alive. I could simply have played the song for them, but I wanted more mileage out of it. I decided to "teach" it in the same way I got my other class to learn "Momma, Look a Boo Boo." After a few tries we were belting it out like the Salvation Army, and everyone in the class knew the song *by heart*, a profoundly different way of knowing than by rote. Not only did they know the idea of the song, but they had also actually *experienced* it. It wasn't just a theory. When you know something by heart, it is internalized; it bounces around in your head; you hear it in your nervous system. Schools need to tinker with ways to make that kind of understanding likely.

That Voice

These experiences with music changed the tone of my classes. A class that was merely prose was no longer acceptable. Communication is a commingling of spirits, not merely the transmission of information. The art of teaching now became finding a way to make whatever we were doing—melodic, poetic—an act of creation. The power of the sound envelope was brought home in force when I experimented with the sound track of *Hands of Maria*, an eleven-minute film that shows Maria Martinez going through the process of creating her exquisite pottery. The film shows her working the clay in her home in the pueblo of San Ildefonso near Santa Fe. The visual part is wonderful, and I wanted the students to see her quiet authority, the simple beauty of her art. But the sound track had that voice. You know the one I mean. From the time I was a kid in the 1930s, they have used the same narrator for all instructional films. There must be a studio somewhere that clones this hideously dull voice. The instant you hear it, you know it's nap time.

So I decided to make my own sound track, and I pieced together several melodies from that era. The movie starts with a long shot of the Jemez Valley at dawn and zooms in on the pueblo and then Maria rolling clay into a coil for forming a pot. The new sound track starts with Cat Stevens's "Morning Has Broken," continues with Donovan's "Someone's Singing," and the Beatles' "Lucy in the Sky with Diamonds," and ends with Don McLean's "Vincent." When I tried it out the first time, I was astonished. The new sound envelope had transformed the film! It was downright lovely. Before, it had been a "lesson"; now it was something beautiful in its own right. And we really looked at the hands of Maria with our own eyes, not through the eyes of the living dead. We were free to roam around the scene, seeing much more than what the narrator instructed us to see. It went from a dull institutional film to a piece of art. We got an absorbing investigation from that accident that led to discussion of what it is to create, why we bother, and what dues we have to pay for our "sanity."

I had not guessed changing the sound track would have such remarkable results. I had not planned "appropriate" music. Mainly, I wanted music, and I needed enough to match the time frame of the film. But its unintentional serendipity profoundly affected my awareness of the effect of environment on experience. It had a direct influence on the atmosphere in which my classes functioned from then on. That's why students would arrive sometimes and hear Louis Armstrong singing "What a Wonderful World" or Joni Mitchell singing about the sun pouring in like butterscotch and sticking to all her senses.

Classes in any discipline could easily add a sound track. They could all include the largo movement of a symphony and a minute of relaxation. Imagine setting up a whole college that recognized the powerful effect of environment on learning. Imagine an entire faculty committed to students' emotional well-being. It would be a good experiment.

The Sound Envelope

Every class—hotel management, welding, police science, physics—ought to be more than instruction. It ought to be a spiritually satisfying event in its own right, like a symphony or a poem. Experiences that touch the soul have an afterlife. I remember using *Hands of Maria* at a workshop I gave for the nuns teaching at Marillac College in St. Louis. We had been exploring the differing effects of the musical version—which I played first—and the original. After lunch, as I was walking back to the workshop, I heard the silvery voices of the nuns in the chapel singing "Morning Has Broken." The spirit in those voices! I don't think any "instructional" film has ever precipitated such a response.

Natural Music

Music isn't something we add to a learning experience. It is something that has been taken away and needs to be restored. Learning does not take place in the conscious mind, albeit most classes are conducted as though it does. We simply do not learn that way. We learn poetically, metaphorically—that is, musically. We are designed that way. What goes on in most academic classes is unnatural, and that is what makes them seem arduous. When conditions involve the whole being, there is no grunting, no drudgery. We simply absorb—just as we always did before someone turned off the music. Whatever teachers want students to learn, their efforts will be more fruitful in a melodic envelope. That can involve actually playing music, but it is the inner music that has to be revived. Not much will happen if the mind is not tuned in and tuned up. It is simple enough to arrange. It does seem self-defeating not to take advantage of it.

8

The Structure
Keeping the Party Going

I wished to live life deliberately, to front only the essential facts of life, and see if I could learn what it had to teach, and not, when I came to die, discover that I had not lived. I did not wish to live what was not life, living is so dear. . . . I wanted to live deep and suck out all the marrow of life, to live so sturdily and Spartan-like as to put to rout all that was not life. . . .

—Henry David Thoreau

Getting Started

Soon after Bill Niland took over as president of our college in 1966, he sat in on one of my classes, and of course we had a little chat afterward about what I was up to and why certain things were done. My intention, I told him, was to cut away anything that didn't look like Chief Crazy Horse. Not in those terms, though; I didn't know him very well. What I did say was that I wanted every thing we did to count, to be vital, necessary, as important as anything a student would do anywhere else in life. And as full of feeling and spirit. Teaching took up most of my day—I even dreamed it—I had no intention of living a passionless life. The moments ticking away in our classes are *life* flowing by, not a rehearsal. I wanted our classes to get right to the heart of the matter and live there. Anything that distracted us had to be cut away. By the time Bill Niland showed up, a lot of baggage had been tossed overboard. Lightening the load has continued to this day; *living is so dear.*

So it was clear to me that even the first day of class was the *only* day, not a throwaway. I suspect that one of these days I will die. Why would I want to subject students and me to one moment of tedium?

That's the aim of the artist, conscious or not: finding a way to realize life *while we are living it.* Teaching has to go that deep; the work cannot be superficial and trivial. There is nothing wrong with practicing the times tables or musical scales—provided the drills are experienced as deeply pleasurable acts.

That said, what's the first thing a teacher says to a class? How about, "What's for breakfast?" What's for breakfast in an English class is English. In trig it's trig. In history it's the structure of our past. But that is metaphoric. The idea is to plunge right in. I have seen teachers spend half the class taking roll and the second half explaining the syllabus. What sort of message does that send to students? There are lots of ways to find out who's there—if you are required to do so—without wasting a minute of class time. The syllabus can be read elsewhere and the fuzzy stuff explained later, if need be. But a third to half of most sessions is wasted every day on such matters.

You can start right in: "The title of our course is Trigonometry. What do you suppose that's all about? [*What's for breakfast?* Get it?] What do you guess we will be doing? How do you think we should go about it? I'd like you to get into groups of five or six and talk about it. We'll get back together shortly and see what you came up with. Remember, we're not after *the* answer right now. We'll be figuring that out throughout the course." Then turn them loose, no assigning to groups, no group captain, no instructions on how to carry on the dialogue, nothing about taking notes. They will work all that out themselves. It's their job. Right away they have to think, really, not just pretend. They have to be alive, awake right from the start. Learning how to do that for themselves is part of why they are in college. Teachers should mind their own business. If a teacher wants everyone thinking about the course, this beginning is surefire.

That's the first part. The teacher is now free to go around and get the feel of the class, to sit in with a group or get out of its way. After ten minutes or so, it may be time to say, "OK, let's see what you're coming up with." Whatever gets fed back to the class as a whole becomes the raw material for that day's session. This dialogue will set the tone for the entire course. The students will know by the end of the first day whether the teacher gives a damn about them and their ideas. Geometry is really about human beings: this student in this class at this time. Anyone who doesn't know that will always be a lousy teacher.

Working up the raw material is tricky, and there are precious few places to witness the process working well. So a new teacher will have to screw up regularly. The clearer the central purpose, though, the faster an appropriate manner will emerge. No matter what ideas are tossed into the dialogue, however poorly or cogently phrased, however limited or complete, an overview of the course can be worked up, and everyone will be interested. The teacher simply explores whatever comes up, "Let's see. Is this what you're saying?" Or, "Does that fit in with the idea Mita just gave?" Or, "But what if blah, blah, blah happened? Would that idea take care of it?" The dialogue amounts to a genuine examination and an expansion of the ideas and a tendency toward integration. If the discussion seems to be flagging or too narrow, the groups can start up again and then get back together. By the end of the first day of class, a pretty good introduction to trigonometry (or English or accounting) will have been generated.

In this way the entire focus shifts from the teacher to the students, students who are immediately transformed into active participants instead of a passive audience. Starting with groups is critical. It takes the pressure off individuals and gives them time to work up their confidence and test out their guesses. When the class gets back together, individuals can present the group's idea—even though it might indeed be their own—with more ease and assurance. Usually, if a teacher wants class response the approach is to ask leading questions of the class *as a whole*, and maybe a brave soul or two will haltingly raise a hand. It is a highly stressful atmosphere. No wonder so many teachers complain, "I just can't get these kids to talk in class. They just sit there." Well, sure. Who wants to look like a fool or a kiss-up in front of the whole class? Letting students talk things over *first* is a simple shift in focus from teacher to students, but it makes all the difference.

This approach can be used throughout any course, from poetry to quantum mechanics. It shifts the emphasis to exploration, investigation, and experimentation—necessitating active thinking by everyone involved. It encourages and rewards mutual aid rather than competition. Students help each other clarify their thinking and make discoveries. Doesn't that sound great? Most teachers *say* that's what they want. This is a way to get it.

What next? Sometime before the end of the session, before students are looking at the clock and gathering up their stuff, would be a good time to tell them, "I'd like you to think over what we've talked about today and try to pull it all together. Jot down your reflections as you go along. It will take twenty to thirty minutes or so. Don't waste time editing. This is a rough draft. It won't be graded. I will read and respond to it, and you can save it in a folder." They can also be invited to relax at home over a beverage of choice and browse the course requirements and the text and see if what they find fits in. Keeping track of what's going on and constantly trying to make sense of it puts each student in the center. It becomes each one's course, not the teacher's. Traditionally, teachers do this *for* the students—with the inevitable ennui.

The idea of the first day is to put the students solidly in charge of their own learning, give them some experience of it right off, and set up an investigative structure for the whole course. Lengthy instructions will only muddle things. The students will be too nervous to register what you're going on about anyway; "Words are the source of misunderstanding," says the Little Prince. So cool it. Let the students lead; try not to step on their toes.

The Second Day

Start in the middle, of course. Always. And then work your way out, gathering attendant elements as you go along. The students' minds, being connecting organs, will organize the bits and pieces right there in class or in reflections later. If you want students to think about a trig concept, let them work it out in groups using whatever resources they want. When they think they've got it, let them explain it to everyone who doesn't. Goal: *Everyone* gets it.

> English: "Everyone give me one thing that *doesn't* belong in an English class." Get a list. "OK, get in groups and figure out a point of view from which each item *does* belong."

> Critical thinking: Write on the chalkboard: *Koan I : Whatever you say a thing is, it isn't.* "In your groups, figure out from what point(s) of view this could be a correct statement."

Move back and forth between groups and the whole class and work over the concept until its implications are revealed, or until it gets boring. Of course, the students will be connecting this with previous work, too, all the time, in and out of class.

What a teacher can do is take an interest. That shouldn't be hard to do. Anything seen clearly is breathtaking; but seeing clearly requires paying plenty of attention to whatever is being looked at, and this can't be faked. The hardest thing in the world, though, is giving up, or at least setting aside, preconceptions. Everyone knows racism is a bad thing, or cruelty or murder and so on. So if a student is all for gay bashing or carrying assault weapons—anything you happen not to approve of, it's hard not to blast back. But if you want a class to examine ideas and think about them, all ideas must be treated with equal respect. And they deserve respect. What a student truly thinks is a best guess, based on the input and circumstances available. It can be fascinating to trace out an idea and discover how it came into being, any idea, not just "great" ones. Examining an idea that favors murder can only broaden one's sensitivity to emptying the life out of living things. In any class there will be a wide spectrum of views; the devouring of the flesh of animals—or *any* life form—for example, is viewed by some as cannibalism. Whatever the topic, a genuine examination of any student's perceptions can only strengthen one's understanding of, say, integrals or fractals. So the wide range of viewpoints in any classroom is valuable and worth nurturing. The effect on a class is immediate and positive. When students know they will be heard with compassion and genuine interest and are not being conned, there is no holding them back. That's what makes such classes so noisy.

The trick is to really mean it. If teachers want to foist off their viewpoints as the only acceptable ones, however clever or forceful, it ain't gonna fly. Students can smell the artificiality. Of course, this means students have to be valued as remarkable creatures. They are, and it doesn't take more than a couple of genuine classes to realize that. An idea is an extension of a human being. It's a package deal. Attentiveness to each other's ideas ends up being attentiveness to each other. And how does that make the students—and the teacher— feel? Everyone feels burnished, shimmery, worthwhile. So not only is the academic intent fulfilled but the human being gets a boost, too. The point is you can't teach your subject in a vacuum. Learning is a holistic, whole-person activity. That's not a new idea. It's a fundamental principle of education.

There really isn't any art to question asking other than turning loose insatiable curiosity. It's simply a matter of taking a good look. That shouldn't be too hard to do. All of us have been fascinated with *something*, so we ought to be able to examine the mechanics of that process and apply them deliberately in the classroom. The scary thing is to take a chance and try it. Shifting the emphasis from teacher to student is learning to ride a bike. Before, it's scary; just after, you wonder what all the fuss was about.

Wait. No, what's really scary is giving up our expertise. The whole society, graduate school and everything else, supports the view that the teacher is the one who knows. Of course, we all know there is nothing like an expert to shut down a learning lab. If you are in the middle of a messy learning process, a supercilious eye can make you feel like a damned fool. So the teacher-as-expert can only interfere with the students' work. I remember in the early days doing a math calculation on the chalkboard and a student in the back raising his hand to correct an error I had made. Later he wrote that it was the most eye-opening event of his schooling. Until then he had never seen a teacher make a mistake. Teachers were gods; students were nothing. His being able to correct me was a turning point. Usually, a teacher comes to class with everything all worked out, all the screwups taking place off stage. The "lesson" is a closed sphere with no way for students to break in and get their hands on damp clay. A sloppy teacher needs help; I needed lots of help. Making mistakes in public turned out to be an asset, and luckily it was one of my talents. Typically, teachers show students the results of thinking, but rarely do students get to see it in action, much less participate in the process. So it's a good idea to do something together that's not too well worked out, or to rework it somehow, and leave lots of room for the teacher to struggle along with the students.

Day Three, ad Infinitum

Keep the party going. Sift the gravel and see what nuggets need attention next. If one is not used to seeing a course generate itself as it progresses, it is hard to imagine things working themselves out over time, but they do. My student teacher Charlie Dodt thought trust and courage were prerequisites of good teaching, but they are learned on the job. If you've done it a few times, you know the students will be fine and the course will pattern out. There is no danger—perhaps at first but not once things get rolling. There is tremendous support right there in the classroom. Casting out artificial authority only strengthens authentic behavior. What has to be learned is to be one's own self right out in public. It only looks scary; it's really a glide. Students, too, need to learn this about themselves. The less they fake it, the closer they get to educating themselves. Naked selves commingling is what education is, isn't it?

> Basically what we do is throw stuff around, then gather it up, save the good stuff and toss the rest. Play again, gather the good stuff and toss the rest. When all that gathering and tossing is finished, we root through the garbage and finds the jewels that make the good stuff shine. The game is in shuffling the garbage and the good stuff. If you play your cards right, you can shine in the end. We've got a box full of gold. Just needs polish.
> —Eileen Giaquinto, student

Units of Study

To my friend Cynthia from a neighboring college, my classes seemed like a herd of mustangs. I didn't control them but eased them away from the cliff's edge. It's true; healthy, free individuals surging along full of spirit and energy do not corral easily. That is as it should be, but it scares most teachers. I suspect that is why they have lesson plans, quizzes, tests, and term papers: to keep the lid on, to scare these free spirits into submission. These devices are not really for educational purposes but for control. Because I could see clearly that these tools actually interfered, I began casting them away one by one.

In some colleges predetermined units of study and time frames are so regimented that you can visit any section on a given day and find every teacher at the same place in the course outline, *covering* the same material. In our college we had considerable latitude, but even so, there were required texts and units of content we were all expected to "cover." Often my students and I had other fish to fry, but we were straightjacketed. Such packaging ignores how we assimilate new experience. Learning is not linear. Even in supposedly sequential courses like chemistry, accounting, math, and the like, units of study are arbitrary and artificial. Suppose you are to study trigonometry for a semester. There is no pedagogical justification for starting thirty-five uniquely furnished minds at the same place and dragging them along at the same pace through a predesigned course of study. That is not how the mind works.

For example, instead of explaining the slide rule to students of logarithms, Karl Staubach got the kids to invent their own and teach the whole concept to each other. An economics teacher got the students to purchase some stocks and follow their interests thereafter. Another teacher got kids to make flutes out of drinking straws; imagine the effect of that experience. Instead of teaching the history of the electron tube, a teacher whose students wanted to know how a radio works let the students ask their own questions; that is, he started where *they* and their interests were, not where he thought they should be. Most people who use computers start where they are, usually in the middle, and learn as much or as little as they need, any way they can. Their progress toward mastery, as they determine it, is a good lesson for any teacher in how we learn—if not too blinded by intention.

When I got this problem worked through, I put it together in an article published in the November 1965 *English Journal.* Following is an update. Even though the message was for English teachers, a unit that generates itself as it goes along works just as well for any subject. It simply means we start where we are and work our way outward.

A Generative Unit

English courses are organized around just about anything. They focus on history, region, genres, psychology, sociology, gender, or on some fragment like literature or on skills like reading or writing. One problem is that such divisions are teachers' emphases, not students'. More fundamental, though, is a confusion about what an ongoing English program is all about. What it is all about is an investigation of the native tongue. Whatever fragment a student might be pondering, it is always in the context of the entire spectrum of language phenomena. English teachers must have a deep sense that language is the basis of all that goes on in every English class. The subject is not philosophy, poetry, male dominance, history, or journalism. Classes may explore these and anything else that transpires in a culture, but they do this to see what might be revealed about *language*. (The subject in the math department is not differential equations, algebra, or probability but *mathematics*. And what all math students are learning to do is talk like a native speaker of that language, the language of mathematics, to talk math, and to be able to witness the world through that lens.)

My classes and I found conventional study packages distracting and confining. Sometimes we needed to go over to the mall and tape-record dialects or watch paralanguage. In the process someone might feel a poem coming on and decide to write that instead of the department's required 500-word theme—or maybe a letter to the *Contra Costa Times*. Or maybe a headline, or maybe make a flag, or play the guitar. The damned course outline was always butting in. And when we heeded it, it was always a wet blanket—the plan, the time frame, the required readings! We needed a unit free to capitalize on the moment, able to move in any productive direction in space or time, a unit that was inclusive, not confining.

What we needed was a pattern that comes from within, not one imposed from outside. Clearly, a unit of study *was* unfolding, a spiraling open-ended idea generating in each student's mind, the same process that we all go through as we try to make sense of the blur of data that confront us at birth. We all try to order the data, to make a picture that fits all the pieces together. It's always a self-portrait. That's what the reader of these words is doing this very moment. Life and learning are ongoing projects, not units one finishes. All things are related. All things need to be connected, not pigeonholed, not wrapped in a red ribbon and stored in a trunk somewhere. But the real fault of conventional units is that they are created by teachers. The teacher does the one job that must remain with the student. If teachers think *for* the students, what is the message? We see the results every day.

If ideas are feats of association, as Robert Frost said, we can see the problem with conventional units. They are teachers' related facts, their insights, their ingenuity. No wonder they report them with such pride. But if individual thought about language is to be encouraged, students must create their own units, lifelong units of their own insights, awareness, relationships. Their minds yearn for a piece of the action. To pass the fun around, teachers get to continue their own projects. There is always more to see and discover.

When a course is subject-matter oriented, it is impossible to tailor the semester to each student's measurements. It is a principle of education that learning begins where you are, not where someone thinks you ought to be. Individual organisms simply cannot be brought along at a lockstep pace. We can see to it individuals get every opportunity to reflect penetratingly on their language experience. An organic, continually developing investigation of language from kindergarten through graduate school and onward is the best program of English possible.

Such a unit *is* sequential and *does* integrate with the rest of a student's work but not in the usual sense. The continuity of English study lies not in a body of material but in the students themselves. The sequence lies in their growing control over and awareness of the processes of communication. (This is true of the sciences, too.) We need not be concerned with items of information (academic trivia) but with students being able to perceive whatever chunk of communication lies before them—in other words, with gaining command of the language. When we use language blindly, we are its prisoners.

Ongoing individualized study does articulate with previous and succeeding years. Because it is student-made, student-centered, always focused, and always flexible, it easily integrates bits and pieces conventionally associated with English programs: reading, writing, listening, speaking, vocabulary, grammar, literature, rhetoric, and so on. When something happens in a generative program, a student's problem is always the same: "Does this stuff fit what I already see? Can I make it fit? How? Does my picture need to be reworked?" So the ongoing job is to reflect on experiences as they come along and try to fit them together meaningfully. That's what the mind likes to do anyway, so it's no big deal. It is a piecing together of individual experience with new adventures the class shares together—but from each student's unique vantage point.

In an investigating, experimenting, examining class, the teacher can come off it. Instead of jimmying facts into heads, the teacher can join students in *examining* these facts. Instead of saying, "We are here to study English because . . . ," one can say, "Why *are* we doing this?" Instead of prescribing usage, one can examine usage, turn a curious eye on the entire spectrum. "What's this all about?" There are infinite baubles to examine and limitless lenses to look through. Almost anything a teacher is sure everyone must know can be turned upside down. *Should* they know this? Why? Is there a point of view from which we need not know it? And so on. What teachers do in class, then, is exactly what they do behind the scenes, only now they do it in public. The artificiality evaporates and elaborate machinations become irrelevant. The teacher is right in there doing honest research along with everyone else. That is why a stranger might sometimes have trouble finding the teacher in these classes.

When an ongoing study is open-ended, investigators can take full advantage of chance occurrences. Whatever is going on in the culture can be tapped. The raw material is continually updated. Over time most elements of a good language investigation get dragged into the dialogue in a very natural way. What this means is that the mind engages in its usual processes but notices itself at work as it goes along. The mind reflects on what it is doing.

Of course, if the process is working well, no two students will be arriving at the same view. Since no two beings consider the same aspects of an experience significant or compelling, they will piece things together differently. There is no way to test for uniform content, since there is none. The course consists of different processes going on simultaneously. Paradoxically, even though they become more divergent as they proceed, students report feeling like part of a warm and friendly family, something they rarely experience in conventional courses.

In a generative approach to education, students never start a new unit. They are always working on the same one. It is not a sequential course of study or steps in a curriculum—there is no curriculum—but a picture forming in the mind which becomes sharper and clearer from year to year. The artist considers all the phenomena, not a predetermined handful. Sometimes a teacher-artist must go back and take another look because some new discovery makes that aspect seem out of harmony or because a new lens has been fitted. Though teachers and materials change, the same quest is under way. This is the way thinking people always proceed, so the hardest thing about this teaching approach is to get out of the way. The sooner the students take over as their own guides, thinking up genuine questions, finding ways to resolve them, creating meaningful relationships, the better.

How different it is to experience such vitality in a classroom. Conventionally, the message is that things are known; in time all will be revealed. Be quiet, be patient, memorize, take the test, forget it. Most classes leave students with the feeling of having completed something. The generative unit engenders the feeling of having *begun* something. For educated people life itself is open-ended. It is a closed system for others. Which is better? Life is growth and change. We all know what the opposite is.

9

The Manner
Rhythm and Blues

I am not I.
  I am this one
who goes beside me, whom I do not see;
whom, sometimes, I can visit,
and whom, sometimes, I forget.
He who is quiet, calm, when I talk,
he who forgives, gently, when I hate,
he who goes where I am not,
he who will remain standing when I die.

—Juan Ramón Jimenéz*

Eighteen years after I started teaching at Diablo Valley College we were still debating the nature of the job, but there was lots more gray hair at faculty meetings and the dialogue was slowing down. It seemed to me we still hadn't gotten down to the nubbins about lecturing, so in March 1981 I took a crack at it in the *DVC Forum*, a publication for the exchange of information and ideas among faculty and staff of the college. It still puzzles me that research on the educational limitations of lecturing is ignored. Anyone who does it regularly, unless that person is a master showman, must surely know how depressing it is to go on and on to a numbed audience. You don't even have to read the research. It's just plain awful. Here's why.

---

*1973, Heredos de Juan Ramón Jimenéz, Madrid-España.

Lecturing Is Not Teaching

Lecturing well is an art. Teaching well is an art. Other than that they have hardly anything to do with each other. It's a matter of definition, not a criticism. It's like comparing film making with typography, two different kinds of activities. If you want to talk about the art of film making, you will have to discuss trucking, montage, camera angles, cuts, framing, close-ups, bridging. For typography, leading, type face and size, margins, line justification, bleeding.

When a terrific lecturer says what's going on is not teaching, that is not false modesty. It is simply a clear understanding of the difference. If you want to talk about the art of lecturing, you will need terms like stage presence, voice modulation, tone, paralanguage, pacing, props—and I would include costume and lighting. Effectiveness is measured by audience involvement, its degree of enthusiasm, the emotion one is able to stir and control. Lecturing is usually a one-person stage show, a performance, and must be judged on that basis.

Lecturing is not directly involved in the processes teaching focuses on: growth and change, learning to learn, mastering of material, processing of data. *While* the lecture is going on, such behavior is inappropriate. Indeed an audience that set about *learning* during a lecture would unnerve the coolest speaker. What people do learn during a lecture is how to behave as an audience. In lecturing, it is the speaker's show; in teaching, it's the learners'. If you observe a group of people together, you can tell right away which is going on.

Suppose you hear a lecture on being assertive. During the talk the examples make sense; you are stirred. The arguments given are persuasive. Yes, you think, that's right. I *should* be more assertive. But have you learned to be assertive, have you changed? The answer almost invariably is no. Within a day or so almost everyone in attendance will have forgotten nine-tenths of what was said. Even if they could recite the lecture verbatim, no learning could be said to have taken place *until* the listener becomes more assertive. If that ever happens at all, it will be the result of individual acts of mind and body the learner performs himself or herself, *chooses* to perform, over a period of time until the behavior has become a part of that person, *is* that person. Only then can we say something has been learned, and it should be obvious who is doing the teaching.

If 250 people sat through the assertiveness talk, the most accomplished lecturer can have no certainty whatsoever that any of them in the weeks to come will change at all. I can think of few so smug as to think that change takes place *while* they are jawing. One can admire a great lecture, but one would be naive to expect to learn while it is going on. The restructuring of one's mind takes time and experience. This is not a criticism. It is a description.

On the other hand, if you want to teach people to become assertive, you will have to involve them in situations in which they can act assertively enough that it becomes part of their behavioral structure. Likewise, if you want people to be mathematicians, you will have to structure an atmosphere in which they do math, think mathematically, until it becomes part of their nature. Talking at them about math—lecturing—will not guarantee this.

If you would like people to think in a certain manner, you will have to set up situations in which they will have to perform frequently enough to get the hang of it.

While it is clear that learning is something an individual chooses to do or not do, it is possible to provide environments in which most people will choose to do so. That is the art of teaching. I see nothing wrong with people getting really good at lecturing and doing it in classrooms. But if what has been identified here as teaching is not central, then the institution is not a school but a theater.

The Name Game: Who Are *You*?

The Name

Do you know a word that doesn't refer to something?
Have you ever picked and held a rose from R, O, S, E?
You say the NAME. Now try to find the reality it names.
Look at the moon in the sky, not the one in the lake.
If you want to be free of your obsession with words
    and beautiful lettering, make one stroke down.
There's no self, no characteristics,
    but a bright center where you have the knowledge
    the Prophets have, without books or interpreter.
                                —Jelaluddin Rumi

When emphasis shifts from teacher to student, priorities change. In a humanistic college each student is the center and the whole human being, too, not just a placeholder. Who *are* you? We all know our name is not the answer, but it is our handle, our access code. So as soon as possible my classes set about learning each other's names. Some teachers do try to learn all their students' names, but that is only part of the job. Everyone in the class is a resource person, so to make full use of the "Internet" everyone needs to know everyone.

At the beginning, though, everyone is hiding out; a classroom can be dangerous to your GPA. So the word is *watch out*. From the first moment on, the style and tone of a student-centered class are a clear message, and the interplay of groups with the whole class moves things along. But by the third or fourth day, it's time for a name game.

There are many variations. The first time I tried it, we formed a large circle. The object, I said, was for everyone to know all the class by the end of the session, and I would have to do it, too. Knowing all the names would be a requirement of the course—just like terms in biology or art history—and we would have a "test" a couple of weeks later. I asked someone to start:

"I'm Heidi Klinger."

If it was a small group, there might be time for Heidi to tell us something about herself or to answer a few questions, if she felt like it.

"Next."

"Hi, my name is Hae Lee. I'm from Hong Kong. I've been here two years. I like computers."

"OK. Say your name again and then the first person's."

"I'm Hae Lee, and this is Heidi Klinger."

"Next."

"I'm Gloria Pelayo."

We go through the same routine, and then Gloria gives all three names:

"I'm Gloria Pelayo. This is Hae Lee. This is Heidi Klinger."

And so on around the circle, adding one and saying all the others each time. Of course, the game gets more challenging as it progresses. At the end, I was supposed to say my name and give all the others. The students always loved to see me squirm. The first time we tried it out, I was nervous, but I did manage, and each time got easier, because I knew I could do it. After all, in a class of thirty-five people that's only seventy bits of information. (I like to point out to those who think remembering academic trivia like biology facts is hard that it's the same thing, the same skills.) If a class was large, we might work on ten people at a time or use any other approach that would allow us to give our complete attention to every student. But whatever the approach, I wanted all the students to feel responsible for entering all the others into their memory banks and to be fully engaged throughout the session. Everyone knew it was a game, but they played seriously, and that made it exciting and fun.

The best classes have layers of meaning and multiple aspects. And so it is with the name game. Some students, of course, would have been asking why we had to learn everyone's name. What did that have to do (in our case) with English? So they got to think about that in their daily reflections. What did the classroom feel like before the game? How did it feel afterward? Do you feel better with a shell around you or out in the open, knowing lots of people and lots of people knowing you? And so on. There are all kinds of implications. How does a name, a label, work? Do we use it to access the area of experience it represents—so that we can open that "file" and renew our acquaintance and expand it? Or do we use it to settle things, file, and forget? Why do people call it your "handle"? Will knowing everyone's name help you study English (or history or computer programming)?

And there is more. A name, as Karl Staubach's classes discover, encapsulates the individual's personal history, a genealogy, and ethnic and cultural panorama. Even when he gave workshops for teachers, Karl would always begin by casually asking somebody in the group about his/her name. Jim Daley, Kabir Arghandiwal, Kathleen, Clark. Right away you're into all sorts of things. Kathleen means "pure." Clark is "clerk." Kabir was a revered Afghan poet, and Arghandiwal is actually a region from which Kabir's family took its name. Which part of Ireland did the Daleys come from? Moore means "black." You already know about Millers, Stones, Fords, Masons, and so on. Mc or Mac means "son of." Karl would have everybody fascinated within minutes.

The name game is multifaceted, layered, poetic. In fact, when a whole class is the resource and not just the teacher, there are endless surprises. You get into things like letting children choose their names, taking the husband's family name, naming a person for an event or a situation, even the deeply metaphoric implication of all naming of all things. It is an extremely lively topic. It can lead to the heart of things. But the immediate effect is profound. When a whole group concentrates its attention on one person, that human being is illuminated, no longer anyone but someone. And when a whole group has been highlighted in this way, it becomes a warm and friendly place, no longer a roomful of strangers.

There are other pedagogical benefits. People's minds work better when they feel safe and relaxed. When they are anxious, the corpus callosum slams shut, and it's hard to move information between the two hemispheres. So if the group is more at ease, even those teachers who don't give a damn will be able to do conventional things more easily. If they are among friends, students will be able to handle whatever comes at them easier. A good experiment for a college would be to agree to have students and teachers in every class learn each other's names. Some doctoral candidate ought to set that up.

Once they do the name game, students realize how unnatural conventional class settings are. Human beings are gregarious, but students report sitting in a class all semester and not even knowing the name of the person next to them—or even the teacher's name! Often our name-game class is the only one they have in which they know lots of people. They go around campus greeting each other. "Hi, Heidi Klinger." "Hi, Hae Lee. How's your computer class?" Some of them know more people from this one class than from their entire college experience. Lots of students feel isolated when they go to college. It is one reason they drop out. So turning the college into a community makes a difference, academically as well as spiritually. One experiment to the point was set up at the checkout desk of a college library. When some students presented their library card, the clerk ever so slightly touched their hands. With others, the clerk did not. Outside, the students were asked how they felt about the library. The ones who had actually touched the clerk's hand thought it was a friendly place. The others thought is was rather formal and cold.

Ministers like to press the flesh as their parishioners depart. They would find more response to their sermons if they greeted the congregation as they entered. If I don't make contact with every student, I know the class is not as good as it could be. Even eye contact or a smile, some recognition, will do—just so that organism is brought online. When I see students greeting each other, I know their thinking will be more productive.

If they feel comfortable, teachers perform better, too. There is a well-known story of students in a behavioral psychology class who wanted to see what they could accomplish with a warm response versus the cold shoulder. When the teacher made any motion toward the door, they would sit up, be attentive, smile, nod their heads. Any other behavior would be met with dead pans, slouching, no eye contact. Of course, as the story goes, the teacher ended up lecturing out in the hall. I tell my students they could make almost any stuffy teacher into a pussycat just by giving lots of strokes for desired behavior and ignoring the rest.

Karl's Christmas Party

Whether we know it or not, we are always using behavior modification, teacher to student, student to teacher, students to each other, everybody and everything in the whole culture constantly massaging each other all the time. I remember Karl Staubach's annual Christmas party. We used to crowd three or four classes in a big room just before the Christmas break and do T. S. Eliot's "Journey of the Magi." There was food and drink and sometimes music. Our dignified-looking and -sounding British colleague Bill Sparke gave the proceedings a touch of class by reading the poem out loud. Then we'd hand out copies of the poem, and Karl would start in with the trivia game. (His own students were shills; they had had a chance to look at some of the questions earlier.)

Journey of the Magi

'A cold coming we had of it,
Just the worst time of the year
for a journey, and such a long journey:
The ways deep and the weather sharp,
The very dead of winter.'
And the camels galled, sore-footed, refractory,
Lying down in the melting snow.
There were times we regretted
The summer palaces on slopes, the terraces,
And the silken girls bringing sherbet.
Then the camel men cursing and grumbling
And running away, and wanting their liquor and women,
And the night-fires going out, and the lack of shelters,
And the cities hostile and the towns unfriendly
And the villages dirty and charging high prices:
A hard time we had of it.
At the end we preferred to travel all night,
Sleeping in snatches,
With the voices singing in our ears, saying
That this was all folly.

Then at dawn we came down to a temperate valley,
Wet, below the snow line, smelling of vegetation;
With a running stream and a water-mill beating the darkness,
And three trees on the low sky,
And an old white horse galloped away in the meadow.
Then we came to a tavern with vine-leaves over the lintel,
Six hands at an open-door dicing for pieces of silver,
And feet kicking the empty wine-skins.
But there was no information, and so we continued
And arrived at evening, not a moment too soon
Finding the place; it was (you may say) satisfactory.

> *All this was a long time ago, I remember,*
> *And I would do it again, but set down*
> *This set down*
> *This: were we led all that way for*
> *Birth or Death? There was a Birth, certainly,*
> *We had evidence and no doubt. I had seen birth and death,*
> *But had thought they were different; this Birth was*
> *Hard and bitter agony for us, like Death, our death.*
> *We returned to our places, these Kingdoms,*
> *But no longer at ease here, in the old dispensation,*
> *With an alien people clutching their gods.*
> *I should be glad of another death.*

"Can anyone tell me the name of the poem?"

Someone would answer. Everyone would laugh, and Karl would fish out a piece of Christmas candy from his big grocery bag and toss it over to the brilliant student.

"Who wrote it?"

Another correct answer and another piece of candy tossed over.

"What do the letters *T* and *S* stand for?"

"They're his initials." This was probably one of *my* smart-aleck students.

Another piece of candy for this ingenious answer.

"Thomas Stearns."

More candy.

"Why are there quotes around the first lines?"

"Because it's a quote."

"Because someone else said that, not Eliot."

Two more pieces of candy.

"Who is the quote from?"

"Bishop Lancelot Andrewes." This was on the cheat sheet Karl's kids had.

"Who was he?"

"He was one of the people who wrote the King James version of the Bible. The quotation is from one of his sermons."

This was no doubt Bill Sparke. This was *not* on the cheat sheet. Bill gets a piece of candy.

"When *is* 'the very dead of winter'?"

"Winter solstice." Candy.

"What's that?"

"How many times is death mentioned? Why is it capitalized sometimes? Birth, birth? Feet kicking the empty wineskins? What's 'folly' rhyme with?

'Singing?'" And so on for most of the hour, people getting out of their seats, shouting out answers without taking turns, really into the game.

And so it went. Citing trivia may seem silly and immature, but the effect was immensely pleasing. It boiled down to more than 100 people intensely examining the surface features of a many-layered poem, and as that was going on, the beauty of the poem emerged on its own. Karl knew that would happen. That's how the mind works, after all. Gradually the imagery revealed itself, the sounds of the words, the intrinsic associations, the repetitions and variations, even punctuation and stanzas—all from taking a good, playful look. At the end Bill took the podium again and did a final reading of the poem for a very attentive, appreciative audience. They will probably never forget "Journey of the Magi." It's one of my favorite poems, too.

Normally, I prefer everything to come from the students, but this event showed vividly how powerful behavior modification can be. They went after the candy in exactly the same way B. F. Skinner's pigeons did learning to play Ping-Pong. For human beings the candy was only symbolic of our inner pleasure in noticing, seeing, un . . . covering. It was fun to be fully engaged in mind, body, and spirit. But you don't have to give out candy to elicit peak performance. The experience itself is the reward. Just remove impediments and pay attention. It is that simple.

Postscript: Before I had the bugs worked out of behavior modification, I tried Karl's candy routine on a disruptive student, and did it backfire! Maureen was a woman who demanded lots of attention. No matter what we were doing together, she would turn and talk to another student, challenge whatever we were doing, offer her "expertise," and in general shut down the proceedings. I was young at the time and was stymied. So I figured, "Well, Maureen wants attention. She wants everyone to notice her. OK, whenever she does something for attention, I'll toss her a piece of candy." I'm sure you can see how dumb that was. Now she really did it up brown! Boy, was she playing Ping-Pong! That sounds like a failed class, doesn't it? However, I would say it was one of my most valuable lessons. I got a firsthand experience of how conditioning works. It has stood me in good stead ever since. Whenever I ask students to do anything, I think *What kind of behavior is this really eliciting?*

Students should know they can affect their learning conditions. In fact, they have complete control. A teacher in the sixth grade, for example, had been yelling at everyone and giving lots of time-outs, and everyone was feeling bad. So the kids got together and wrote her a note: "Dear Mrs. Agnew, We really like you, and we're sorry you are feeling bad. We will try to be good. But would you please stop yelling at us?" Mrs. Agnew read the note, put her head down on the desk, and cried. Classrooms are assemblies of human beings. We all need to remember that. Barbara Stevens, a first-grade teacher, used to start by asking, "Does anyone need a hug today?" College kids need hugs, too, at least verbal ones. The learning curve would soar if everyone in every class felt thoroughly hugged all the time. Efficiency experts would find time spent on the name game to be a good investment. And students invariably report it is one of the best things about the class. It costs so little to make learning inviting.

Test Day

I quit giving tests altogether seven or eight years into teaching. I would have quit sooner, but I'm a slow learner. I thought I had to, even after I realized how destructive they are. I didn't have to; I got along just fine for the next thirty years without them. But I always gave a name-game "test." I would tell the students they have to know everyone's name, one of the few specific trivia requirements of the course. There will be a *test*, I would tell them, in a couple of weeks. They knew very well I wasn't *really* going to give them a test, but they acted like it anyway, doing all the stuff I used to hate about test games. "Do we have to spell them all correctly?" "How much time will we have?" "Can we just give first names?" "Can we have more time to get ready?" I pretended it was all very serious, too. I did want them to know each other's names, but I certainly wasn't going to grade them on it.

So one sunny day the students arrive, and it's TEST day. As they file in, each student gets a number to wear and a roster. There is music playing, and the teaching assistants and I have set up a table with things to eat and drink. The "test" is to match the person's number with a name on the roster. They have to get 100 percent or they fail.

Of course, it doesn't take a minute for people to start cheating. They start going up to each other and asking their names. (Big surprise: Lots of them haven't studied much.) The first thing you know the whole class is milling about, talking with each other. It turns into a jolly good time. Everyone is thoroughly enjoying the "test." More than once I found a couple of guys erasing numbers from their rosters. That way, they had an excuse to talk with someone they were attracted to. Pretty smart, eh?

The one-and-only test day turns out to be one of the best days of the semester, and everyone knows everyone else much better by the end of the hour, wonderful enthusiasm, lots of positive energy. What's amusing is that people actually turn in their "test paper" at the end. They really know how to play the school game.

As always, students think about the event in their reflections. Often we talk about whether that really was a test. Then we get a chance to explore what a test is, what it is said to be for and what it actually is for. Is the name-game test a good test? If tests are learning tools, did everyone know *more* by the end of the test? Sure. Should you be allowed to cheat on a test? Depends on how you define *cheat*. Should the atmosphere be formal or informal? Which elicits your best performance? Should it be fun to take a test? Should it be on how much you know or how little? Is it really necessary to scare the pants off everyone in order to advance understanding of the periodic chart or whatever? Do you get to cheat in real life? And so on. Students are subjected to tests from the time they set foot in kindergarten onward. For many, reflecting on the name-game test is the first time they ever take a good look at what is going on.

So the name game and its test accomplish exactly what any traditional teacher would want and a whole lot more. It is only one example of what a multifaceted "lesson" can be. All classes can learn that way. Everyone, including teachers, would actually enjoy coming to class and experiencing what Goethe described as "a rich, manifold life, brought close to the eyes."

Paying Attention: Surface Features

> To see or to perish is the very conditon laid upon every creature....
> —Teilhard de Chardin

It is impossible to bring a rich, manifold life up close and not be dazzled. In the midst of such wonder, "What's the point?" never enters the mind. Just being there, witnessing, without ulterior purpose is enough. "Does anyone ever realize life every, every minute?" asks Emily in *Our Town*. "No," says the stage manager, "The saints and poets, maybe. They do some." Certainly such clarity is rare in classrooms. When a math concept is explained to students, they know about it, but it is not their *experience*. They have not merged with it, as the thinker did who originally discovered that concept. But it is this very co-mingling of spirit with matter that art and education are all about. The moment of that intersection is the artistic experience. For the artist it lies in the process of creating. For the witness, it lies in re . . . creating. I remember my wife marveling at the minute details our little granddaughter found in the smallest snail, piece of bark, or speck of lint. "Emily, that's fascinating. I never see those things." "Grammy, you don't *look.*"

Whatever life is or is about, it surely calls for a close look as we go along. Having a look is central to a learning environment. It isn't something nice that can happen once in a while. It is what we are up to all the time, both in and out of class, throughout life. Paying attention is a habit that can be valued or, as in most schools, ignored. But if it is not a habit, what is the incentive to take a good look at the skies? When Whitman heard the learned astronomer, he hurried outside and looked up at the stars. It reminds me of the time our friend Gert came to visit California and spent most of her time at the postcard rack, instead of stepping outside and seeing the real McCoy. School is not *about* life; it *is* life. We learn what we do. If every class is a paying-attention class, that is what we will get good at.

I don't remember how this idea became so clear to me, but no doubt it evolved from letting students have their say and my being so absorbed in their reality pictures that I myself got better at paying attention. It's a transferable skill, as educators might say. One experience does stand out, though, as a turning point. I forget the original purpose of the "lesson"; but we were looking at Pieter Brueghel's painting *Children's Games.* Everyone had a copy, and I said, "Let's see how many things we can notice about the painting. Everyone give us something, no matter how minute, whatever you see, and we'll keep going around the class till we run out."

We never did run out. Every time someone pointed to something, it was as though a light had been turned on over that detail. The painting got more vivid with each new discovery. There was an uncanny sensation of the lighting being turned up; the painting kept getting brighter. I can't describe it better than that, but I am sure any reader who tries it will have the same experience. We illuminated this painting by concentrating our beam of attention on it. We spent the whole hour, and I am sure not one of us was bored. What an art lesson! But during the process, we were simply *seeing what's there.* We were eating the banana because it tasted good and getting the full flavor of it, not because of the potassium.

Most people I know feel compelled to glance at a painting, a dress, a poem, and judge it immediately. It seems a point of honor to have an opinion about everything, to come down on it, pro or con. In our Brueghel investigation the idea of judging the work never even came up. That wasn't what we were doing, and evaluating it at any time during that session would have been a terrible intrusion. In fact, it would have killed the painting, like sticking a pin through a butterfly and fixing it in the collection box. No one wanted to do that. Think of the implications: Think of how often in classrooms our natural curiosity is shut off by expert opinion. Think of how much we don't see in life because we already "know" it: a person, the sidewalk that takes us to the store, the taste of this particular Concord grape. If there is someone in a classroom who knows things, it is going to harm us.

The Brueghel did-you-notice game left us all with such an "appreciation" that none of us, I am sure, could ever look indifferently at his work again. In fact, a student later sent me a card from the Kunsthistorisches Museum of Vienna, where she saw the original painting. But she said she recognized his hand in other of his works long before she went there. When teachers know what they want students to get from a music-appreciation class, a lab experiment, or an electronics lesson, that will severely limit what students—and teachers—will be able to "see." The message is that education is enhanced, not diminished, by the suspension of judgment.

What does happen to discrimination, recognition of quality, critical acumen? What if there is a contest, and you have to choose the best wine, car, painting? Isn't there an objective set of criteria? Usually, such questions do come up after a good paying-attention session, either in class or in reflections later. One response is like that of John Cheever when he was asked to compare the quality of his work with John Updike's: "Writing is not a competitive sport." Someone who knows how to take a good look can enjoy even a "bad" wine. To a little kid, sail-toads (squashed and dried-out roadkill you can throw like Frisbees) are just as fascinating as spring blossoms. Who wants to be so discriminating as to be self-imprisoned? Julia Child enjoys a McDonalds hamburger and french fries. I have an acquaintance who will eat only in restaurants with tablecloths. She never gets to go to the best Mexican restaurant in the county—which happens to be in a run-down neighborhood in Pittsburg, California. Seeing what's there doesn't mean you can't judge things as better or worse. It just means whatever you are doing you do as well as possible. It means whatever is going on can be thoroughly enjoyed.

Beginning with surface features shifts the sequence, that's all. I've been to galleries with people who make snap judgments of everything they lay eyes on. It certainly takes the fun out of it. I want to say, "Just tell me what you see. We can talk tomorrow about whether it's good or not." Schools foster this urge to reach a verdict. It's so grown-up. But as usual, the emphasis is on the results, rather than the process. It ignores the structure of the brain and the tasks handled by the two hemispheres of the new brain. We don't think much at all, it turns out, in the conscious part. That part can set things in motion and gather and sort data and handle routine matters, but the real piecing together of data takes place off stage, out of awareness, in the nonconscious. We do not critique a poem or a used car with our conscious minds. The nonconscious mind is brilliant at taking care of quality control and needs to be allowed to do its job, thank you very much. Do a few did-you-notice games, and you soon learn to trust your nonconscious mind. Applying critical standards before taking a good look prevents anything from being fresh. "There are a lot of completely educated people in the world," said Robert Frost, "and they are going to resent having to learn anything new."

It turns out that starting with surface features has broad applications. It can be applied consciously to anything one wants to "know," be it computer science or a short story. It is a way of fiddling around and then along the way discovering how much you have learned—without even trying. The mind loves to make sense of things; it doesn't need to be intimidated or forced. My students and I have learned what is suitable for conscious attention and what must be left to the nonconscious. Once it figures things out, the right hemisphere faxes a printout for the conscious mind to record. "Did that come from me?!" Yep.

Here is one of scores of examples: The spring I first got a computer, the apparatus felt like a foreign country. With great effort I was able to get my word processor program going. I could use it but only by-the-numbers, so to speak. It was mechanical and awkward. Everything I wanted to do was laborious; oh, how I longed for my typewriter. In June I went away for three months. I was busy all summer and never consciously thought about computers at all, not at all. When I turned on the computer that fall, everything that had been so effortful was easy. It all fell into place; it all made sense. I'm sure this sort of learning had been happening all along, but I hadn't noticed the process. It's the same with typing, driving, using chopsticks. What I realized was that I needn't have fretted so. It would have come. I have since watched the mind set things up, and sure enough, it's the same process every time. Only now I know not to worry, and that makes it happen better and faster. I can actually enjoy the mess-around part, knowing tomorrow morning I will understand much better than I did when I went to bed.

Once they became aware of how natural learning works, students and friends began giving me examples from their own experience. Patty, who had been away from the business world for ten years, got nervous talking with a sales manager who snowed her with technical jargon. But when she got off the phone, she remembered how we had looked at surface features in our classes without express tendency and how easily she had learned then. She decided to let things take care of themselves. Sure enough, the next morning, with no studying in-between, it all made sense.

Brain structure has powerful implications for students and teachers. It means the puritan work ethic is strictly for masochists. Control freaks have been scaring kids half to death about how hard they have to work, how valuable it is to be bored out of your skull. It's simply not true. Motivation is intrinsic, as are span-of-attention, enthusiasm, and creative behavior. These are all natural traits in any human being, and probably all creatures. What I discovered in my classes is that the conscious mind can deliberately set the stage for the nonconscious to do its work. Fiddle around with surface features and almost anything will soon become absorbing. And once absorbed the organism "learns" whatever object it looks upon.

> *There was a child went forth every day,*
> *And the first object he look'd upon, that object he became,*
> *And that object became part of him for the day or a*
>   *certain part of the day,*
> *Or for many years or stretching cycles of years.*
>   —Walt Whitman

Discipline cannot be imposed; it comes from within. It is the thrust of mind and spirit toward realization. When you see students' vitality engaged, with no external prodding whatsoever, you realize how counterproductive and stifling all the teaching paraphernalia are. They simply get in the way. When education is in the learner's hands, the amount of learning increases dramatically.

When I realized the implications of the surface-features game, I began applying it, one way or another, every chance I got. The "lessons" got turned on their heads. Leafing through John Dewey the other day, I saw that he was saying the same things in 1900. That is, it is stupid to try to explain a concept to people who have not had their hands on the stuff first. If you want to discuss the principles of carpentry, do a lot of measuring and hammering and sawing first. Someone who is actually building a set of stairs will be much more interested in the mathematics of it than someone for whom it is an intellectual exercise. If someone doesn't *want* to know the mathematics, let that person alone. This organism may have another agenda, and it might be better than the one you have in mind. You never know. Learning is a hands-on activity; the whole being has to be involved. That includes mind, body, spirit, and emotions. Dewey had it all figured out. But it seems nobody pays any attention to him. Pity. Without this awareness, teachers impose dreary exercises on their victims and go home worn out day after day. No wonder they are burned out.

Chapter 9

The Brain

> "Reason only functions when the emotions are involved."
>
> "Reason is supposed to be logical."
>
> "There's no logic unless the emotions are involved. You want to do something, so you do it. That's logical. You want to do something and don't do it, that's a breakdown of reason."
>
> —John LeCarre, *The Tailor of Panama*

No one is sure how the brain processes information, but a workable model is now available that helps illuminate how we learn. Before we knew about hemispheric tasks of the cerebral cortex, we relied on creativity studies that worked from the outside, seeing what people did and then trying to apply it, without knowing the actual mechanics. Before that we worked with a metaphoric-processes model. Before that Zen understood perfectly how observer and observed were one thing going on. They are all metaphoric variations of the same process. But for teachers the biological model is the most useful schematic so far. Even a rough understanding reveals what works in a classroom and what is useless.

We are mainly interested in the new brain, the wrinkled outer layer with the fore-and-aft split. But the primitive cold-blooded hind brain and the fiery mammalian midbrain are wired together with this outer cortex so that all three function together, multitasking *par excellence*. The organism can put any of the three in charge at any time. Teachers need to know what behavior of theirs might trigger that shift of authority. Abject fear can trigger reptilian behavior. Invasion of a student's space can bring online fierce mammalian defense. Neither is hotsy-totsy for self-actualization.

Typically in the left hemisphere of the outer brain, there is a wetware chip, about the size of a half-dollar, that comes formatted for language. Babies program into it whatever language is in use around them. Since almost all of the thinking we are *aware of* is closely linked with language, schools operate on the idea that this part of the mind is all there is. (*Brain* is the physical machine, and *mind* is the nonphysical thing it is doing. But then, how can we know the dancer from the dance?) This part of the brain is like a color TV. The mammalian brain could be likened to black-and-white TV (or maybe just red!), and the hind brain could be a classy calculator. There are about 20 million pathways that connect the language side with the right hemisphere. And what do we find there? *Laser holography!* It is this fantastic computer teachers need to be aware of, for it is what will make their job a joy. It is tremendously swift and powerful. It works *holistically* (as a whole, all at once). So putting things together *iconically* is the specialty of this hemisphere. Since we don't have a clue about how it actually does its work, we can't monkey with it. We don't know, but it does.

What we can do is throw some switches in the conscious sector (the left hemisphere), define, describe, count up, sort and file, check out and test results, and put things into logical order. But that's where we have to butt out and let the holographic right hemisphere take over. The left brain takes things one at a time; the right processes bunches and *gives them meaning*. Meaning comes from the nonconscious, nonlinguistic mind, not the part we're aware of. Usually the printout from the right hemisphere is in the form of a metaphor, *motherboard*, for example. Now, *where* did that come from?

What seems to happen is that the conscious mind messes around, doing administrative work, office management, pencil sharpening, and so on and at some point downloads investigative data through the 20 million pathways to the right hemisphere. While the organism is doing all sorts of other things, the right brain gets busy creating patterns (solving problems) with lightning speed, making what appear to be leaps of insight. What's neat for teachers is that they don't have to worry about getting every detail of a concept *expressed*. This computer is perfectly happy with sloppy, incomplete, or even "wrong" data. It is smart enough to sort all that out. It can even use hunches, guesses, and feelings effectively. There is nothing teachers can do about this anyway, so they may as well relax and enjoy the surprises: delightful or shocking metaphors that suddenly pop up on the screen. A class in this phase of the process overflows with marvelous associations, many far-fetched, bizarre, and totally illogical. When a class shifts into this mode, the wise and grateful teacher gets out of the way—or joins the dance.

A classroom can actually be a splendid place to learn—if teachers allow the nonconscious hemispheres to operate according to their nature. We all know what classrooms that ignore this process are like. Most responsible teachers feel they haven't done their job if they don't have all the kinks worked out for whatever they hope to teach that day. Knowing how the brain works makes it clear that that simply is not their job and indeed is obstructive. We can earn our money by going with the way the mind works instead of constantly getting in the way. There is plenty we can do and then step back and enjoy the remarkable results.

10

Teaching Reading
Turning Prose into Poetry

An intense vision of the facts.
—William Carlos Williams

Reading is extracting meaning from anything written down. That would have to include mathematical shapes, chemical formulas, and road signs. Indeed, for teachers, reading could be stretched to include acquiring the *message* of anything human beings put out there in a physical form. *Do you read me?* It is all a reading problem: How to get what's there? If we want students to be good at that, nothing would prepare them better than development of their poetic faculties: being able to bring mind and heart to bear on what lies before us. There are hundreds of books on how to teach reading, but no one knows better than that individual does what needs to be done. Once we have cracked the code of reading, the rest is problem solving. *The Wasteland*, the WordPerfect reference manual, or a paragraph in a chemistry book—it is always the same question: What do I need to do to extract the metaphor embedded here? "Let us go and make our visit."

An experienced reader knows what to do. If you get into enough jams and find your way out, you develop a knack. Reading a technical manual and reading *Dubliners* both require us to extract the writer's metaphor. The reader sets up a dialogue with the writer. Each writer shapes a word painting of the perceived world, and the manner of painting does influence the matter. *How* the WordPerfect writer means—style, selection of examples, tone of voice, sentence length, word choice—affects my understanding of what's said; I have to get the feel of how it is said. Of course, this is the blueprint for reading poetry, too. So if I really do want to understand something, I treat it as a poem. I'm not "on" all the time, but if I want a full experience of a newspaper item, then anything short of a poetic reading is insufficient.

This process can't be forced. Ideally, it is ongoing, from the time a child begins to play with sounds on throughout life. There is a need-based way to proceed: See as sharply and attentively as possible, and then let the mind do its sorting and classifying. Let it generate its own synthesis. This takes time. Meanwhile, we wash our socks, wait on tables, and chat with friends. Sometimes we go back for another look. Sometimes we sit. If not distracted, the mind continues to work toward a synthesis. It will flesh out what it can from the food available. If these adventures are approached with heart, the mind flourishes. Too much protein can overload the system. It needs roughage, too, and lots of variety. Biking and dancing can do a lot for a reader. After all, we're talking "human situations" here, and we approach reading as whole human beings. There is no mechanical way to go about it.

Reading Programs

For a long time, though, I thought we really could teach reading mechanically. When I first started thinking about reading, the word was that *Time* magazine was written at about a sixth-grade reading difficulty. I suppose that was figured out the same way IQ was—which is pretty nutty when you think about it. (We now recognize different *kinds* of intelligence, and considerable skepticism abounds about the concept of an intelligence quotient and the validity of the tests.) It was also found that most grown-ups read like sixth graders. Newspapers reported Americans, by and large, could barely read the backs of cereal boxes. When I came into teaching in 1957, I was all for remedying this deplorable situation. There had been oodles of research about the reading process, and there were lots of books on teaching reading. So I was all set. I had even taken a speed-reading course at the Pentagon while I was dawdling as a liaison officer at the Navy Training Publications Center in Anacostia. I was ahead of the game. Schools all around the country were putting together remedial reading courses, even whole departments. At Stagg High I was asked to create a speed-reading course and was happy to give it a go. As usual I learned on the job.

We set up a reading room equipped with scanners, a tachistoscope, timers, materials from Science Research Associates—color coded for difficulty—

workbooks with number-of-words provided for each article, a collection of novels (there were formulas for determining grade level), *Word Power Made Easy*, and placement tests, progress tests, speed tests, and final tests. There were also charts to keep for each student. And so on. It was scientific, so it seemed, a lot more so than anything else in my discipline. I felt like a real teacher. Things were being accomplished; you could *measure* results. It was great. You could see where a student started, typically reading with understanding at between 180 and 250 words per minute, many ending up on a posttest at 350 to even 400 words per minute. I thought that was grand, and I continued in the program for six years.

When I started teaching at DVC there was a Reading Development Department with more than twenty sections offered every semester. It emphasized efficient reading (getting what one wanted from print with the least wasted time). That was even better than speed reading, so I got right into the program. Other colleges all over California had established *remedial* classes. I did not like that idea at all. Kids couldn't get into freshman English until they brought their reading level up to college standards—however that was determined. Often they languished in purgatory for several semesters or got discouraged and dropped out, but DVC was more enlightened. The reading courses were satellites. Students were not forced into them and could choose to take them at any time. If they wished, they could take a developmental reading course while enrolled in mainstream English courses. That seemed sensible to me. What's more, the philosophy was that students could start at their own levels. The course was individualized. I liked that, too. It was student-centered; it respected the students' ability to make decisions; we didn't humiliate them by dumping them in lower-track programs. Even our best students could enroll and work on developing even more reading power. And it was scientific.

I taught a section of developmental reading every semester for several years, but there was always a nagging uneasiness. For one thing the reading classes were never as spirited and joyous as my other classes. The work was sweaty and pedestrian. We also had trouble qualifying these courses for college-level transfer. Students could put in considerable time and effort, and even if their reading did get better, it was hard to get any credit for it. When a student was struggling to stay afloat, it was a real sacrifice to add on a reading course. But we had seemingly solid evidence that the course worked. Some of our teachers were officers in the International Reading Association (IRA); we knew our reading theory. Still, it was a burden for students to take reading development. I hate teaching in a negative environment.

Meanwhile, the insights I had been getting in my other classes began filtering over into my thinking about developmental reading. I began asking myself what the underlying message of such courses was. It was widely thought, as I have said, that lots of people simply didn't read well enough for college work. If our college district had thought otherwise, the Reading Development Department would have evaporated. We had set it up as developmental, but it existed in an atmosphere of remediation. Why else pull out one aspect of the language continuum and teach it as a separate subject? Why do that? I taught everything developmentally anyway.

It was clear to me that troubles people had with reading were not in the printed materials but elsewhere. I knew of lots of instances of "poor" readers rising to the occasion; for example, Malcolm X or my nonacademic niece who tracked down her birth parents through a maze of bureaucratic double-talk, did excellent research into her dad's multiple sclerosis, and did herself proud reading the fine print in real estate contracts. It happened over and over in my other classes. Under the right circumstances, anyone can read anything. But there's no law that we all have to read everything brilliantly. We all could, if we wanted to, but who needs it? I hate reading sociology or economics texts. I could read them, but I don't wanna. My friend in the Physics Department prefers murder mysteries to Faulkner or Updike. So?

Meanwhile, in my mainstream English classes there were people of all kinds of background and experience. That wasn't a problem; it was a plus. We read and wrote all sorts of things all the time, but I never taught those things, and students progressed at their own rates in a whole spectrum of language skills. Facility wasn't my purpose in teaching these classes, anyway, but it was definitely a by-product. So I began to realize my teaching philosophy was at odds with what I was doing in reading development. When I thought of changing the course, I realized it would end up looking like every other course I taught, holistic and whole-brained and poetic. I felt like a traitor. The IRA did know a lot about what goes on when people read. We knew about eye movement, regression, breadth of information in each stop across the page, vocabulary, and level of difficulty. Did I want to abandon all that? Not at all, but maybe it was getting too much emphasis. Maybe we were using the information in a way that wasn't productive.

Once these issues surfaced, other information began popping up. I started looking beyond the IRA and discovered the National Reading Conference (NRC), made up largely of teachers from schools of education who taught prospective reading teachers. The NRC did not have the slavish missionary zeal of the IRA; they were willing to doubt. It was refreshing to read "There is no such thing as a good reader. Some people are good at reading mathematics books; others are good at reading books on anatomy or literary criticism or books about painters." My sentiments exactly. Someone else wrote, "We do not read reading. We do not write writing. We read about something. We write about something." Think of the implications of that observation. What were the course materials for our reading classes? They were all dragged in so that we could teach reading. When we read about ants, we didn't give a damn about ants. The print was just for working on reading skills. We had changed the subject! This was a key to the lackluster mood of the classes. No wonder students couldn't work up enthusiasm. All the materials were mere fodder for another purpose: reading development. The material and the purpose were at cross-purposes. It wouldn't have mattered if we were reading the most choice prose in English. Developing reading skills would still have been the purpose. When we read about African termites in my other classes, it was a poetic experience. I was *not* teaching reading. A taste for well-written articles on biology was a likely by-product, but that was never our purpose. Self-directed active reading, without ulterior intention, seems to me a much, much better way to develop reading power than noticing how many times the eye regresses per paragraph.

As for tests, in my other classes I no longer gave them. But we had all these carefully prepared standardized reading tests to help students see where they started and where they ended up. On closer examination, though, the only thing you could be sure they measured was skill in taking tests. For example, one series provided a timed reading sample and then twenty multiple-choice questions. Karl Staubach and I took the tests without reading the selections. Karl usually scored 19 or 20 out of 20. I typically scored 17 or 18. In my college skills classes I showed students how to take a test without knowing anything, and they started scoring higher, too. It turned out there was plenty of research to corroborate my skepticism about tests. Clearly, I could no longer blindly trust the results. In fact, the tests proved to be beside the point. They assumed uniform purpose, attitude, and interest. That was the opposite of what I wanted to see in my students. It would have been amusing to see the test makers grapple with questions my students might have asked about those articles.

And what about speed? When someone ended the course reading 350 words per minute, what did that mean? Did that person read *everything* at 350 words per minute? For myself, it could take me half an hour—maybe days, even—to "read" a fifteen-word poem by William Carlos Williams. I could get everything I wanted out of some newspaper articles in less than a minute.

A reading-speed score is meaningless. What are you reading? Why? What do you want out of it? How absorbed are you? How familiar are you with the topic? Rather than reading speed, the issue is Who's in charge here?

Some of our teachers were rather smug about the scores, though. They could not be persuaded that the reading tests were seriously flawed and irrelevant. But then some disturbing data began to emerge. Even the "improved" speeds and comprehension became threadbare within a semester or two. The edge soon evaporated. Speed and comprehension tests showed no significant difference between people who had taken such courses and those who hadn't. I no longer put any stock in such tests, but by their own measures, reading advocates were stuck with these findings. These results turned out not to be a big problem, though; they were simply ignored.

Throw Out Reading Programs?

> The idea that the level of literacy will be raised, and learning to read made easier, by the development of new materials or a more complex technology is in fundamental contradiction to everything that new knowledge and common sense tell us about reading and learning. Man had never journeyed to the moon before technology took him there, but children have been learning to read for centuries. We have failed to even consider the possibility that when children learn to read today it may be despite all our sophisticated educational gimmickry, rather than because of it.
>
> —Frank Smith, *Psycholinguistics and Reading*

As they are structured, most reading programs aren't viable. They do not do what they purport to do. But should they be tossed out? Not necessarily. I am sure the apparatus could be dismantled. We could certainly get rid of the tests; they don't work. At least some people have become good readers by any standards one might choose to invoke, and they have done so without taking reading courses. How does that happen? It's clear we don't need the machinery, either. If one wants a pacer, moving a hand along under a line of print is plenty good enough. Nor do we need specially prepared reading materials. Reading difficulty is more a function of the reader's passion than of vocabulary and sentence structure.

Most people read as well as they need to, considering their circumstances. When they change their lives, their values, and their interests, then their self-esteem and their reading needs and behavior change, too. Most reading courses approach the issue backward. Genuine interest in the ideas stored in the print must come first. But all that information about how we extract meaning from print is valuable—for all teachers. Every teacher is a teacher of reading—of the literature of the discipline. If chemistry teachers know a little bit about how we get meaning out of a chemistry text, they can arrange a warm and friendly environment in which students will develop that skill. Certainly, English teachers will do a better job if they understand something of the psychology of reading and the mechanics of it, just as understanding how language works keeps us from torturing students with meaningless lessons. So whatever we can find out about how reading works helps. It would even discourage testing for trivia or requiring miserably written textbooks. Find a well-written chemistry text and most reading problems will disappear. Use art.

But despite all the research, we do not really know how the mind is able to translate print into meaning. People have been doing it for a few thousand years, but no one knows just what the mechanics of it are. It's been progressive, too: A seventeenth-century monk was astonished one day to come upon a brother reading *without moving his lips!* When and how did silent reading click into place? We don't really know what the brain is actually doing. Try it yourself. Go back and read the first sentence in this paragraph. Can you really say what happens as you move your eyes across the line? Of course not. No one can. It is a profound mystery. So we can't be too cocky. We know some of the circumstances in which people somehow acquire this strange power, but we can't get inside the box to examine the coding and decoding. So our remedies for "poor" reading are no more reliable than bloodletting. There is far too much intrusion, far too much instruction. We do know kids in a literate environment pick up reading ability almost as unselfconsciously as they pick up language facility. In a genuinely literate environment you won't find eighth-grade remedial reading classes filled with rebellious boys.

Reading and Therapy

Unfortunately, though, lots of kids do make it to college with a reading problem —or a problem reading. But on closer examination, decoding print is almost never the problem. I can't recall any college student who couldn't decode print. Once one has cracked the code, as I have said, the rest is psychology. It's like Henry Ford's observation: "Whether you think you can or whether you think you can't, you're right." That's mainly why we might as well have our reading classes out on the lawn or up at the park—without any books at all!

How people feel about themselves—even people with dyslexia—is always the problem, not lines of squiggles on wood pulp. "Poor readers" usually have a crummy view of themselves and their abilities—at least regarding the reading of academic books.

So it made sense to me to discover the best reading specialist I know is a psychologist. When I met Tony Manzo at a reading conference, he directed the Reading Department at the School of Education of the University of Missouri in Kansas City. He told me he had come into the teaching of reading through the back door. He had discovered, for most of the students in these programs, reading difficulty was a symptom of something else. Training teachers to recognize and deal with *affect*, with feelings and emotion, was a service he could, as a psychologist, provide directly. But *affect* isn't what everyone noticed. What everyone noticed was the symptom: lousy reading. And that was why reading programs existed. If you want to help students prevail in their studies, you will find a ready audience in reading classes. Tony may not agree with this simplification, but the work he and his colleagues did with students almost always involved revealing to readers their capacity to solve a problem. There was modeling and oral dialogue back and forth until the reader "caught on" and took over.

Tony described working with a middle school student on a story they were reading together. They would each read the same sentence or paragraph. Then Tony would ask a question. They would settle the answer one way or another. Then it was the kid's turn to ask a question. Pretty soon it was a good give and take, the kid's eyes would light up, and reading suddenly turned into a spirited game, like checkers or chess. The key here is that the student became an active participant in the reading process. That's all it took and that's all there was to it.*

There are all sorts of ways to stimulate that kind of participation, but in my view these activities are always self-esteem sessions. More important than anything happening with the print was Dr. Anthony Manzo giving his full attention to this scruffy reject. Here was this grown-up matching wits with a kid, and this kid getting the better of him sometimes, in a friendly atmosphere. Imagine what that did for this student's feeling of self-worth.

How to teach reading? Pay attention. Witness. Keep your eye on the ball. In the reading game, what's the ball? The teacher's wonderful knowledge and

---

*This is just a glimpse of a reciprocal questioning procedure developed by Tony called ReQuest. Documented results show that students exposed to ReQuest develop sophisticated inquiry techniques significantly superior to those of students in control groups.

superior skill? The stuff there on the page? The student? If you want to teach reading the ball is the student. Teachers who become fascinated with students will be good teachers of reading. And we develop respect for students' intelligence, too. When we really listen, we become (sometimes painfully) conscious of the usefulness and reasonableness of students' questions. Until our educational systems value and cultivate self-esteem, independence, and self-direction, there will be lots of students who have difficulty with reading. Enlightened reading teachers in such institutions can help restore these essential traits. In that sense developmental reading is therapeutic.

Teaching Literature

Our second-semester English course at DVC concentrated on short stories, poems, and novels, but to my mind we had been doing that all along. Those forms simply came to the fore, whereas they formed a backdrop in my other courses. Even *Thinking About Thinking*, a book I wrote for critical thinking courses, has a score of poems and half a dozen short stories and lots of essays in choice English woven into the chapters. And the critical thinking course always included at least one novel. I can no longer imagine teaching anything in isolation from the cultural context. So when we shifted our attention to literature as a subject, we were simply continuing with our work. The way we looked at a poem or story was the way we had looked at mandalas, roadkill, and Phil Harris.

The tendency to treat literature as something elevated or removed from eating grapefruit or picking huckleberries only makes it inaccessible, for literature is all about huckleberries and grapefruit, CD-ROMs, and MSG. Separation of heart and state is a disastrous schism. Schools might get the idea that the spirit is dispensable. But one can't be much of a technician if not a *poetic* technician. It all goes together as one whole context, and as I have said throughout this book, we behave awkwardly and inefficiently when we ignore our spirit. It takes the whole being to drive a car, and literature is there to keep the driver tuned up. Not in any sort of fancy way, of course. That would only kill the pleasure of literature, as its deification has for so many.

There is something sad in people who have been denied their spirits. In his book *Working*, Studs Terkel concluded that most people lead impoverished lives. Their spirits are too big for the jobs they do. And literature reminds us of how we are—if we don't make too big a deal out of it. A woman in her seventies told Terkel of her involvement in the labor movement when she was young and of picketing and of clashes with the establishment. When she listened to the tape Terkel had made of her narrative, she exclaimed, "I never knew I felt like this." Literature is a way of letting us see what is going on under our very noses. It lets us live life while we are living it. When my classes studied literature we reclaimed our spirits—which too often had gone underground or had been suppressed. I have never met a student who did not think revitalizing the spirit was a splendid endeavor. Nor can I imagine any reader who can look into his/her own spirit and disagree. "So that's what's going on!"

Little More Than Seasoning

Leafing through a back issue of the *San Francisco Forum*, I ran across an article about parents and teachers in Berkeley trying to patch together an arts program in the aftermath of a tax-reform initiative that depleted school funds. Nowadays, they are having to set up programs themselves out of their own hides and pockets. When the money dried up, arts and letters were the first things to go. Who needs 'em, after all? Just the other day I read that three-fourths of teachers surveyed in California thought we could well do without literature classes, especially if they competed with computer science. "The arts, once seen as an integral part of a well-balanced educational diet," wrote Dashka Slater in the *Forum*, "are now considered little more than seasoning." I can picture a future someone sifting through the rubble of our lives at the end of the twenty-fifth century and fishing out a training manual for Windows 95: "What savage place was this, inhabited by automatons!?"

> The desire to make and experience art is an organic part of human nature, without which our natures are coarsened, impoverished, and denied, and our sense of community with other citizens is weakened.... When you boil it all down, the social purpose of art is the creation of mutuality, the passage from feeling into shared meaning.
> —Art critic Robert Hughes,
> *The New Yorker*, May 27, 1996

And so on. Human beings who live poetic lives would never fall for the false separation of things of the spirit and things of the physical world. I remember taking students up to Paso Nogales Park near the college and doing a drawing experiment. After our music and relaxing routine each person sat alone and paid attention to something nearby. Then I asked everyone to keep looking but to draw what they saw and not to look at the sketch, only what was in front of them. After everyone looked at each other's drawings and patted themselves on the back, we talked about it. Most couldn't believe what they had done to a bit of unexclaimed nature simply by shining the beam of attention on it. The quality of the drawing wasn't the thing; the experience was—and the use of the human mind to vivify life: See? Literature! Then we decided to try it in a linguistic mode. Under the drawing everyone wrote a verbal version in seventeen syllables, as we had done before. Then we compressed the haiku even more into a title, a metaphor.

Here's one:

This

*Here near where I sit
two five-inch pine needles lie—
oh, here's gravel, too!*

Little more than seasoning? On second thought, that Windows 95 manual is literature, after all. A poetic archeologist would see that right away. Human spirit is in there, but only someone whose metaphoric faculties were engaged would notice. Of course, that's the point: We realize our situation only when the nonconscious is invited to participate in reading a training manual. Otherwise, we will read mechanically, like an inhuman machine. When we read with passion, what we read becomes literature. If I read a math book that way, then I will more likely be formatted to read a poem that way. So the process is reciprocal. We really don't have a choice. "Practical" things can only be done well when we are passionate, poetic. Poetry can only be fully experienced when it is restored to the "practical" world. There is not separation; there is no choice.

Getting What's There

So releasing the spirit in matter is the quest, and that means engaging the spirit of the observer with the spirit of the observed. They become one. While I was writing this, people were trying to figure out who the anonymous author of *Primary Colors* was. One analyst, Donald Foster of Vassar College, had used a process of lexical overlay that reminded me of a game my classes sometimes used. He had examined such things as sentence structure, word choice, and sentence length, and then compared that with the prose of a dozen writers he suspected might have been the author. With the advent of computers—God bless their poetic little hearts—this sort of attributional study has been made ultraeasy. We had set up our own game simply to get a good look at what was on the page, and we had used rather crude measures, but our results were surprisingly revealing, even so.

One variation I remember was to examine three separate paragraphs one at a time and see what was there. The writers' names were not given until afterward. We concentrated on the first one and did not look at the second until we finished. Were all the sentences of about the same length, or did they vary? We counted words. What kinds of sentences—simple, compound, complex? Periodic? Balanced? These terms were defined during the process. What era? An experienced writer? Educated? Vocabulary? Man or woman? What sorts of interests did the writer reveal—philosophical, practical, scientific, adventurous? This was a variation of the did-you-notice game. I got it going with a few questions, but then small groups worked together to see what they could uncover. Finally, I asked, "How would you describe the person who wrote this? Any guesses about the name of the writer?"

Once they figured out the first sample as much as they could, we looked at the second paragraph, and when that was done, we took on the third. One set of paragraphs dealt with the sea, and the passages were revealed later to be by Jack London, Herman Melville, and Richard Henry Dana. I did the same thing with paragraphs about baseball from John Updike, Mark Harris, and Bernard Malamud. Sometimes, we would look at just one piece, perhaps by Woody Allen, Mark Twain, or Danielle Steele. From time to time I might bring in a passage and ask, "Do you think any of the writers we've looked at so far did this?" These investigations were always carried out playfully and usually in groups. Nothing was tested. But a direct outcome was that we all experienced how much was there before our eyes, on the surface, available to anyone who chose to have a look.

What we were doing was what we had done with paintings in the art gallery, with our own mandalas, and with objects brought in from a slow walk around the campus. So our "literary criticism" was not really a departure from our way of going about our business. We could even take samples from the students' daily reflections. Blank out the name: "Is this reflection a verbal mandala for the writer? What is the person like?" And so on. What happens when we fiddle with surface features is that we are obliged to keep paying attention to the object, painting, prose, or whatever until the spirit of the piece emerges. Seeing ceases to be mechanical and passive and becomes active and attentive, full of the viewer's spirit—which in turn releases the spirit within what's being observed.

As I have said, a thing has not really been "read" until that spirit is experienced. We haven't really got it at all. Remember what Tennyson said about the flower he plucked from the crannied wall?

> *—but if I could understand*
> *What you are, root and all, and all in all,*
> *I should know what God and man is.*

It's the same thing.

Millie Martin, in her graduate seminar at Bucknell, was doing something like this back in 1956. I remember our spending all the time we wanted taking a look at one page of Thomas Browne or John Donne or Robert Burton. We looked at balanced and periodic sentences and other surface features. What I remember most was how comfortable Millie Martin was spending half an hour or even an hour going over a page and how stimulating it was to see the abundance of what was there. In *How to Read a Page*, I. A. Richards shares the attitude that there's no hurry. This posture runs counter to the zeal to "cover" material. Throwing a cover *over* things is indeed what happens when we are in a hurry. If we keep in mind what education is for, we are not so likely to rush.

When it came to reading a novel together or a short story, it was not uncommon for us to examine the surface features of a page. The medium really is the shape of a writer's mind. One pleasure of reading is in being able to enter another person's world and walk around in it. Superficial reading simply won't do. It is like looking at a blueprint and not the building. Sooner or later we have to take a good look and catch on. Once we do "get it," the reading can often proceed rather quickly. But not always: A close reading of a page may show that it will take longer to get the fullness of a work. That is what the phrase "efficient reading" means anyway, taking whatever time is necessary.

As for literary criticism it always seems premature to me to evaluate a work before we take a close look. For my students the tendency to evaluate diminished the more we simply looked. As John Cheever said, writing is not a competitive sport. Seeing what's there is usually enough. If one wanted to judge, though, this sort of "intense vision of the facts" would certainly provide a much better foundation for doing so—but afterward, afterward.

The Best American Short Stories of 19___

> *Some judge of authors' names, not works, and then*
> *Nor praise, nor blame the writing, but the men.*
>
> —Alexander Pope

I used to wonder why students weren't excited about classic stories and novels commonly read in literature classes. I think it was the dust. The whole business seemed so settled. The critics had had at it. The issue of quality was dispatched, so there didn't seem like much for students to do but be a receptive audience. That's hard to fake, though, and most students found "studying" these classics analogous to sitting in church. The joy in these pieces of art was all but smothered. Then in 1984 I noticed that John Updike was editor for *The Best American Short Stories* of that year. That piqued my interest, and I decided to use the book in my second-semester freshman English class. That decision turned out to be good for us all. These stories were fresh, and, better, they had not been vivisected by scores of critics. We were on our own.

I made it my practice to read the assigned story once-through the night before, the way I imagined my students would. When we all got to class we proceeded to fiddle with it till it came alive. By noticing this or that we began to savor nuances. Not one of our sessions with these stories was a passive experience. When students got to class they *wanted* to talk with each other about these stories. I didn't care how superficially students read the story before coming to class, but they did have to have read it a little bit. Typically, the day the first story was to have been discussed, a third of the class might not have read it. As gently as possible I would tell them they couldn't be in on the discussion. I allowed them to go off somewhere and read the story and, if they finished in time, come back for the rest of the discussion. That's all it took. There was no punishment involved; I didn't pay any attention to who left. The next time everybody stayed.

It was a teacher's dream. Sometimes I would start out by asking, "Someone recount the story. Just tell what happens, the plot." Someone would start out only to be interrupted by someone else blurting, "Oh, no! That isn't really what happened." "Well, what, then?" Before anyone realized it, we were examining themes, tone, setting, characterization, word choice, rhythm, even sentence structure—all the stuff that usually goes on in literature classes. But it was all spontaneous, and those literary terms were rarely invoked. The fact is, if you really are fascinated with a story, poem, or novel, it is almost impossible not to talk about these matters. So along with the surface-feature game we usually played, we were also in the midst of literary criticism without even noticing.

The bottom line, of course, was the experience of a work of art, the realizations it evoked, and the joy we felt in the craftsmanship. It was a pleasure to read these stories and discuss them in this manner. The difference in using these uncataloged works compared with the usual fare of introductory courses was astonishing.

The Safe and Settled

This procedure let students use their own resources to "read a page." They got better at it and more confident with each new investigation. But the technique didn't work at all when we tried it out with teachers in our English Department. Prior to a workshop weekend, everyone was given a copy of a story from *The Best American Short Stories* of that year. It was "Unknown Feathers" by Dianne Benedict, a beautifully written story, delicious in detail and metaphoric implication. (John Updike had thought it was one of the best stories of 1984.) The idea was that teachers would approach the story the same way students had, fooling around with it, looking at surface features, seeing "what's there." But, my, my, it was hard sledding. Right off the bat a number pronounced the story inferior. No one had asked, but they felt they had to get their judgment on the table right away. If you want to kill a dialogue, start with a judgment, a pronouncement, or an assertion. My students wouldn't have dreamed of starting that way. I certainly hadn't when we explored that story in class, and by the end of the session I was glad I had withheld evaluation. With the help of my fellow explorers, it had popped into vivid relief, and afterward when I read it again it was as if I had been blind the first time through. The second reading was a poetic experience. I saw so much of what the artist had done, the economy, the choice language, the delicate symmetry. It was a joy. But that was not what happened at the workshop. Once the teachers had staked out their positions, they set about ridiculing each other's critical judgment. The discussion became a clash of expertise, making it almost impossible to look at the story itself. It was dramatically clear to me that starting with a bias prevents our seeing anything as it is, in its own right. The teachers' literary credentials turned out to be blinders.

Something else was at work, too: fear. The teachers were nervous. This was something they had never seen before. Our teachers were already completely educated, as Frost would have put it, and this new stuff was a royal pain. No wonder students find literature classes so tedious. Only the safe and settled are examined. If there is any one thing that might let a breath of fresh air into discussions of literature, it is recognizing the deadly effect of the "expert" in any dialogue. Expertise has its place and is often valuable, but not up front. The biggest barrier to communication, as Carl Rogers eloquently argued years ago, is the tendency to evaluate without first seeing the message from the sender's point of view. Without lots of experience in first seeing clearly what's there, students will have little incentive to take the reins.

But teachers will have to kick over the traces themselves first. Unless they themselves are used to exploring uncharted terrain, how could they possibly provide students with investigative environments? Exploring has to be something they do regularly. They will have to learn to take chances, and they will have to forget all their hard-won training, or at least set it aside. The apparatus with which to evaluate anything new has not yet emerged. It can only come after the art, to describe it, not beforehand to destroy it.

I love working with new material, without even the opportunity to refer to some comforting pronouncement. But it is possible to look at classic works, too, without first announcing their superior quality. I. A. Richards's *Practical Criticism* shows some possibilities. His students wrote evaluations of a series of poems without knowing the authors' names. He didn't evaluate their evaluations, nor did the students critique each other's, but all the responses were made available for reflection and contemplation. That's really all it takes. Over time responses became more thoughtful, more astute, more penetrating. Richards's approach isn't exactly like working without a net, but it does put the students more in charge. I prefer to let the "great" mingle with everything else and let nature take its course. Whereas Richards's students prepared their responses elsewhere, my students usually approach an investigation as mutual-aid groups and get immediate experience of a wide range of observations. The key to developing refined perception is hearing lots of unendorsed viewpoints. Evaluation takes a back seat in our classes, but I think students develop true critical acumen simply by using their own beams of attention. They could tell exactly why they like a work of art, if they wished, but they rarely find that part important. The visit itself is the thing. The rest is for chatting around the hearth on cold winter evenings.

Why Teach Reading?

I prefer to think of "reading" in the most general terms, for in educating ourselves we are always obliged to "read" our environment. In the academic world, however, the most common activity across the disciplines is reading printed matter. So, as I have said, like it or not, every course is a reading course, and getting the fullness of what's there is the challenge every student encounters. In this sense, education is a process of getting better at communicating, and in schools that mostly means communicating with writers.

Paradoxically, the way to facilitate acuity is not to explain how to read a page but to read the page—and chat about what each participant sees there. Of course, what is read does have to be of value in its own right; its content must be something everyone *wants* to understand. There is no dearth, though, of such material. In fact, groups generate common interests as they go along, and for active minds, material a passive group might discard will come alive with possibilities. Almost anything becomes useful. The right hemisphere is brilliant at making connections.

The major barrier to an investigative and exploratory atmosphere is the tendency to prejudge. This tendency is natural and no doubt instinctive. Prejudging is a self-protective mechanism, the moat around our fortress. But education is the process of moving the moat outward farther and farther so that ultimately the entire universe is the fortress and nothing within it is alien. Everything becomes part of the empire of the mind. Surely every educator would agree a liberated mind is the ideal toward which all learners strive. There are no completely settled assumptions. There is always some niggling little thread that might unravel the whole tapestry. If we haven't invested too much in our idea of what's what, that prospect will not be too threatening. We will be able to say, "Well, well! So that's how it is! What a surprise!"

From one point of view a course in physics is a reading course. Students in a mutual-aid group going over a physics chapter to get "what's there" are refining their reading skills. The tendency to prejudge is replaced with the urge to understand, and this mode of thought is the same for a lab experiment, a poem, tea leaves, or a therapy session. What we are doing when we read anything is getting into a suitable mental condition for receiving what's there. As usual, what is out there is not the problem; it is the way we structure our thinking, *how* we think, that must be honed. To read well is to understand. And understanding is always therapeutic.

If all teachers provide therapeutic situations in which students consider their subject, then reading courses are superfluous. A student who finishes a mathematics course will have become a more proficient reader of mathematics books and more capable of getting the fullness of a paragraph on the binomial theorem. And so it would be with other courses. Over time the commonality of all reading problems would become apparent, and our students would be able to approach new subjects with assurance. It is a matter of enlightened practice. The question isn't whether we should *all* teach reading but how. The subject of each course is in the print, and extracting it with as much understanding as possible is good reading. Reading is a fundamental skill across the curriculum. Its development is a by-product of good teaching, for good reading is the active engagement of the mind with what it contemplates. If we provide a positive learning environment for our subjects, our students will strengthen their reading skills.

In the end the despair over students' rotten performance is misdirected. If anything needs remediation it is the school programs. Students don't have reading problems; schools have teaching problems. How about setting up remedial teaching courses? In these courses, teachers would come to recognize their role in teaching the literature of their subjects and discover how easily that can be done. Patch-up reading courses would evaporate overnight. Thank goodness that's cleared up.

Postscript:
A complicity in the creative process

I used to tell students, "Don't waste your time reading." That was to get their attention. Once they got to thinking actively about that koan, they figured out the translation for themselves: "Reading passively is a dumb way to treat our gorgeous selves." But I wanted them to realize that themselves. Admonishing people to read actively might be swell advice, but it falls on deaf ears. We have to think these things up ourselves for them to have any effect. And there has to be experience that active reading really is worth the trouble. In a human-being-centered classroom, that is the only kind of reading that goes on anyway, so there is plenty of positive reinforcement. Students know a good thing when they see it, and they know what it feels like to read poetically. The Russian poet Marina Tsvetaeva wrote, "Reading is complicity in the creative process." Comprehension *is* complicity. When that link between print and the self-actualizing human being is forged, we will not need to fret about reading development. It is implicit in every humane classroom.

Ars Poetica

*A poem should be palpable and mute
as a globed fruit.*

*Dumb
As old medallions to the thumb*

*Silent as the sleeve-worn stone
Of casement ledges where the moss has grown—*

*A poem should be wordless
As the flight of birds*

*A poem should be motionless in time
As the moon climbs*

*Leaving, as the moon releases
Twig by twig the night-entangled trees,*

*Leaving, as the moon behind the winter leaves,
Memory by memory the mind—*

*A poem should be motionless in time
As the moon climbs*

*A poem should be equal to:
Not true*

*For all the history of grief
An empty doorway and a maple leaf*

*For love
The leaning grasses and two lights above the sea—*

*A poem should not mean
But be*

—Archibald MacLeish

11

Mandalas: Who *Are* You?
Thumbprints and Weather Reports

"Who are you?" said the Caterpillar.
"I—I hardly know, Sir, just at present—at least I know who I was when I got
   up this morning, but I think I must have changed several times since then."
"What do you mean by that?" said the Caterpillar sternly. "Explain yourself!"
"I can't explain myself, I'm afraid, Sir," said Alice, "because I'm not myself,
   you see."
"I don't see," said the Caterpillar.
"I'm afraid I can't put it more clearly," Alice replied, very politely, "for I can't
   understand it myself, to begin with; and being so many different sizes
   in a day is very confusing."
"It isn't," said the Caterpillar.
                                        —Lewis Carroll

The curricula of most schools are based on logic, sequence, and order. Never mind that that is only the tip of the iceberg, the result of thinking, a way of tidying up, not where the action is at all. But the right hemisphere of the new brain, so central to learning, is invisible. For students to take deliberate control of their own learning, they need to know what they have going for them. That takes a little tinkering, but the time spent pays off. In the long run, it's "cost effective." Clearly, this power center does not speak English—or any of the hundreds of human languages. It uses verbal symbols sometimes and pictures; that is, metaphor and icons. We don't know what's going on in there, but we do know some tricks for getting a printout.

When I first tried out mandalas with my classes, I didn't realize the manifold implications for education. For example, I hadn't read any of the research on the two hemispheres of the outer brain. It was new stuff. I didn't realize how profoundly knowledge of this separation of tasks would affect our understanding of the learning process. By this time, of course, I knew every class activity would end up multifaceted and many layered. Nothing was ever for just one predictable outcome. Something I had in mind was likely to come out, but not always, and there would be things I never dreamed of as well. That was standard operating procedure. I did know about the significance of children's art from the work of Rhoda Kellogg and others. I had also read of Carl Jung's study of mandalas and his analysis of their powerful messages. One thing I wanted to explore was the difference, if any, in someone's verbal and visual outerances. What did each reveal about the artist? That was an academic sort of question. Another purpose was to pay some more attention to the individuals who made up our group, to warm each one up with our beam of attention. Another was to let them get their hands on some crayons and colored paper, to create some art of their own. We are more responsive to other people's creations when we have experienced the process ourselves.

At first we set up our workshop right in the classroom, but later it became more theatrical. We would meet up on the hill at the science museum, a big space we could reserve all for ourselves with neat displays from the physical and life sciences. (Our college professed a philosophy of integrating the disciplines, so this was also a good excuse to be up there.) When the students arrived, there would be mellow music—Vivaldi, Corelli, Handel, Bach—and they were told to help themselves to a piece of colored construction paper and box of oil pastels. They were to spread out and make themselves comfortable.

Next I asked them to close their eyes and listen to the music while we went through a brief relaxation exercise. Sometimes we would add a poem or a bit of prose that seemed to go with the mood of the day.

To Draw Pictures

Draw what you see just how you see it,
strings of trees or hills with faces. So much
depends on where you live. Name what you draw
by where it is: Utah scape, or Texas scape,
or scape of windows and the sea. Draw
horizon right up front and put the sky
on top. Draw fast, past your vocabulary

> *and hope of some eventual display.*
> *Let things have conversations and connect*
> *them with your lines: typewriter to curtain*
> *rod, fireplace to davenport, vegetables*
> *to moon. Forget what you don't know, or do,*
> *of composition. Just fill the space and use*
> *all the colors as you guess they were.*
> *Don't keep your pictures. Give them up*
> *to children and their friends. For them,*
> *put in something that does not belong.*
> —Maggie Anderson

Then I would explain the activity: "When you open your eyes, please give yourself plenty of space and start working on a drawing. You can draw whatever you feel like, but make sure it has a center and everything you draw radiates from that center in some way. Toward the last third of the hour, we'll want to see what we can discover without knowing who drew the pictures, so try not to look at each other's work and put your name on the back. When you're finished, give your drawing to one of the TAs."

That's it, as little explanation as I can get away with. I try to minimize my influence on what they draw. I don't say, "Draw what you're feeling now," or anything like that. I don't even tell them they will probably end up with a mandala. I want them to draw as spontaneously as possible. I don't even say, "Be spontaneous," because then they wouldn't be.

Then the teaching assistants and others who finish early begin preparing our exhibit. The drawings are clustered on a wall, tastefully spaced so that they make a nice display. Students begin standing around chatting about the various drawings as they are mounted, one by one. When everyone is finished, I say, "I'd like to introduce you all to our class." And with a flourish I point to the display. "Aren't we a gorgeous bunch?! How about all this variety?! Are any two just alike? Would you want them to be? [Absolutely not!] Let's take a closer look. Someone pick out a drawing for us to examine." No one is supposed to know who the artist is, and the artist keeps it a secret until the end. Then we begin a surface-features session, just like the approach we used on Brueghel's *Children's Games*.

I ask various students to pick out one detail they notice. We keep that up till we get a pretty good look at the drawing. We try to keep it at a descriptive level with as little interpretation as possible. "There's a four-inch red line that curves to the right in the upper left corner." "Yellow dot in the middle." "There's a flower in the bottom right." "Describe the shape, color, size of the flower. Pointy or rounded edges? Is this drawing representational or abstract? Geometrical? Complex or simple? Symmetrical? Color choices? How heavily did the artist press on the oil pastels?" And so forth.

After a while it's time to say, "Now let's see what we can guess about the artist. When we finish, the artist can tell us how close we came." Students start spontaneously offering observations, and I ask questions that occur to me: "Would this person like going to parties? Why? Easy to talk to? Why? Keep a neat room? Make a good architect? Prefer people or things? Prefer a life of the mind? Prefer the received world or one of his/her own making? More visual than verbal? Worried? Serene? Assertive? Shy? Confident? Religious? Spontaneous? Humorous? Used to drawing? Sensuous? Male or female?" After a while, I ask if anyone would like to guess who the artist is. Some people are amazingly good at this. Why aren't we all? "Grammy, you don't look," maybe? Then I ask the artist to come forward and rebut or confirm our observations.

You can bet that person has been all ears and is tickled to have been so thoroughly attended to. Here, literally, is a student-centered "lesson." When the student is *the* subject, attention is complete, authentic, and intense. A student-centered trig class will have the same impact. The teacher's artistic effort every day is to find a structure so compelling that every student feels central to whatever is going on all the time, as though it is his/her "mandala" being explored.

Usually, the interpretations are uncanny and the artist is amazed, but it doesn't matter if we've been accurate or not. What we try to do *through language* is describe what our nonverbal mind actually does see accurately. The colors, lines, shapes, and sizes are themselves the nonlinguistic message. The naming of details is just a way to make us look. It is as useful to mess up as to score a bull's-eye. Our dialogue is a casting about to find a verbal equivalent of what's there. (In fact, that is the art of the writer, finding words to match what is already seen—or to pay attention long enough to bring the message to the conscious level, to unmask the hidden beauty.) The mandala experience could provide a splendid entrée into the art of the writer. This aspect is often a by-product of our reflections.

So now one student in our class has been elevated to the status of Brueghel, getting just as much attention as any other great artist. That person has become illuminated by our attention, our welcoming. Clearly, it's OK with us for that person to be him/herself. The difference is valued and appreciated. The artist then picks another drawing for us to examine, and we get in one or two more by the end of the session. Of course, we've been standing before the entire display all this time, so when we leave that day, everyone feels good. What marvelous creatures we have revealed ourselves to be, all this while masquerading as ordinary students.

Meanwhile, we have arranged to come back for another session and see to it that every drawing gets a thorough look. When we go back we put on music, and students work in groups of five or six. They take up the drawings of their group one at a time and give each one the same kind of attention we practiced as a whole. We put the drawings back on the wall, and they become another exhibit for the museum for a few weeks. One time my TA Carol Stout made up a plaque to go with the display:

MANDALAS

Instinctively spontaneous drawings done by students in Clark McKowen's Critical Thinking classes with a minimum of direction. All have a "center" representing the "self's" center, with other aspects of self emanating outward from it.

Various insights to the artist's self can be interpreted by observing colors used, character of the lines, use of shading and space, subject matter, and so on.

But there is, of course, much more to it—and much less. I have examined thousands of these drawings, and I know you don't have to be Carl Jung to get value from them. Most of us have an idea of ourselves that isn't quite accurate. In fact, getting our self-image and our self to match up is one of the ongoing quests of education. Most students are surprised at how well others can describe the artists' nature by looking at their drawings. The naked self is displayed without the filter of language. Most students are glad finally to be out in the open. But it is surprising that others notice traits the artist had never realized. It's like those aptitude tests counselors give. Through the class interchange students become conscious of inclinations they hadn't realized. It's a real "I" opener.

One incident made me a true believer. We were looking over a forceful, colorful design Jamie Wilson had done, and someone blurted out, "Oh! It's a clown!" Huh? "Tilt it a little. See?" Sure enough it was clearly a representational clown, a good one at that. Jamie was as surprised as the rest of us. He had had no conscious knowledge that he was making a clown, but there was no doubt that he had done so. He had thought he was making a design, but part of him was making a clown and concealing the act. A postscript to this story is that Jamie happened to be the son of a colleague who told me that Jamie had had brain damage some years earlier that had caused some learning glitches—the left-hand-not-knowing-what-the-right-was-doing sort of thing.

We are all like Jamie, only most of us are more adept at the deception, so we are really hard cases. Jamie, at least, was right out in the open. Lots of times students will insist that everything in their drawings is deliberate and conscious and there is a reason for everything they did. In truth, though, these explanations are more like alibis. When we take a good look at our art—any outerances—we don't need to explain. We are simply looking at that-which-is. It is a step toward self-acceptance, and the integration of the hemispheres enables the two parts to work harmoniously rather than at cross purposes. That's when we become *brilliant*, an apt term for what it feels like to live in the golden light of the new brain.

Mandalas are a spiritual weather report. Jung used to draw his own mandalas and observe the changes in himself as he grew older. I've done that, too, with my own drawings. "So *that's* how I am now, eh!" To paraphrase Alice, I know who I was when I was twenty, but I must have changed several times since then. It isn't necessary to do anything about what is there, but it does seem like a good idea to see it as it is, not through the overlay of what we were taught.

A Few Words from the Students

To lots of people, messing around with mandalas sounds fishy. We are a pragmatic society. So some students of course, while they enjoy the parlor game, remain skeptical about what can actually be observed in a drawing. I'm skeptical myself, so I have sympathy for those with their doubts. But it is delightful to witness a student discovering some of the magic in ordinary life. Here's Robert Press:

> Today was a very strange day, and I was very surprised at the outcome. I changed my attitude toward my art creation that I made last week. I decided the quality did not lie in the physical appearance but in the beauty and the amount of me that was put into it. When someone does something with some concentration, a portion of that person is expressed in the creation.
>
> I did not believe the previous statement much at all prior to today's class. I kind of thought that what is created on the paper is just a random drawing that has no individual characteristics. Even when we analyzed a couple of mandalas in the class as a whole, I was not taking the experience very seriously.

But after we split into groups and after my mandala was evaluated, my attitude changed drastically about what the whole thing was about.

At first as we began going through each mandala in our group, I was just playing the game, but as we began to discuss my own mandala, the others pointed out many things that were very true. I learned a lot about myself and I saw how others were seeing me. I was impressed by the accuracy of their observations through the use of the mandalas. I really began to get into the interpretation. I think maybe we really do store some of ourselves in the things we create.

At about the time Robert wrote his reflection, Valerie Turner, my teaching assistant, made some observations, too:

There are a few things I want to note about mandalas before I close this reflection for today. In the past, you gave each group several mandalas to examine—none of which were their own. This new way of having the artist hear the comments and interpretations of his mandala by the small group is much better. I think everyone had a great time doing it—I certainly did. And I'm getting pretty good at it, if I do say so myself.

What happens in an oh so subtle way is that the person being observed gives clues about the mandala, favorite parts, what he/she was thinking at the time. When you begin interpreting the picture, they are anxious for you to grasp what they were feeling and tell you things about their private selves and natures that they would normally feel uncomfortable sharing. It's really quite beautiful to see people let go in that way. (If I get a chance, my Sunday school class *will* draw mandalas!)

Did Carl Jung write a great deal about mandalas and his work with them? I'd like to read more about how he could see the connection of all minds to one eternal mind. Perhaps over the summer I can explore his world.

The Art Gallery

Once students catch on to the surface-features game, it's fun to take a field trip and try it out. So sometime during a semester, we would meet at the college art gallery. There were usually five or six exhibits there each year. At least one would be student work, and one would be by faculty members. The rest would be guest artists. "There's an exhibit of mandalas down at the gallery this week," I would say. "Let's meet there Thursday and have a look." When everyone was assembled, there would be soft music, just like at the museum, and I would say, "Stroll around and look over everything and then pick out one mandala to become an 'expert' on. Pick one you wouldn't usually be attracted to. The way you become an expert is to do the detail game the way we did up at the museum. Later you can tell us what all is there, and we can guess what the artist must be like, just the way we did with your own drawings." No one ever said, "Hey, these aren't mandalas. They're paintings and sculptures." By this time it was becoming second nature to make connections, and in the broader sense, these were indeed mandalas, as is everything a human being creates. You just have to tilt it a little to notice that.

I love to see people looking at art in this manner. They don't feel compelled to render judgment. It doesn't even come up. We simply enjoyed seeing what was done, figuring out how, and guessing what the artist must be like. It didn't matter what was displayed or how "talented" the artist. It was all equally exciting. I must note, however, that there was a distinctly different feel between the faculty exhibit and that of students. The faculty work as a whole was much more polished and professional but not nearly as vibrant and free. The student work was more various and vivacious. You can sense the excitement and energy the minute you enter the gallery, and the work seems more accessible. The craftsmanship of the professionals set up an invisible barrier that was harder to penetrate. Nonetheless, paying close attention made both exhibits equally pleasurable. It isn't what's there but what we do with what's there that makes the difference, as any good Taoist would know.

Of course, it is a short step to tell students that everyone's persona is a mandala. (Indeed, nature's skin is *its* mandala.) Sometimes we would bring in a specimen. I'd have an artist come to class, and we would do the surface-features game to see what the persona might reveal. My artist friends always got a kick out of being under the microscope. "Now that we've had a pretty good look at this person," I would say, "Let's guess what the paintings would be like." Then we would unveil some of the work and see how close we came. The artist would throw in observations as well. We were honing our skills. Think what good readers these students became when we looked at verbal mandalas.

Or we would do it backward. We would bring in several paintings or sculptures or whatever and observe all the trivia we could, and then guess what the artist must be like, just as we had done with our own stuff. What sort of furniture would this person have? Neat, messy? Colors? How would this person dress? Is the artist a man or a woman? And so on. Then I would go get the artist, and we would see how close we had come. We usually nailed 'em. Even though the artists were used to making things, they were often surprised at how much their lives revealed their art and how much their art revealed them.

We had the excuse of integrating the disciplines, as our college philosophy espoused, but our field trips nonetheless often occasioned raised eyebrows. Many serious teachers considered the whole thing frivolous. Some art teachers were aghast that we would look at paintings without expert guidance. English teachers wanted to know exactly how this would be made to fit the course outline. "Do you give them a writing assignment?" they would ask? "Do you have them critique a painting or write a review?" (Wouldn't that be a splendid way to kill the whole thing? Geez!) "No. I don't have them do anything different from what they always do. They just reflect on their experience and connect it with anything else we've been doing, as they see fit."

Verbal Mandalas

What would happen if a piece of writing were treated as though it were a verbal mandala? In Millie Martin's graduate seminar at Bucknell in 1956, we did something like that, but she would, of course, never have pushed a metaphor that far. We would spend an hour just looking at how John Donne put a sentence together or an hour or so on Thomas Browne, looking at periodic or balanced sentences. What we were doing implicitly then was what the surface-features game and examination of mandalas brought to the fore decades later. How might my TA have put it?

VERBAL MANDALAS

These prose passages and poetry samples all have a "center" representing the "self's" center, with other aspects of self emanating outward from it.

Various insights to the artist's self can be interpreted by observing length and style of sentences, choice of language, subject matter, and so on.

Sure enough, it was indeed possible to get a bead on the artist. Taking a close look gave the nonconscious time to get the feel of the artist and the work. In fact, the two are the same thing. Literary criticism involves this sort of close reading, but genuine apprehension of any linguistic structure requires full attention, too. Noticing what's there on the surface provided a general approach—to anything, really. We could see vividly the difference from writer to writer, each occupying a unique niche. Era, social class, schooling, philosophy of life—along with personality, self-image, and so on—are embedded in our language. Put Nathaniel Hawthorne and John Cheever side by side, Melville and John Updike, Woody Allen and James Thurber and Henry David Thoreau, Richard Henry Dana with Jack London and Herman Melville: fascinating revelations. To be sure, prose or poetry analysis on this level is more difficult than examining drawings. Because we are so used to looking at the "message" rather than the structure itself, the pattern is taken for granted. But McLuhan was right in saying the medium itself is *the* message, as we discovered—much more so than any content.

The message is never an objective abstraction. The pulp is not the orange. That's why Frost would get annoyed when someone would ask him to say what he meant in a poem. "You mean you want me to say it less well?" An utterance is a hologram that can be read only by a computer with the all-at-once power of the right hemisphere of the new brain. But the right hemisphere needs the conscious mind to hold the wiggly creature still and pay attention long enough for the holistic brain to do its work. Given the chance, it *will* do this for us, guaranteed.

Sometimes I took a page or so from some writer or other and asked the students to do a structural examination of it. They would work in groups for a while, feed their observations back to the whole class, and repeat the process. No interpretation. At some point we would guess at a profile of the artist—and indirectly, of the work. Then I would tell them the name of the artist and what information I might have and things others had said about the work. Once we had mopped up that one, we would lay another passage beside it and work on that a while. At some point I would ask, "Do you suppose the same person might have written both passages?" They could work in groups on that and then come back together with their responses and their reasons for their views. Of course, being right or wrong was not the point. Looking closely with the conscious mind allowed a chance to experience the passage more intensely. Reading that way we get more of the flavor; we understand more accurately; we get a more complete experience. Unless the sensorium is engaged, reading is quite literally *sense*less.

Student Writing

It is only a short step to the utterances of students and teacher themselves. Taking a good look at each other's language package was just as rewarding. We never evaluated; we witnessed. *Witnessing* makes all the difference. You can see the little bubble in the diamond in the lower right quadrant, but that diamond is just as wonderful as the one without a bubble. Framed and matted color enlargements of cancer-cell photos are beautiful. A witness can indeed see what the critic sees but rarely finds it necessary to take sides. The manifesting earth is too beautiful for that.

If you want to make yourself throw up, examine in this manner passages from five or six randomly selected textbooks. You will experience for yourself why analysts have said textbooks are among the most excruciatingly tedious scribblings in print. Harlequin romances look good next to most sociology texts or books on how to write. Looking at what's there on the surface exposes rambling, contorted sentences full of needless jargon, lengthy explanations of the obvious, and scarcely any editing for readability. But examining textbooks in this manner is fun, too; seeing is always fun.* It's refreshing to see what's putting kids to sleep and to see clearly how it's done.

Implications

In our classes nothing was ever about just one thing. The class dialogue and structural examination turned up all sorts of ideas about verbal and visual messages—even that print is itself a *visual* medium—and the question of how spirit can be deposited *in* matter. Through hand or mouth, the writer or painter encodes stuff from mind in some medium. Then that has to be retrieved somehow—or just lie there undeciphered. And there is the problem of getting it right, of getting not only what the artist thinks is there but all that he/she is not conscious of as well. Frost said a poet has a right to anything someone finds in his poem. That brings up the wedding of sender and receiver. No matter what's "there" it is always altered by the viewer, a Heisenberg effect that applies to mind and spirit as well as physical phenomena. Of course, human creations *are* physical, so they all fall under laws of physics. We don't eat our breakfast in a vacuum. All things are connected.

A student who learns inclusively makes a better mathematician than one who pigeonholes knowledge. A whole-brained humanities major will enjoy Patsy Cline as well as Carreras, computer science, cooking—the whole spectrum, not just one band of color. It's simply a matter of knowing how to enjoy

---

*When I say *fun*, I mean the condition in which a person is fully present in the moment, all the faculties harmoniously engaged in that process; that is, fully alive. That's *fun*.

whatever one is doing and insisting on it. The full engagement of spirit in matter is another way of saying *education*, the self or spirit at the center with all the implications.

> *If you are walking*
> *around the planet and see*
> *what you are looking at*
> *you will discover*
> *a poem.*

Nature, too, is a mandala to be decoded by the witnessing spirit, the self looking at itself.

12

Teaching Writing
Spirit in Matter

Words are the windows of the soul.

Teaching writing. That's like teaching infants to talk. No one knows enough to teach those things. And there would be no point. Teaching doesn't have anything to do with it. In fact, research on language acquisition shows that attempts to teach only get in the way. Fortunately, most adults don't try to teach kids to talk. But they do enjoy chatting with them, and the babies are delighted. Who wouldn't be? We all love that kind of undivided attention. The best place to learn is a snuggly nest—or cuddled on someone's lap. Ask any baby. Clearly, spoken language is acquired, not taught.

Acquiring literacy is no different. Put human beings in a fertile literate environment, give them warmth and friendliness and lots of attention, and they will learn to read and write. If everyone around is writing and reading in real situations, we are of course going to do that, too. We learn whatever is needed in order to participate. But most schools do not provide such an environment. Instead, the *teaching* of writing begins with kindergarten or first grade and continues throughout most students' schooling. The result of all this sweaty instruction is that, once they escape the schoolroom, most adults want nothing more to do with writing. That's not the end of the world; we can live fulfilling lives without ever putting words on paper. It is a shame, though, that what could be a radiant and enlightening resource has been shut off. In a literate world the person who does not write is maimed and is reduced to finding other ways to engage in the cultural dialogue. At the least it is inconvenient; sometimes it is a major barrier.

English teachers are always saying things like that, of course, but then they try to do something about it. That's where the trouble comes in. In their zeal they drive students nuts. Meddling in this natural process starts with the first correction. I still remember what happened to my daughter's essay on flowers in the second grade back in 1964. She had a caring, well-intentioned teacher, but look what happened. I saved Kathy's paper and later published it in *Montage: Investigations in Language*, a freshman English text Bill Sparke and I did in 1970. Here's the essay, with her teacher's corrections, just as it was written. If you were the teacher and wanted someone to enjoy writing, how would you have responded?

1. Titles start with capital letters.
2. Daisies — not daisys.
3. They're — not there.
4. <u>Don't</u> starts a new sentence so make it capital.
5. <u>Don't you think so?</u> is a question so use a question mark.

daisy   violet

F(l)owers   Try harder

I think flowers are (Try harder Kathy. There's no hurry.) pretty, violets (daisys) and all. (there) so very pretty. D(d)on't you think so.?

by Kathy

What can we suppose sixteen years of that sort of help will do for one's inclination to pick up a pen?*

What bugged me the most about the teacher's response wasn't the corrections. It is not very encouraging, of course, to have more red marks on your work than there are words of your own. I don't know why teachers are so slow to realize what a blow to self-esteem correction can be to a tender spirit. Nonetheless, if a teacher is really a caring person, kids know it and make allowances. They are unaccountably forgiving of our ineptitude. The important thing—which they are expert at ferreting out—is genuine warmth and love. In our society we are used to this impulse to correct. We develop thick skins. No, what annoyed me no end was a simple omission: Kathy had asked, "don't you think so.?" *The teacher had not answered her question.*

That omission encapsulates the trouble with the teaching of writing. What is written is treated as an exercise, not a real message. And that makes all the difference. If we want students to get good at writing, we must respond authentically to authentic messages. The first order of business is to establish a channel of communication between writer and reader. We must try to understand what has been written to us. We must use our best reading skills. And let's stop pretending the message is unclear simply because it is in a different variety of English. Nitpicking only muddies the process of getting what the writer intends us to get. Reading a student's message is the same as reading a newspaper article or a poem. As a receiver of a communication my job is to "get it," however I can. It is not to tell writers the way they wrote it is crummy.

That Impulse to Correct

Most English teachers, indeed just about everyone involved, think the whole idea is to eliminate error. English teachers spend most of their lives finding fault. What a wonderful life. Maybe their martyrdom would be laudable if it had any positive results. The evidence is all to the contrary. Studies keep coming up with the same results: Correcting does not improve students' ability to get their minds onto paper. It only makes them nervous and their prose awkward and in general makes them more reluctant to try.

---

*John Fowles, author of *The Magus, The French Lieutenant's Woman,* and *The Nature of Nature,* had prep school masters who told him, too, *to try harder:* "British reviewers make me remember my own reports as a boy, which always had on them that awful phrase, 'could try harder.'" Had he tried harder in the conventional sense, Fowles believes, he would never have become a novelist.

That's the research, and my own experience bears it out. For a long time I had the usual English-teacher mind-set and spent a number of years trying to help students improve their writing. It didn't occur to me to ask if they wanted me to do that. I would correct the same comma errors in May that I had corrected in January. I would show how a sentence could be rephrased. I would circle spelling errors. I would question the logic. I would write encouraging notes at the top of the paper. I would even explain how to compose an essay and show where I wanted their names, date, section, to be placed on the papers they handed in. I read the professional journals, went to conferences and workshops, tried tape-recording my responses, tried individual chats.

But I wasn't getting anywhere. The kids weren't buying any of it no matter how sugarcoated. I wasn't alone, either; the whole English-teaching establishment was stumped: How can we make the kids shape up their writing? Eventually, I developed my own plan: If it doesn't work, stop. If it doesn't make you feel better, stop. I wanted every motion I made in my teaching to count. So I began thinking about why there was so much passive resistance to my ministrations.

It took me an embarrassingly long time to wake up to why all our effort had no noticeable effect: No matter if the essay was brilliant, what we always got down to was what was wrong with it. "Yes, yes, swell paper, but see here: Look at this usage. Maybe a comma here would make it clearer." And so on. Sooner or later we had to get in there and clean up. The mind-set of the whole damned English-teaching establishment was on the negative. Most of us could not bear to let a mistake go unnoted, as if someone might come across that essay and see that Clark McKowen had let a boo-boo slip by. The horror of it! One must protect one's reputation at all costs. Vanity. But I would rather suffer censure than persist in futile behavior, so I was willing to toss out what didn't work, even if conventional wisdom did pronounce my behavior wrongheaded. After a while I stopped teaching composition altogether, and wonder of wonders, the students started writing beautifully!

In retrospect, when I think about why creatures learn and how they learn, it seems so obvious. As I noted earlier in this book, we learn because we want to, not because someone holds a gun to our heads (a grade, ridicule, negative criticism). The natural way to learn is *on the job*. That's a basic, too. We learn best in real situations, doing authentic things. A letter grade on a paper is a way of forcing the teacher's will on the student; it's a power play. Students perceive corrections as paper cuts. No matter how much we wail that we are just trying to help, it simply won't wash. Who asked for our help, and what makes us think there must be something *wrong* with students' compositions? When Kathy says, "don't you think so.?" for God's sake answer the question.

When I told my colleague Tony Calabrese I wanted to eliminate fear as a motivator in my classes, he said, "Then you are going to have to give up intention." If my intention was to improve students' writing whether they liked it or not, I would have to knock it off. Grades on papers, corrections, evaluations—these turn a message into a specimen. The written word becomes an exercise in etiquette. Did I want authentic writing? Then I had to respond authentically. If I was willing to unclog the channel between students' minds and mine, I had to pay attention to their messages, or to put it more accurately, to the self that produced the message. The self is in hiding, but it wants an outing; it wants a witness. It wants to be *comprehended;* it wants an accomplice. The first job was to see what they wrote from their point of view, and thereby to see *them*. There isn't any second job. When we shift how we respond to students' writing, everything else falls into place. In other words we have to read students' messages poetically, just as we have to read everything else in the universe. Unbelievable as it may seem, all the things English teachers cherish—correctness, precision, clarity, consistency of voice and tone, and so on—resolve themselves incidentally, for the most part, in the give and take of understanding each other.

So, eventually, I stopped putting letter grades on papers. Then I stopped correcting them. Then I quit offering unsolicited negative comments and then the unsolicited praise. Once the extrinsic reward and punishment were gone, what was left? Only the written communication between two people. Instead of hunting for error, I looked for nuggets of gold and responded not as a teacher but as myself. Anything I didn't like I ignored. I made no attempt to show a "better way." I simply tried to understand. I expected a hullabaloo, but it never came.

Everything changed. Abruptly, the students were eager to read my responses and, when they got their papers back, went through them then and there, reading every single word I had written. There were a few wary students who held out for a week or two or even most of the semester. I figured they were licking their paper cuts and let them alone. The issue usually resolved itself, and a barrier to my happiness as a teacher disappeared overnight. It is so much more fulfilling to read for ideas, not errors. The more I noticed, the more there was to notice. Now I actually enjoyed reading students' papers.

Of course, when I read this way, I could read more papers and walk away refreshed. I looked forward to students' responses. Their individuality blossomed. In a half-hour of enthusiastic reflecting, most people write two and a half pages or more. If that is done five days a week, imagine how much composition practice that amounts to over a semester's time. These writings were accumulated in folders the students kept.

Radical as this approach may seem, it was not a new idea. It simply put learning theory into practice. The general concept is in John Dewey's writings of almost a century ago and in current learning theory: Provide the right circumstances, and creatures will teach themselves. Throughout the decades evidence supporting autonomy and self-actualization piled up. For example, in England, from the time they could write, students in some schools kept journals. They wrote regularly. Teachers read these journals, but never required revision or editing. When students were ready to move on, each would be invited to the headmaster's office and ceremoniously presented with his/her accumulated journals all nicely bound up in a bright ribbon. In those journals there was, of course, a steady progression toward assurance and command of the written word. Speech and writing, if not tampered with, reflect the mind that shaped them and that they shape.

Looking at a semester's work, I could see remarkable changes—even though most of my own students had never been involved in such hands-off programs. When there was no penalty for writing in one's own voice or for nonstandard spelling, punctuation, and form, the awkwardness and childlike styles so common in freshman writing vanished. The prose matched the intelligence and the perception latent in these young minds. Now that it was safe, students were saying what was on their minds, not just what they were supposed to say. Their thoughts came out in all sorts of delightful ways. I never required a specific form; I wanted to see what would evolve. Over a semester a student would use most of the forms that rhetoric texts usually solicit (inductive, deductive, causal, argumentative, comparative, contrastive, sequential, spatial, and so on). A reflection might include a drawing, a photo, or an audiotape. No doubt students chose these structures and materials unselfconsciously and out of awareness. The force of the message seemed to dictate what emerged. Unless totally other-directed, that's the way most of us go about it.

I had given up trying to get everyone to submit their writings in ink on 8½-by-11 lined paper or typed and double-spaced, so I was treated to all sorts of variations. Most were indeed in ink or typed, but there would be the occasional *oeuvre* on the back of a lunch bag or a McDonalds napkin, maybe a piece of cardboard if that was all that was handy and a reflection needed to get written down then and there. Sometimes these came in from people who never, ever wrote anything, so I was happy to get them. It was no time to get picky; it was good to hear from them. I never knew what might show up, but that made it all the more intriguing. I loved the spontaneity. I can imagine my tidy colleagues cringing at such messiness, but you can't have it both ways. If you want students to develop their writing skills, you will have to accept them as they are. I soon came to prefer sifting through the ore. There had been precious little pay dirt in graded and corrected papers.

Other infelicities English teachers fret over fell away, too. Coherence, unity, emphasis, organization, economy, consistency of voice, tone, tense, and so on are all functions of authenticity and passion. When writers mean what they say and have a burning desire to say it, stylistics take care of themselves. It is the same in conversation. Come off it, get real, and silly, rambling, garrulous chatter stops. Whether we realize it consciously or not, we all want to live poetic lives, and when the coast is clear we do. Much of what teachers correct is there because of the way the writing was solicited and/or the way the task is perceived. Remove the artifice and you discover a roomful of poets.

Editing

There remains the matter of standard spelling, conventional punctuation, and academic diction. I suspect most of the brouhaha about the lousy way college students write is really about unedited compositions. Students' indifference to proofreading and copyediting is seen as evidence of ignorance or stupidity.*

Most English teachers are really editors. Even those who know it's a losing battle persist. I know why: Happy as I was with my students' writing, I would cringe a little to think of their papers falling into enemy hands. The composition teacher's pride is at stake, and that is more important than engaging students' minds. But to get the kind of reflective thinking I wanted, I told the students to consider their daily entries unedited drafts. "Get it down any way you can. We'll worry about proofreading and copyediting some other time." We hardly ever did get around to it, though. For their final syntheses, I did ask that they clean up their drafts and make them look nice but to write the way they wrote their daily entries. I read syntheses the same way I read all their other work, so I never did get serious about editing.† It would have changed the dynamics, so my students didn't get much practice.

---

*Reading this section, my own copyeditor—more valuable to me than precious stones—wrote, "Much to my amusement I recently discovered a derisive term for a copyeditor is 'comma chaser.' Oh, my . . ."

†Why not have students save their unedited writings in folders and then offer an elective course, Editing 101, in which they could spend a semester on just that? They could be working on authentic material they had really wanted to write, not some school exercise. Somebody ought to try it. It would make the public happy, and it might even clear up the confusion between editing and composition.

There was an indirect kind of editing going on, though, including spelling and punctuation. One student captured the idea years ago:

> I didn't regard punctuation as important at all before I started writing down exactly what I think. I don't think I really cared if my writing was confusing because of wrong or left-out punctuation. But now that it is really me writing I want to be sure the reader gets the point exactly, stops when I stop, pauses when I pause, laughs when I laugh.

That seemed to me a succinct primer on editing; it still does.

But what about the poor souls who wandered off to other schools or jobs and never did get in the habit of checking over their work? Weren't they in for trouble? Rae Cecchettini, whom I mentioned earlier was a teaching assistant for me and is now a college English teacher herself, spoke to me about that recently. It is OK with her if the students don't edit their work, but she tells them they could get into a jam later on. She asked me if maybe I should have forewarned my students of all the perils awaiting them? Well, no. I haven't any idea *what* perils await them. I told her about Mike Muccigrosso. He was a Vietnam vet who had taken several classes with me and had become a friend. He had had almost no experience writing when he started with me, but had become comfortable with words on paper by the time we said goodbye. I was delighted with his work. He was, too, but when he dropped by after a semester at San Jose State, he said, "McKowen, you left me flapping in the breeze. I got a D on my first English paper."

"Gosh, Mike, that's terrible. What did you get on your second paper?"

"B."

"Gee. How did that happen?"

"I figured out what to do."

No one knows what's ahead—for ourselves or anyone else. But what does comfort me is the idea that my students may be more adept at figuring things out. Even though they may have had little formal work in copyediting, they will meet that challenge if they need to. Rae Cecchettini herself is a case in point. When she entered my freshman English class at DVC, she had been out of school twenty years and had two grown children. Starting college after so long a hiatus is scary. One's self-esteem can be shaky. Though her sentences were conventionally structured and the words properly spelled, she was not an experienced writer. At first, I know, getting anything at all on paper was painful. But I never offered her advice or told her how tough those UC Berkeley teachers are (I suppose some are, some aren't). While she worked with me, her writing became more and more assured and fluent. A couple of years later I read her master's thesis, and it was just fine. She had the whole business of composing under control.

"So, Rae, look at the first reflection you wrote for me and this thesis. What do you think you'd have done back then if I had shown you the gap between the two?"

"I'd probably have dropped out of college."

It was the same with Dennis Sullivan. He was a street-smart kid on the lam, so to speak, from the streets of Detroit. He was staying with his sister Rosan and her husband, my colleague Karl Staubach, and had decided it might be a lark to hang out in college a while. He was not what you might call academic. For weeks he sprawled in his chair on the sidelines and scoped me out. He was prone to tossing in some wise-guy comment from time to time. I think Karl put him up to it; there was always a twinkle in his eye. When he did write it would be a few words in pencil, mostly misspelled, rough and crude. I never did know what went on behind those eyes, but I'm sure when he finished my course his written work would have appalled most college teachers. Nonetheless, a few years later I was at Karl and Rosan's and saw a letter he had written them from graduate school in San Diego. It was fine: articulate, spelled and punctuated appropriately, intelligent.

Recently, I had a chat with Steve Herrmann, who had been in my classes twenty years ago. He is now a psychotherapist and is writing about the quest for self in technological America. He is *writing* a book. He writes all the time, poems, articles, whatever. "The journal experience," he said, "with feedback from other students—getting to know each other through language—was a fabulous mirror-reflection experience; even if most of us, myself included, didn't realize the full implications of what we had discovered until much later in our lives." I never tried to make Steve—or anyone else—want to write, much less to be a writer. It was the authenticity of the dialogue, written or oral, as Steve and many others pointed out, that did the trick. "If you had given us drill in grammar or mechanics," he said, "I'd have been turned off. I had had my belly full by the time I got to college." When he went on to the University of California in Santa Cruz, he had no trouble fixing up his writing so that it would be acceptable to the academic community. He enjoyed getting his self on paper, so he was willing to do the editing. If people don't enjoy the work, they will not enjoy the editing either and will never become adept.

These are not isolated instances. A normal self-actualizing human being can and will master necessary skills when needed. But even if the dangers are real, we cannot anticipate them, for they are ever changing. Nor could we protect the young, however concerned we might be. A teacher works in the present, and everything that can be done is done there. Anyway, when a genuine need is recognized, most people can learn to edit passably well and rather quickly. It is not as difficult as computer science. So I didn't worry much about my students' indifference to proper form.

What Makes Students Want to Write

> there so very pretty. don't you think so.?
> —Kathy (age seven)

Teachers like to exaggerate their influence on the nuts and bolts of writing. The most they can do is act as a catalyst. That is, they can set the stage, but it is always the students' show. We need to get out of the way. When I was chairman of the Instruction Committee of our college, we asked students to recall any positive writing experiences they might have had. In a 1982 article for our staff publication, I summed up my impression of what the responses might mean. A more deliberative person might see the implications differently, but I still think my title, "The Human Factor," embodies the common message of those responses.

We had asked students to recall a writing experience that they had enjoyed. In every instance they liked getting their own hands and minds on the stuff. If that happened, they remembered the experience warmly. Just about everybody could recall at least one such experience, but one student wrote that he *never* once enjoyed writing. Almost no one liked writing just to meet a requirement. Teachers need to think about that. Students perceive schoolwork as something they have to do. But learning will be optimal only when mind and spirit are committed. That explains the wheel spinning. Students resent busywork and wasted time. They want something educational to happen when they sweat.

Teachers are always talking about killer assignments that capture students' minds, but the survey showed what worked was different for each respondent. The survey reinforced my own experience: Each entity connects with the environment uniquely. Uniformity produces passive resistors. Students have to connect with the assignment: "Big Whoppers" in fourth grade might have been the hook for one student, but a sixty-hour research paper might be the turning point for another, or even weekly 500-word essays. It could be daily ten-minute free writing for one person but book reviews, short stories, or a scrapbook for another. So any common assignment had better provide room for many approaches and lots of escape hatches. If there is not room for every single student to interact, then the assignment, investigation, or exploration needs tinkering. Good teaching is sloppy teaching.

As I have said, what caught up one student bored another, but an assignment in almost every discipline had clicked with at least one of the respondents. Some music, biology, math, or business assignment had done the trick. An essay on Handel's *Messiah* was thrilling for one student. Another was eternally grateful to his eighty-year-old teacher of classical guitar for having him research and write about various fingering techniques. Twenty-nine other people might well have found it tiresome. For one it might be a paper on tension for health science, for another the plight of whales for marine biology or an anthropology paper on Atlantis. One even cited a composition for a calculus class. That's the point. We never know in advance what will work or for whom. It isn't the level of difficulty or the field or how formal the work. Any of those might be right for somebody but definitely not for everybody. We cannot think for other people.

What did matter every time was whether students became absorbed in the task. Something had to happen inside while they were working—or afterward. The common, recurring theme was that the students' own spirits were enmeshed in the product; the mark of their own hands was upon it. I don't see how there can be a more powerful message to educators. Such involvement must be the mode, not the exception, throughout an institution. This revelation was not surprising to me. It is remarkable, though, that absorption is the exception, not the rule.

Perhaps the reason is that make-work is the common assignment. We all hate that; if we invest our lifeblood we want something for our efforts. A letter grade is not spiritually nourishing, nor is avoidance of the whip sufficient compensation. Bliss will do nicely, but teachers can't provide that. Not one student listed fear or extrinsic reward as a catalyst. Deep pleasure is not associated with either. In the end intrinsic pleasure is the only common motivator identified in the survey. Think how useless our pep talks and threats are, how much energy is wasted.

That does not mean, however, that students want to write in a vacuum. I have noted how important a witness is to writers, and these responses bore out that observation. Respondents were not interested in criticism; not one cited grades or evaluation as a motivating factor. But someone's interest or attention was indeed valued. It was important to be understood.

Many respondents resented doing a lot of work and getting a terrible grade. Students want—as do all of us—a day's pay for a day's work. They like to know the score. They don't like vague or ambiguous assignments. If they can't figure out why the grade is low or if they think the teacher doesn't like their ideas, they are angry. If your pay is docked you want to know why. They don't like having to do menial work, either. Some wrote about assignments that required too little thought to be interesting. But a writing assignment during which a thought got clarified or a new one emerged was great. Any assignment in which students use their own minds is almost sure to be viewed positively. We all do like to be gainfully employed.

Assignments fail when students don't see the point. One respondent wrote that she hated the daily writing until she realized the purpose was to provoke thought processes. Then she was enthusiastic. Apparently, just clarifying our assignments is magic. Picking a paper apart usually interferes with growth, but thoughtful, considered uncritical response is welcomed. When respondents saw value in a reader's comments, they were grateful, but they hated faultfinding.

So the kind of writing task isn't nearly as important as the students' involvement in it. The teacher's personality isn't critical either. But the assignment does have to be clear, and room must be left for all sorts of human beings, all thinking uniquely and all approaching tasks in their own individual ways. Heart and mind have to connect with the work. And someone must witness the product, but that can be a teacher, other students, a senator, a boyfriend. Feedback keeps the process flowing.

Responses to our survey went beyond the issue of writing competency. We had of course asked about writing experiences students had enjoyed, so it turned out they were really identifying the components of joy. The elements of joy include learning, growth, and adventure: heartfelt experience. An assignment with the opportunity for individual input, one that encourages unique thought and has a recognized and accepted purpose, has an excellent chance of being educational.

Every writing assignment has to be a *human* assignment. We have to consider the human factor. Nature has designed us, as it has other mammals, with feeling. Emotion is the sensor that guides and directs us; its role in education is not negotiable. We do think by feeling, through feeling. In fact, what we have learned to call thought—which seems so mechanical and matter of fact—is never objective, and in the biological sense objectivity is impossible, for the heart of the mammalian computer is spirit. Until spirit is engaged the biological computer stays "down." In that context National Education Day is February 14.

Honing: Correctness and Precision

"You know," I tell my students, when I try to talk them out of being scared of their teachers, "these people in front of the class are just like you and your classmates—only older. They had the same problems you do when they were in school. In fact, some of you here will more than likely become teachers yourselves." So when the Instruction Committee was surveying the college community about their writing skills, we decided to ask people who had been through the mill—our faculty—how they themselves had gained competence. Some of them wrote for our staff publication, some had written for professional journals, and others had written textbooks. Many were accomplished stylists. None of them were obliged to write; it was something they chose to do. We were not a publish-or-perish institution. So how had they become good at it? Would they applaud their English teachers? Would they cite 500-word themes? Would they credit drill in mechanics?

Many of our teachers said that as undergraduates they had had trouble writing and had left school insecure about their abilities. So how did they develop the control, assurance, and competence? They learned on the job. That could be working one to one with an adviser on a doctoral thesis, to fill a practical need, or to do some personal work that called for words on paper. It was comforting to realize that most of these writers, when the time was right, had found a way to get as good at it as they needed to be. No doubt, if these are typical adults, it is normal for writers to develop their skills as they go along. In nature's time schedule the writing level of our students is probably right on target. If they have not been traumatized by some zealous missionary, they are at exactly the place they should be.

Like students, teachers have all sorts of writing needs. Some don't need or want to write brilliantly, but they can say so in reasonably error-free sentences. One wrote,

> My writing is mediocre. I can organize and express thoughts clearly, but my literary style would be considered boring! I have no need to write a book, so I am content with my present boring style.

The survey gave us a chance to measure schooling against practical needs. It was evident that when we actually use writing in our adult lives, our emphases shift. Our students value assignments that engage their minds and spirits and enable them to become fluent. But later on, as the comments of teachers show, there is more focus on correctness and precision.

> An adviser in grad school helped me tighten my writing. . . . An editor removed about 30 "which's" and "who's" and "that's" from a manuscript. . . . Practice helped, and close critical evaluation. . . . Greatest help and sharpest criticism came from friends and political allies here at DVC—people who paid attention to the purpose of my writing and forced me to do the same. . . .
> Proofread + proofread + rewrite + rewrite. . . . My positions in the United Faculty and in the Senate required me to write for a wider audience; as a result my writing has improved and my perception of my ability has changed, too, in a positive direction.

Some did mention a teacher who worked closely with them or a friend who showed them how to do a blue-book exam, but most remembered practical experiences like writing for the eighth-grade newspaper or doing an article for a scientific journal. If the writing had some use it got better right away. Most teachers we surveyed saw their writing as developmental. It is never a fixed or finished skill. For many their most valued experiences occurred after they began working. Writing a book about writing helped, or rewording and condensing a superior's letters, or trying to teach.

> Preparing intelligence reports in military service helped more than my English classes. . . . Writing, writing, and more writing. . . . Writing books, in both monetary returns and satisfaction in a job well done. . . . I really improved when I started teaching Business English. . . . Learned through experience. . . . A lifelong endeavor I get better at year after year. . . . As I teach students to compose, my own composing improves. . . . Four years of working with writing on a day-to-day basis—not learning about writing but just doing it. . . . Writing book reviews.

By circumstance or design we continue to educate ourselves through interest or need. We just happen to get involved in a team-teaching project, or we decide to do something finally about that writing block by taking a consciousness-raising workshop. We get interested in the ERA, or civil rights, or community politics and have to write letters or publicity. And we learn.

Our survey showed that most DVC teachers felt OK about their writing, but many hadn't when they started working. Along the way, though, they figured out how to solve what problems they did have, and none were contemplating suicide—at least not on that account.

Students' writing varies all over the place, and as we should expect, so it is with teachers. In fact, anyone without a vested interest would find all this variety perfectly normal and certainly nothing to be alarmed about. There is nothing wrong—in the scheme of things—and thus no illness to remedy. The behavior of adults no longer in school shows that writing, like any other skill, is developmental; in a supportive environment people will progress according to their nature and need and, with decent luck, will continue to do so throughout their lives. These surveys show that most of the help we offer doesn't help. It would be a kindness to stop that. That would be refreshing. Authentic dialogue is the one sure way to provide an optimal learning environment.

13

Reflective Writing
Living Is So Dear

To see or to perish

—Teilhard de Chardin

In my classes writing was an extension of talking. We wrote back and forth to each other, that's all. I tried to keep the dialogue as authentic as I could. That was primarily my job as a teacher anyway. How is that done? One simply cuts through the kitsch and talks soul to soul, or self to self, directly. I remember Edith Weaver years ago writing in an entry, "You act as if my moods aren't valid." I hadn't consciously thought that, but I realized she was right. My practice was to pay attention to anything true or real and ignore everything else. Moods were like the weather. We pay attention to the weather, certainly; but if it's raining we dress accordingly and go on with our work. I always wanted to go deeper, to go as deep as we could. "I wanted to live deliberately," said Thoreau, "Living is so dear." Our days are numbered, after all; I like to make them count.

That is the key to a teacher's behavior in general, and certainly it is the key regarding written communication. Ulteriority and superficiality, or acting as though artifice is valid, only set the process back. For example, one student said he'd be furious if his girlfriend fell in love with someone else. "But do you love her?" "Yes." "Then, don't you want her to be happy? Is love love if it changes when the loved-one changes?" In other words, what's really going on under all this *sturm und drang*? What's really going on? "'Love is not love / which alters when it alteration finds, / Or bends with the remover to remove'."

I always wanted to explore the implications of such rainsqualls and trace them to their roots. Whatever we were examining we tried to go as broadly, deeply, and intensely as we could. That approach had made the classes sizzle, and when I read students' reflections that way, the same thing happened. I never met a student who did not want an intense relationship with his or her world. To my mind that is all there is to the teaching of writing.

It boils down to unfiltered interfacing of minds. Sometime during the 1970s I gave a talk about this sort of writing at the Conference on College Composition and Communication annual gathering in Cincinnati. In those days I called it journal writing, but there are so many approaches to keeping journals I prefer to describe what we did as *reflective* writing. I have mentioned this sort of writing several times in this book. Here is a description of the process.

> ### *Reflective Writing in Freshman English*
>
> I don't give "writing" assignments or detailed instructions anymore. I say something like, "Think over the things we've been talking about, and as you think about them, jot down your thoughts." If they ask me, I say, "Yes, you can write about anything that seems to be a spin-off from what we've said in class." That permits any kind of tangent, but it always has a connection, like an umbilical cord, to a central focus: our group's interrelationship. From that point they spread out in as many directions as there are students in the class. My suggestions are as brief as I can make them; if I'm more detailed the results are teacher-pleasing. I hate that. The more I explain, the worse it gets. Any teacher knows how that goes.
>
> Once we get going the details take care of themselves anyway. Students begin writing in their own way, usually artificially, about things they do not really care about. At the beginning of each class they turn in a reflection, representing at least a half-hour of thinking and writing and get it back at the beginning of the next class. These are saved chronologically in a folder. I have them do this every time so that the writing becomes a habit. That way, even though every writing session may not be wonderful, the possibility of insight or discovery is more likely. Regularity is an important part of this process.
>
> I do ask them to sit long enough so that there is at least a chance of something happening. Usually when people write they stop just the wrong side of the creative spurt. It takes a little while for things to start happening. We have to stay there playing with an idea until the mind kicks into gear. It takes about fifteen minutes for most minds to warm up. Then, all of a sudden they are really flowing. Once that occurs the writing is a pleasure to read. So I ask

students to stick with it for at least half an hour. Within a week most students are rolling right along—and enjoying themselves, to boot. The regularity and the half-hour on each entry are just about all there is to it.

The rest has to do with my role as a witness. When students turn in their first reflection, it will probably be quite a bit like what they have been writing for other teachers. Instead of responding as a teacher (whatever that might mean), I try to understand the message, as I would with any conversationalist, and I try to be as thoughtful in my response as I can, a lot more thoughtful than "How's the baseball coming along?" If I have been truthful the students will see what kind of person they are talking to and can keep on trying to fake it or come off it and bring our minds together so that we can have a decent chat.

Within a week of this sort of interchange, a good number of the students are writing well. That is, they are writing in their own voices and *metaphorically*. The process is comfortable. They are not trying to please me anymore; they are trying to communicate, and that is an entirely different story. Then all sorts of delightful things happen. For one thing the reflections are fun for me to think about. So their minds get a good workout, but so does mine.

Conventional assignments are usually designed to polish up some aspect of style or mechanics or content. Then the teacher methodically and matter-of-factly searches for what was assigned. If it is there that is good; if not, that is terrible and Fs and paranoia follow. In reflective writing that is all beside the point. Long ago I gave up judging students' writing, and I never assign a grade. So there is never any reason to be writing anything less than one's best, because that is all that either one of us becomes interested in. We are not interested in filling pages with words. Nor are we interested in clever stylistics or ego gratifying, as is the case with most conventional writing assignments: *How do I look? Am I wonderful, or what?* The approval game invites dependency. It sets up a neurotic relationship.

As I said earlier it doesn't matter what students write about. What matters is their purpose. If it is not authentic then our dialogue is second-rate. I don't get upset if a student gets completely sidetracked. It does bother me some, though, if it sounds like a bunch of hooey. I just shift to a different level, to some aspect of whatever's been written that we can talk about seriously. Since their writing isn't constrained I get a tremendous variety from student to student and even within one individual's work. In the middle of an entry a poem might grow out of an idea being worked on. An entire entry might be a poem or a story or a fable—all without any suggestion from me. I think this happens because what they are doing dictates the form it will take. That makes more sense to me than arbitrarily assigning a structure. Sometimes they make lists right in the middle of an entry. One student had a whole page of things a pencil is: back scratcher, weapon, pointer, et cetera. He just got to playing around and that's what came out.

Are there students at the end of the course who still do not enjoy writing reflections? Perhaps a few, but almost none persist in being inauthentic. It just won't wash. When I was still learning how all this works, there might be an occasional student who would just stop writing if the usual snow job didn't work. Sometimes a student would get angry or just drift away. But as I became more perceptive, fewer and fewer took these routes. I hadn't been sensitive enough or attentive enough. Gradually, I learned to take more responsibility for the interplay.

Serious writing isn't necessarily somber, though, and I have encountered intentionally clever writing in the reflections, which I do enjoy. There is room for clever handling of language. If, despite the flourishes and adornment, the communication is still valid and true, then I am pleased. Love of language itself is not enough; there must be authenticity, too. But if the style were taken away and nothing remained, I would have to find some way to change the subject. I recall judging essays for the NCTE annual contest for a few years and finally having to give it up.* All there was was form, no real content. It depressed me to see such empty rhetoric.

As for polishing, I don't do much with that. Get the engine running right, then detail the car. There is a time for correctness and precision, but that time is not the give and take of a semester of freshman English. Copyediting is not as complicated as the palaver about it would make it seem. Most people learn to edit their own work when a genuine need arises. As one student said, "Proofreading and copyediting come when I want to clean up my writing for other people. Then I carefully cut out things, recombine sentences, change words." That is what we do when we want to make our writing public.†

One reason I gave up contriving assignments *(Do this exercise. Write an autobiography. Write about an experience that made a deep impression on you. Write*

---

*Garrison Keillor had a similar experience judging a poetry contest. He got in hot water with creative-writing teachers over his short story "The Poetry Judge" in the February 1996 *Atlantic Monthly*. Give me daily reflections any day. Is there a connection in the fact that inmates in jails turn out far more spritely writings than do inmates in mental hospitals? Hint: Who has more at stake with the keepers?

†I attach a page to the syllabus explaining how to write for the course. I tell the students not to proofread these half-hour reflections: "At this stage, proofreading and editing are inappropriate and counterproductive. If, for your own purposes, you want to work on correctness and precision, do it afterward as a separate activity. Uninterrupted thinking and writing half an hour a day will make the course a rich experience."

an extended analogy. Write an essay about the ocean.) is that the mind ends up thinking about the contrivance as the primary purpose. We can't do that and think about what we want to say, too. The single major objective has to be to say something. Writers want to get out accurately something inside themselves. Why would a student want to do this? Because there is a driving force to connect one's random flow of feeling with some kind of solidity, some physical reality, and words are the most common means of doing that. When one finds the right word or the right expression, it is a release. That feeling of release is why we do it. What we are always trying to do is think something out—think it out of our bodies, pull it out, out of the deep. The more authentic the writing becomes, the more it is oneself, one's story, but it always seems to be simply a chat between the two of us, sometimes a chat between a person's conscious mind and the nonconscious self. (Actually, that is what always happens when we utter a thought. We put something of ourselves into a physical form and then take a look at what we have made. Sometimes our words or actions bounce off another person and bounce back; sometimes the words hit a page and bounce back to our own eyes. "So that's me!") Writing is always the process of getting it out.

I often encounter teachers who think reflective writing is trivial and that such scribbling doesn't really teach people how to write. But it is just the opposite. Most assigned writing, by its very nature, cannot be important. When someone says *Write an essay*, *Do a satire*, the focus shifts. And that destroys the seriousness of the writing. The very assignment makes it trivial. So, instead of a typical assignment, I simply say, "Get it out—any way you can." Everyone in a culture may not have an interest in fine writing, but all human beings are capable of developing their own ideas and of communicating them. It just happens that a pen or word processor is at the extremity of the brain, and what goes on at the tips of the fingers just happens to be labeled *writing*. The less attention we give to the pen in the hand or keyboard, the more likely it is that the ideas will find their way onto the page intact.

Good writers find conventional assignments outrageous. Inexperienced writers become hopelessly confused. But reflective writing is so natural students are surprised at how easy it is. Once they get the hang of it, they love seeing their thoughts emerge, and after the course is over they save their folders. Students come back for a visit four or five years later and say, "I got my folder out last night—had it in the bottom of my drawer—and, you know, I still like what I wrote." The reason is that the reflections are not just an exercise. Aspects of writing that teachers usually emphasize are not assimilated—and would not have much worth if they were. We have such diverse human beings in our classes we have to find some way to meet all their needs.

Reflective writing is the most inclusive mode I can think of. The less specific my suggestions, the better the chances are that most students will be able to respond. The minute I shape the assignment, I exclude perhaps two-thirds of the class, and maybe one-third connect a little bit. But once students get used to doing reflections, the writing begins to take on the shape of the individual. His/her own spirit begins to come through. If the author isn't visible in the writing, it is not much good. Usually within a week or so, each reflection has the distinctive flavor of its creator. That's when my job becomes exciting. To my mind that is what it means to teach writing—by *not* teaching it. By doing it, not talking about it.

The worst thing about this sort of writing is the damage to teachers' egos. There isn't much teaching to do, but the students get better and better. It turns out that reducing our clever tricks to almost zero results in a tremendous surge of vitality among the writers. They themselves are delighted. "Why do you suppose this happened?" I would ask. "You seem very pleased." They would respond, "Oh, I think it was just being able to talk with the other students." No praise for me at all, and I have precious little to brag about to other teachers. I have no brilliant devices up my sleeve, no complicated methods. Quit teaching and things get better and better. Minimalist teaching is not something to write home about. I may never be teacher of the year, but I love it when the students are more spontaneous with each other and more open with me, too. I'm sure it's because I am not perceived as a teacher in the usual sense of the word.

Something else that happens rather spontaneously is students reading each others' reflections. I see them passing their entries around and talking with each other about them. Sometimes they will read excerpts out loud to the class or make copies for everyone. Ideas start flowing. Assigned compositions don't usually elicit such involvement. It's punctuation; it's paragraphs; it's cosmetics. These emphases are barriers to writing. In truth, I hardly notice such matters. I'm interested in something else. I hardly register misspellings, unless asked to check for them. I'm usually reading for the good stuff, and I disregard trivia that might be in the way. Sometimes when a student is on a roll, every sentence requires me to think. The reflection challenges me, and I have to give it the attention it deserves. Usually, when teachers have assigned an exercise, they have put a lot of energy into the lesson itself. When it comes time to respond to the students' ideas, they are all tuckered out. There is no energy left for the mind. It's all been used up on correcting things.

I know a student is authentic when the writing becomes metaphoric. Discoveries often emerge as metaphors. Watch the process: As the mind casts about for some way to say the essential thing, out pops a metaphor. But when I told a student about my observation, she gave me a bushel of metaphors in her next entry, but none of them were authentic. It's risky to talk about good writing with students. Once I told David Malloy his account of his living on the streets in Seattle was quite well written. I said it seemed good enough to polish up and publish. That ruined it. All of a sudden, he decided he was an author and messed it all up.

Assignments such as comparison-and-contrast papers continue to keep students from saying the true thing. We support their addictions. The more we give them help, the less they must discover their own resources. I'm not saying a teacher just sits around and does nothing. One has to do nothing in a very involved sort of way. It has to be straight. Every contrivance throws a wall up between the two people. The simpler and more direct the structure is, the more the writing is going to come out right. *Not doing* is sometimes more powerful than being helpful. Students know there is no point in trying to please me. I'm never going to fall for it. They soon realize I perk right up for their ideas but not their fancy duds. I reach down beyond the ego to the pure self and chat with that. It should be no surprise that they much prefer that sort of interest. But most assignments are based on extrinsic reward and punishment. The more frequent the rewards, the more gigantic the ego. The more frequent the punishment, the lower the self-esteem. There is no need for either. So there are no rewards and no assignments to keep people dependent. The therapy is always the authentic dialogue, always going straight in.

Responses to Reflections

When I began sharing the reading of student papers with my teaching assistants, I had to make sure they didn't start acting like teachers. I did not want them cautioning students or correcting or advising. Most were familiar with the kinds of responses I had written on their own entries, so I didn't have to say much. Mainly, I wanted them to write reflections of the reflections—and nothing more. What a reader does with an entry can make all the difference in a student's feeling about writing another entry. I said, "If you were the writer, what sort of response would you have wanted?" That's all it would take to get the teaching assistants on the right path. The reflection sampler that follows includes the kinds of responses I might make, but they are only possibilities. We all have unique windows on the world, and they will affect what we see and what we say. But it has to be human and honest and nonjudgmental.

A Reflection Sampler

Once, for a teachers' workshop back in the 1970s, I collected some excerpts to give a hint of the range of styles, subjects, and approaches that I happily accepted. It seems to me these samples embody the composition skills teachers try so hard to encourage. Here are students, without any instruction, choosing their words, working out their thoughts, deciding what form they need. It seems self-evident that they are teaching themselves to compose. Here are a few that I saved with the delicious personal flourishes still intact.

- When a metaphor springs up unsolicited, I know it's authentic. It can't be faked, unless it's plagiarized, of course. Metaphors are the vehicle of thought.

  Truth is sort of like light on the eye. If a person is subjected to bright light, his pupils contract so that not so much light gets in. This is what happens to most people who think they have found truth. In letting certain "truths" in, their minds tend to close up; they hold these truths blindly and let nothing else in to disturb them.

  Response: "Neat analogy. That's how bias works, isn't it, and *bigotry*. So how do we knock it off? Maybe knowing about it is a first step?" That's what I might have said, or something shorter if my time was limited. I mainly want him to know I *got* it. Sounds a bit like Plato's cave, doesn't it?

- Thinking about thinking and *capturing* thought. Words like *delicious*, as it is used here, rarely come up in conventional compositions, nor does the sudden insight of "No, I still have it."

  Some people "grok" very easily. It seems to take me a lot longer. I usually don't grok something until I try grokking something else, and while I'm in the process I grok the first idea. A lot of times I don't understand what's going on in class until I think about it quite a bit. I usually get it while I'm at work or in the car, then before I write it here I lose it. No, I still have it, but the delicious words I used while it was still in my head are lost.

  Response: "God, yes! You're singing my song. I hate it when that happens. Those delicious words are what keep what I write from being so damned boring." There is much to respond to in this paragraph. Since I don't have time to pick up on every one of them, sometimes I just touch on one or two. Robert Frost said something like that: Poem B helps you understand Poem C, which in turn helps you understand Poem A. This is a valuable insight the student hit on.

- The desire not to be doing a schlock job of communication, not to mimic: ". . . in my own words and way."

  In class today I understood everything that was said. But it was all new to me, and I was learning. I couldn't respond then and I can't now. To do so would just be saying what we already said, mimicking. I have it all stored, and when I get the fullness, flash, the light will come on and then I can respond in my own words and way.

  Response: "I'm with you, kid. I hate being asked what I think of a movie or concert right then and there. Usually I need time to let it steep." I. A. Richards had the same complaint about on-the-spot criticism as this student, and here is a college kid thinking it up all by himself. I think that's remarkable.

- Modifying a statement by adding on. He thinks over what he has said and changes "no regrets" to "without fighting it."

  I suppose you really don't deserve to have something unless you can leave it. As we discussed this in class today, I *began to wonder* [my italics] something. Is it the same with life? Do you not deserve to live unless you could die with no regrets? Maybe "no regrets" is too strong. Perhaps "without fighting it" would be better.

  Response: "I once told a friend, 'If you're afraid of dying, you can't live either.' 'You mean you want to die?' 'No,' I said, and the idea came to me as I mouthed the words, 'I'm willing to die. I have to be willing to die. That's a condition of living.'" I would have wanted to respond at least this much because the student had hit on an idea I was quite interested in myself. This is real-life investigation, not sophistry.

- Just there in the middle of an entry.

  ### Driving Home

  Down and lonely,
  over the hill
  I came upon
  a road worker
  sitting in the grass
  eating his lunch.

  Response: "Just right! Ain't life grand?" Suppose I had a premeditated idea of what this assignment should be. The poem probably would not ever have been written. To me just the poem would satisfy any half-hour writing assignment I would ever want to make. We should be grateful to have such jewels showing up in students' writing.

- A young woman from Puerto Rico. Is this an essay, a poem, a letter, a log, or what?

    Dear McKowen: I have spent a Sunday up on the mountain of Diablo: Motorcycling up and down, looking at the scenic view . . . I brought back all the world on my face—cheeks set aglow by sunset sky, planes, hawks, people, woods, horses, spring flowers and wind.

    Response: "Oh, Lupe, thanks for that! You've reminded me of what living is all about." Sometimes, when a passage like this appears, I type it up to look like a poem and attach it to the reflection as a way of reframing it so that the student can see her own words stand out in their beauty.

- Aphorisms pop up frequently.

    Removing a waterproof watch before showering is like knowing life but not chancing it.

    Response: "Yep! You ought to put that on the chalkboard." Reflective writing is full of such insights, many as good as or better than things I've seen in print.

- Answering her own questions.

    How come I feel "on" one day and then "off" the next? Oh, it's up to me: I forgot. OK, OK.

    Response: "OK, OK. I love it when people figure these things out themselves." And I do.

- This seems like a complete essay to me, but by conventional rules it's all disjointed. Reading this is almost like getting into the writer's mind and watching it function. What makes it all worth it to the writer is the flash at the end. That's what we all want from our writing, that flash of insight when we've been playing with some problem. Notice how the mind goes on tangents but finally comes back to the original quest.

    I like the idea of making sure our bodies are all scarred and bruised when we die. I know I am always protecting myself when I know that I shouldn't give a damn about the consequences. I should try it anyway—like writing poems.

Reflective Writing

It's nice to be in the middle ground
Between fact and fiction
Where I don't have to rely
On artificial fission
To stay in, almost,
And out, but not too far.
But I could stray
Without a doubt
Without myself
To kick about.

I'm just going to put some thoughts here that I got and jotted down. I'm not going to change them or try to put them in sequence or any kind of order or meaning. These thoughts came to me over a period of about an hour while I was working this morning:

After I "get" something, I don't feel the obligation that the teacher does. That is, to keep things going, to make sure everyone else gets it. How can I get this feeling of contributing a metaphor that might help someone else understand?

All take and no give?

How can I start caring about people I don't approve of?

So what if I don't approve? That doesn't mean they shouldn't be what they are. Unless they are phoney. But then am I just not approving of myself?

I know why I cut out the other poems. So much of the real me shows and I don't want someone I don't approve of telling me I'm wrong. Even if I'm wrong. Truth hurts—me. [Discovery]

It seems like the only time it's the real me writing is when *my nose is running*. [My italics] When I've been doing some crying.

Did I answer my own question? Don't I have the answer to every question I could possibly ask? I create the question and the answer. Any and every idea is completely original.... *It just flashed.* [My italics] If I am to learn anything, I have to get a few or a *lot* of scars.

Response: "You gave yourself a real workout this time—and hit paydirt several times, too, eh! Don't you love it when that happens? Yes, you have all the answers to all *your* questions. Any other questions are none of your business. Would you agree?" I would probably have made some response to several of the ideas in this entry. The thing is, I'm really interested in these ideas, too, so it's no problem responding. I want to.

- Is this practical writing?

> *Walking in the morning:*
> *The gentle breeze stirs a*
>   *leaf.*
> *Hello, leaf.*
> *A piece of aluminum paper*
>   *shuffles.*
> *Good morning, parking*
>   *lot, paper and breeze.*
> *The coffee, hot and rich.*
> *Good morning, coffee.*
> *Good morning, life—me?*

(These are the two minutes from my car to the store.)

Response: "Now, that's the way to go to work! Sorta like Piglet's wondering what's going to happen exciting today. I wonder how many of your co-workers approach work that way!"

- Playing with analogies.

> The journal is a
>   a. doorstop
>   b. diving board
>   c. giant arrow
>   d. harmonizing device

Response: "e. mirror, f. ice axe, g. tuning fork, h. 9-1-1. We ought to try this in class." I get lots of ideas for class activities this way. For example, we could get a metaphor from everyone up on the chalkboard and then try to figure out what the thinking behind the metaphor is. While we were doing that we would also be noticing all sorts of things that can be done in reflections—without my ever "teaching" how to write an entry. It all comes from the students. But, even without that by-product, the fun of playing with analogies is a sufficient justification. (We are also giving our poetic faculties a workout.)

- Just there on the page. No explanation. (The symbol is called an *interrobang*, a combination of a question mark and an exclamation point, suitable for an expression like "How about that?!").

‽

Response: "How about that ❓"

- Thinking about *why* we create.

    One can't be original unless he places his audience in a secondary position.

    Response: "You got it! Everyone knows you can't chew gum and march at the same time. Most artists I know of figured that out. If the artist ain't in love with the creation, it's a cinch it'll bore everyone else out of their skulls, too. I call it enlightened self-interest. Please, please, be selfish!"

- She figured it out herself. Sometimes it takes a few weeks.

    True, I'm really turned on to my journal now. Every night when I sit down to write, I begin learning from a blank piece of paper. [Fifth week]

    Response: "I'm glad you noticed that. I use a blank sheet of paper for this purpose a lot. In fact, if I spend about half an hour on it, I can almost guarantee myself some neat insight will show up." It makes all the difference for a student to make this discovery rather than for a teacher to *tell* her.

- Adding on, modifying, carrying a thought further.

    That's really funny that you're talking about metaphors. I got the idea somewhere that they were bad to use. I sort of think all metaphors are dead metaphors. But—I see that it's like what I've been learning from the book: You have to put life back into it—just like captured snowflakes suffering.

    Response: "Yeah. I think it's mixed metaphors or clichés that people get worked up about. But, really, it's all about using language carelessly, not noticing what we're really saying. It's all about being *alive*, isn't it?" This student is onto a fundamental idea about language.

- A lot of it is defining terms, redefining them for oneself.

    Asceticism? Or is it just proper values and perspective?

    Response: "There you go. It's just living truthfully, isn't it? People who delude themselves think that's so hard-nosed, but to me taking things for what they are makes everything sweeter." This entry makes me think about such things, so I tell her what I'm thinking. It is a dialogue.

- Picking up where the class left off.

    The paradox:

ALL things are significant and important, and I should be totally aware and involved in all that surrounds me.

But

I should remain detached; I should not become dependent; I must partake and enjoy—but never be not able to do without.

Response: "Rats! I was afraid of that. And *not* track it down and kill it? It takes a lot of sitting and being quiet to get used to that idea, doesn't it? I still have some spots that need work! It doesn't hurt for students to know a teacher still has lots to learn—and knows it.

- Enjoying himself, enjoying the process, the metaphoric breakthrough.

I guess you think I'm a nut about avoiding death, but the physical aspect isn't important. I just want to feel up the idea. (Wow! I love that metaphor "feel up." It might be after your time but in our eighth grade vernacular "feel up" meant to caress a girl's breast. Or more precisely in those days, to squeeze the hell out of it. Yes. That's a powerful metaphor. I love it.)

Response: "Yes, it's a powerful metaphor. I love it, too. Ask your girlfriend what *she* thinks about it. Report back." We could get a whole class on sexism out of this passage. I imagine there would be some heated commentary. And we sure would get lots of spontaneous reflections out of it. Almost any entry can have multiple possibilities for response. This one particularly interests me because of the discovery of a metaphor that captures exactly how the writer messes around with an idea. A metaphor is practical: It lets us see what we are thinking.

- Criticism. No trouble at all.

I just read the essay "How Flowers Changed the World." At first I thought it would be just so-so writing, just ordinary. But I really think it's fantastic! It just kind of rolls out very logically and you sit there and say, "Of course. That's it."

Response: "I felt the same way about it, Jeff. That's why I included it in *Montage*. Eisley has a way of making you see what's there, doesn't he?" I never asked him to evaluate this article. I think this a natural way to develop critical acumen, not with a set of received rules, but simply paying attention to how the piece affects the perceiver.

- "Something hit me." I love these revealing phrases. "Hold it!" Reading these reflections is exciting. Notice how he goes over his own work and even challenges himself. No ego interference here. Every defeat of the artificial is a victory for the self.

I just got out of class and something hit me that I don't like to see but I think is there. I was thinking about the reflections and how sometimes they were a drag and I felt committed to write them. I was thinking about the interrobang [‽] and how some people think in periods. I was thinking that when I don't have the time or I think it's a drag, I am probably thinking in periods.

Hold it! I just re-read what I've written and would like to take issue with that because I work some things out in my head and don't need to write them down. (I've not written for ten minutes and tried to condense what I've been trying to say. Here it is:) It's good to be forced to write a reflection.

Response: "If someone forces me to do something, I can make something good out of it—as you certainly did. So whatever happens to me, "good" or "bad" is what I do to the raw material, not what it does to me. Right? Anyway, I like your thinking-in-periods metaphor. That's a neat way to view it." I might or might not say all this, or I might say something else. It depends on what's on my own mind right then, too.

- I like the setting! An analysis of what a book does and what a reader does. I like the tone, too. *Montage: Investigations in Language* is a book Bill Sparke and I did that came out in 1970.

Montage, barrage, garage, collage, and I really super like it, too. I was sitting in my VW reading it, and the sun came out and shone gold on the pages. It's something from almost everywhere. The questions are there to make you give some and not just take some from the book. It takes a bit of getting used to. Only trouble is that you can't browse properly.

Response: "Gold on the pages! Umm! Glad you like the book. We deliberately made it impossible to skim! We didn't want anyone to read it passively." Conventional assignments don't leave room for a paragraph like this, but I think this is the kind of detail most teachers would love to see.

- Ha!

Today we discused diferent ways to use our books. (A friend of mine just came over, and he said *discussed* and *different* were misspelled, so I corrected them for him.

Response: "Your friend probably thinks we're pretty sloppy. I hate it when I show people what I've written and they start out noticing typos or whatnot. First things first! You were very polite." The English profession needs to get its priorities straight. Editing ought to be a separate elective course.

- Unclichéing an old cliché while exploring one's own world.

"Nothing new under the sun" is like saying you never learn anything new, but what you think you are learning is actually awakening something you already knew. I think Socrates said something like that. It agrees with me. Why? It's like saying if you search hard enough, you can awaken knowledge and intelligence and understanding that once seemed dead.

Response: "Yep! Ya gotta look. Then, there's nothing *old* under the sun. We keep freshening things up. It's our job. Right? Gardeners!" I've seen assessment tests in which students are asked to write about an old saying like this one. I'll bet the responses are almost never as much fun. That's because of the way the whole thing is set up in the first place. We get what we solicit. It's our own fault. It isn't so much *what* we ask students to do as *how* we ask them to interact with the investigation.

- Metaphor.

Montage could be used as a very effective door-stop, to keep the entrances and exits of the mind open and unobstructed. These passageways have always existed; it's just that some are never used and have slammed shut. *Montage* should serve to reopen these doors and keep them that way, to enable easy access to the wonders outside and inside myself. If *Montage* can accomplish that feat, then I won't feel so terrible about the eight bucks.

Response: "Gosh, I wish we had used this metaphor in our ads for the book! Now you tell me! Anyway, that's exactly what we had in mind. I think everything we do in college is about the wonders outside and inside ourselves. I hope you always think of that." Isn't this kind of insight into one's own thinking processes what we all want for our students? When I see someone making such a discovery, it makes my day.

- What do you do when this appears in the middle of a reflection? Try it out?

I quite outdid myself this evening. I have prepared one of what has to be the finest pitchers of Kool-Aid ever. [We had read a short story by Richard Brautigan, "The Kool-Aid Wino."] Basically, it is:

1 cup of wine (cheap white)
3/4 cup of sugar
1 1/2 quarts of water
1 pkg grape Kool-Aid
   stirred vigorously
Slightly less than one tray of ice
   again stirred vigorously
1/3 fresh lemon
   squeezed into the liquid (dropping
   in lemon also)
Stirred gently a few times

Definitely a beverage suited only for people like James Bond, Spiro Agnew, my grandmother, Alice May Brock, and the like.

Response: "I know that's a recipe, but it seems more like a poem to me. Maybe you ought to send it to *Poetry* magazine. You'd probably have to explain to them that it's a poem, though. Oh, that's it: Put a title on it. Call it 'Poem.' That ought to do it." This response is simply getting more mileage out of what's there. But I wanted the writer to see what he had produced from a different perspective—not as a teacher, though. I do mean what I say.

- Intellectual autobiography. How reflections work.

Idea about ideas: My ideas are good and right as long as they are completely truthful. Nobody has bad ideas if the ideas are the truth. But our ideas become more sophisticated as we come into contact with more ideas to intermingle with the ideas we already have. The more aware we become, the better our ideas are. The more educated we become, the better our ideas become. I mean, the ideas become better because we ourselves figure them out and analyze them. The more I hash over an idea in my folder the better it is. My writing seems to get better, too. When this folder is done, I would like to think it's a book entitled *Gordon D. Brown*.

Response: "Gordon: You figured it all out yourself. That's exactly how it works. *Whatever* one does is autobiographical, isn't it? If I do a schlock job, my, my, ain't that a swell autobiography! I think yours is likely to be a best-seller." Notice that this writer is witnessing his own growth. He does not need the teacher to tell him. He can feel the growth. He gets intrinsic reward. That's the whole point of student-centered education.

That's why we have to keep our hands off and not intrude. Students have to have lots of experience getting ideas themselves and realizing it when they do.

Syntheses: Pulling the Course Together

"The mind is a connecting organ." Once I realized that, it took a load off my back. I wasn't there to pull it all together for the students. That was their job; it always is. An active mind cannot bear to see two things side by side and not form a bridge between them. That's the metaphoric process, after all. When the mind is puzzled, when it sees two things that won't fit, then it gets busy. My security blanket for our chaotic-seeming classes was that students went home every day and tried to make some sense of it all. I told them every bit of it had to be fitted together—by each one of them—into some sort of a picture, day by day and cumulatively. They were free to explore tangents and could approach the raw material from any viewpoint, but sooner or later they had to connect it all up. If individuals wanted to focus on one thing, that was fine, but they knew they were also generating the course as they went along, so some part of the mind would always be trying to make something out of all the bits and pieces. That is the way we all create our reality pictures, but we don't usually realize we're doing it. It is so natural that most people never notice that they are making it up as they go along. The reality picture they form seems to come from outside themselves and therefore seems immutable.

The difference in our classes was that students were made conscious of this synthesizing process and asked to do it on purpose—every time they wrote a reflection. They were continuously redrawing their received picture —the picture each one of us assimilates, out of awareness, from the cultural womb. If we get lucky we rewrite the dictionary; we redraw and recolor the picture. This synthesizing process went on all semester, so the students were quite used to thinking things over when it came time for a wrap-up. To reinforce this habit, as I have noted earlier, I asked that their final reflection be written in exactly the same way as their daily writing:

Synthesis (two-hour final reflection): *Syn-the-sis* means putting things together.

In a final two-hour reflection pull together and give meaning to the work of the whole course. Write your first draft like any other entry. Spend about two hours in the actual writing process. (This assignment replaces four daily entries.) [I could never understand piling on extra work at the end of every semester. I wanted the final weeks to be business as usual and no more stressful.] Once you have a draft, proofread and edit it. Type the final version, if possible. Ink is OK, but make your final draft look good.

As usual, this assignment is open enough for a variety of responses. I tried to accept just about everything that was turned in. Reading these final papers was like opening Christmas presents. Of course, I didn't grade these papers either. It would have ruined the experience and would have changed the atmosphere radically. No thanks. One thing ought to lead to another. A semester of reading reflections and then the final wrap-up made me intimately aware of how the course had gone for the writer. Each student's folder amounted to a portfolio. I didn't need tests or a grade book to tell how well the students were doing. The "portfolios" told me how I was doing, too. If I had wanted feedback on how well the course had gone, there was abundant evidence in the syntheses.

The Research Paper

When I started teaching, the English profession couldn't agree on "teaching" the research paper or some sort of long paper in freshman English. It still hasn't settled the matter. My own take has been expressed throughout this book: Don't *make up* assignments. Keats had it right. If the term paper doesn't come "as naturally as leaves to a tree, it had better not come at all." I have seen students do the equivalent of researching their interests and devote long hours to their quests, but mechanical response to an assignment results in page after page of bland assertions. Research has to be passionate. It would be more accurate to say not the mind but the heart is the connecting organ. Research skills ought to grow out of need and desire. So I quit demanding research papers early in my teaching, and I knocked off long papers that had no connection with our class. But the syntheses made sense. They were a natural progression of our work. The students took them to be something they did want to do. We all like to think things over, and doing it with a writing instrument at the nerve endings made sense to them. They weren't trying to prove anything to me. They were just sorting things out, as we all like to do periodically. The syntheses gave our course structure a lovely symmetry.

The Last Word on Teaching Writing

In a supportive environment, human beings enjoy putting words on paper. A typical folder of daily reflections contained 20,000 words or more, yet almost no one felt burdened. Most had discovered for themselves that the reflections had a practical use. Their writing wasn't busywork but a meaningful use of their minds. That was the key. Nonetheless, lots of well-meaning English teachers continued torturing students with stultifying assignments. In case anyone didn't know how to do that, I decided to publish a checklist. If the students weren't miserable enough, a teacher could look at my list for guidance. It was published in the *English Journal* in 1980.

> *How to Write Swell*
>
> I have been working on some guidelines for the teaching of writing. The idea started simmering when I heard a talk at a California English teachers' conference. Suzette Elgin was talking about "What English Teachers Need to Know About Linguistics."
>
> > There is ample evidence that improvement in reading will lead to improvement in writing automatically. You can interfere with that. You will never get brilliant writing if you always give stupid assignments under conditions of extraordinary stress and tension. But if you give students a chance, improvement in their reading will improve their writing.
>
> Surely every serious teacher of English knows that. But it was good to hear it said out loud. And without hedging. Bold and clear and with a lilt to it. And so my guidelines began to germinate. But I soon ran into the same old barrier: No two teaching methods can possibly be the same. Just as students must develop their own natures, so must teachers. That shut me up for a while, but browsing through Frank Smith's *Psycholinguistics and Reading*, I saw that he was faced with the same dilemma: You can't tell anyone what to do to teach people to read (no one knows anyway). But he did know some ways to make learning to read harder, and he listed twelve of them. Sure enough, there are at least ten such interferences I can list for writing, too. So here they are:
>
> *Ten Easy Ways to Make Learning to Write Difficult*
>
> 1. Require conscious knowledge of the rules of composition.
> 2. Make error-free compositions the prime objective.
> 3. Give regular grammar drills in class.

4. Correct all deviations from formal academic written English.
5. Work on problems as soon as they appear.
6. Remind students regularly of the severe consequences of weak writing skill.
7. Teach writing in steps: the sentence, the paragraph, the 500-word theme, the long paper. Do not advance until the level being practiced is mastered.
8. Challenge all faulty logic, speculations, vague generalizations, and groundless enthusiasm.
9. Never accept unrevised drafts.
10. Use essay examinations instead of objective tests. Do not accept word or phrase answers. Require answers to be put into well-worded sentences and paragraphs. Set time limits.

Mentors, Books, and Workshops

Minimalist teaching notwithstanding, nothing is wrong with artists looking over each other's shoulders. Every beautiful writer is a mentor, and every lousy one is, too. Truffaut learned what not to do as a director from seeing lots of B movies. So, as has been demonstrated in many studies, reading any old thing and lots of it takes us a long way. Part of the brain is formatting the process. We see sentences unfold across the page; we *see* words bunched together by capitals and commas, semicolons, and periods; and we learn—or we don't. It all depends on what we're up to. There is a deep core of beauty, a ruby mine, in each human being. It is the job of education to make room for it to surface, if it wants to and if it's ready. It can't be forced; it can only be accommodated. Simple as that may seem, it takes a lot of thoughtfulness to come to that realization. Once there, though, teachers can toss out encumbering bric-a-brac. That would be a kindness.

In the normal course of events, most students' writing skills will match their thought processes. Writing is simply something they do under appropriate circumstances. Sometimes talking is better. Sometimes writing is. For some of us, however, writing becomes more than a facility; it becomes an art. That is when all those books and workshops come into play, not as classroom prescriptions or drills but resources for tips or insight. Writing like someone else will never do, but one can see how to tighten a paragraph or compress a sentence, how to rearrange phrases, how to find the exact word—in short, how to take charge of the process.*

The first several years of teaching, I usually required resource books, at first because I thought they might help and later as security blankets. But when I saw we got on better without them, I left them on my shelf. They, too, were distractions. To be sure, people learning their craft will devour any nourishing morsel, but there must come a time when no one else can help. What goes on the page has never been done that way by anyone else. When a writer arrives at autonomy, there are no mentors, only fellow artists. I analyzed how I went about my own writing, how I ended up with a page of prose, and I read about the physical conditions in which professional writers went about their work—Kurt Vonnegut, Graham Greene, Ernest Hemingway, W. C. Williams, John Updike, John Cheever, scores of them, really. Common among all of them was one thing: *habit*, day-to-day ingrained habit. I wanted to give students the experience of such artists every time they wrote their reflections. If ever there came a time for deliberate artistry, they would have had experience of it already and would see how to go about it on purpose. So we did our investigations and explorations, thought things over, and sometimes jotted them down. That was all it took.

---

*I gotta million of 'em. All of these and dozens more contributed something or made me think about the approach to student writing described here. Ira Progoff, *At a Journal Workshop*; Ken Macrorie, *Searching Writing* and *Uptaught*; William Zinsser, *On Writing Well*; Strunk and White, *The Elements of Style*; Peter Elbow, *Writing Without Teachers*; Brenda Ueland, *If You Want to Write*; Natalie Goldberg, *Writing Down the Bones* and *Wild Mind*; James McCrimmon, *Writing with a Purpose*; Sheridan Baker, *The Practical Stylist*; Frank Smith, *Writing and the Writer*. Then, too, there are all sorts of handbooks. My own feeling is that for most writers handbooks are only occasionally useful. A good dictionary is good to have, and maybe the *MLA Handbook*, and *The New York Times Style Manual*. The copyeditor for *Teaching Human Beings* uses the University of Chicago Press *Manual of Style*.

14

Mutual Aid
The Gene Pool

We may be brothers after all.
—Chief Seattle

My students worked together. Almost every session they would be in groups of five or six some of the time. Even when they were working alone, there was usually a hum of comments back and forth, consultation, an ease and fluidity. They liked being there and working on things together and passing what they had done separately to each other. "See what I whipped up!" "Listen to this." I loved coming to those classes. There were often quotes and drawings on the board, things going on before I got there. They were warm and friendly places to work, and during our sessions my mind was about as good as it gets. Even when we failed it was better to be there than in most other places in our society. The students liked each other. In fact, the feeling of family was one of the things they valued most, year after year.

Most of their other classes were not like that. Often, my friendly students would go to their next class and not even know a student sitting next to them. More often than not, those students wouldn't even nod to each other. I don't have to describe these classes; we have all done time in them. But the difference is dramatic. It boils down to the old arguments about mutual aid and competition. Do we grow and change better in a competitive environment or in one that fosters networking and dipping into each other's minds and spirits? Will you be a better chemist by competing with other students for top grades or by working with all the other students and helping each other out?

A Mutual-Aid Investigation

Is there a way for individuals to actualize themselves without going for the jugular? If I am to excel, doesn't that mean stepping on others? How can I get to the Olympics? More to the point, can a classroom with no competition work? Is a mutual-aid classroom a better learning environment? A pattern-recognition investigation we often did bears incidentally on these questions. You could use any drawing, photo, or painting, but I liked Charles Demuth's *I Saw the Figure Five in Gold*. There was a full-page color reproduction in one of my textbooks, so I cut that into 1-inch squares. Each student got oil pastels and a square to enlarge onto an 8½-inch square of yellow paper. They didn't know what the original painting looked like, only the little square each had.

As the enlargements were completed, students began figuring out how the pieces fit together. Once it was assembled they turned the whole thing over and taped all the edges. Then they hung their 4-by-5-foot mural on a wall and made whatever observations occurred to them.

The composite is always astonishing. What a blaze of color, what a conjoining of spirit! I can think of no better demonstration of the power of mutual aid, the intensifying of individual effort into one grand surge of meaning. What a sum! I had thought up this exercise initially to explore how the two sides of the brain divide and combine tasks: the oh-so-careful left-brained precision and the oh-so-playful right-brained hunches it took to make everything fit. A number of related topics emerged, too, but I was fascinated by the dynamics of individual and group effort.

Students worked intently on their squares and then would gather around to help piece them together. I never assigned tasks; I wanted to see how they would manage to get it all together and up on a wall. Sure enough, various people took over various jobs. They were all curious to see the result. They always liked their mural, even when a few squares didn't come out accurately. The project warmed up the room. Everyone's contribution was important, but they saw they were making something *together*, too. Every classroom, not just the rare mutual-aid kinds, is a gestalt in which the group makes *something* together.

We discovered a number of implications. We could always get a pretty good picture of the picture—what it could be—even when several squares were crummy. Some students were color-blind. Some were not used to making pictures. Some didn't realize how important their drawing would be to the whole picture and didn't do their best work. You can see where this is leading: It's just like daily life. In life there is always the problem of time, too, so we set a time limit just so everyone would be on the same footing. Even so, some refused to be hurried, and we had to use their bare-bones product. How each one approached the job revealed what that person thought life was all about.

Nevertheless, a picture does emerge, and the mind stitches over the rough spots to produce an idea of what the picture could be. That's to say, the idea of reality in every mind is more complete than the physical representation. We teachers don't have to spell out everything. We don't have to fill in every detail. We don't have to jabber on. Leave blanks, leave holes. Don't give the punch line. Human beings are expert at working with incomplete, even faulty data. That is all that's available in life anyway. What is on the page is not where the action is; the mind is where beauty dwells.

Our classes soon realized each of us does contribute to a general idea of what is going on on this planet. We do that with our own unique skills and commitment. The more accurate our own square, the truer will be the composite mural. We are indebted to the truth each one of us can dredge up. We tinker with our own part, step back and look at the whole picture, go back and tinker some more. Dialogue and reflection help us fix up the squares that are off the mark. We *need* that piece. Sometimes a square will be missing for some reason, and although we can still stitch together the big picture, we certainly miss that piece. Clearly, the group as a whole and the unique individual are equally vital. I may not have an inkling that what I am doing has anything to do with a big picture or even that there may be one, but there is no doubt that I am contributing to it. My fine-tuned, precise, and careful work are valuable.

> *Task: to be where I am.*
> *Even when I'm in this solemn and absurd*
> *role: I am still the place*
> *where creation works on itself.*
> —Tomas Tranströmer*

This level of commitment is central to education.

---

*From "Guard Duty."

Competition

Our dialogue and reflections cast a new light on competition. Our project made it obvious we *have* to wish our associates all the best! Your sloppy work diminishes me. When you do well, I benefit. If I help you do your best, I help myself. That goes for my relationship with all other creatures and things, too: healthy self-interest. Competition can be a means of getting everyone closer to an accurate composite picture, closer to recognizing the pattern. It isn't just Joe Montana's teammates who benefit by how far he extended the art of quarterbacking. His skill at passing enriches all of us. In Special Olympics competition participants encourage, even assist, each other to a goal. Competition is giving ourselves *to* something, not fighting *against* something. Mutual-aid classrooms are productive for all concerned—and far more pleasurable. Your success, your unique ideas, enrich me.

A Leap of Faith

Even with incomplete, missing, or crummy data, we can get a good idea of how things are. That should be encouraging. To be sure, each life is infinitesimal in the scheme of things, but it is wrong to think that the pursuit of enlightenment, of clarity, is hopeless. Our mural suggests it is not hopeless. We do have to take flying leaps in the dark, but that gives us the excitement of entering the unknown, of living life instead of passing through it. If wonder isn't the daily fare in our schools, our graduates will be zombies. The staid certainty of conventional wisdom is a sleeping pill; the next moment is *not* predictable. That's why we get up in the morning. Open-ended class experiences nurture the romance of being alive.

To put all this in brain imagery, the thrust for meaning comes from within, from our guts, or we could say, the feeling centers of our mammalian brain. Our cold-blooded persistence against seemingly indefensible odds is reptilian, or we could call it our genetic programming, our DNA. When our picture is developed our neocortex is shot full of brilliant light, perhaps even enough to see in the dark.

> At the back of the brain there is a forgotten blaze, or a burst of astonishment at our own existence. The object of an artistic and spiritual life is to dig for this submerged sunrise of wonder.
> —G. K. Chesterton

The mind thrives on doubt, on taking chances, on leaping into space without a net. The enticement of science is the process itself, the thrill of discovery. Thinkers would rather join a circus than be part of a science that is merely a compendium of data. My classes discovered this distinction by comparing how they felt while working on a linguistics problem with their feelings trying to figure out who dates the minister in a complicated puzzle.* On the face of it the two "research" projects called for pretty much the same sort of skills. In the linguistics problem twenty phrases were given in English, German, Persian, and Hebrew. The analyst had to sort through the data and determine the equivalent in the other three languages for ten English words. This is a challenging task, and I did find it fascinating. But we all agreed that it didn't have the kick we got figuring out who dated the minister.

On closer examination the difference seemed to be this: You *could* figure out the correct vocabulary items through a systematic, conscious approach. You did have to fiddle around, and you couldn't be sloppy. But the work was straightforward, and once the procedure was figured out, success was inevitable. On the other hand the puzzle of who dated the minister had no more variables, but you had to mess around with the variables all at once. There was more guessing and trying out of hunches. No safety net. But coming into the solution at the instant of insight there was a surge of pleasure. So for educational purposes the experiment with the puzzle was more valuable in promoting the full use of mental powers than was the more respectable linguistics problem. The kick in the discovery is what enables a Leakey in Africa or a Salk in San Diego to work days and years on minutiae. If the results were certain and inevitable, the most important element of being alive would be missing.

---

*In the following situation figure out who takes ads for the *Berkeley Barb* and who dates the minister: There are five apartments, each with a different colored door and rented by women with different occupations, tastes in music, hobbies, and husbands or boyfriends with different work. (a) The seamstress lives behind the gold door. (b) The feminist lecturer dates the filmmaker. (c) The woman behind the magenta door paints for a hobby. (d) The model golfs. (e) As you face the doors the magenta door is immediately to the right of the pink door. (f) The woman who likes blues music is married to the teacher. (g) Jazz is preferred in the apartment with the brown door. (h) The woman in the middle apartment likes to water ski. (i) The nurse lives in the first apartment on the left. (j) The woman who likes honkytonk lives in the apartment next to the woman married to the grocer. (k) Jazz is played in the apartment next to the apartment of the woman who dates the lawyer. (l) The classical music buff likes to hike. (m) The belly dancer likes country western music. (n) The nurse lives next to the apartment with the green door.

Schools must provide such intellectual stimulation. Most teachers I know try to take the guesswork out of their "lessons." The job of the teacher is to disturb settled ideas, not to set minds at ease. Without the chance of failure or surprise, life is a museum. Viewed from this angle, failure is pretty exciting. Process is everything. What happens later has nothing whatsoever to do with it. They are two separate things. Certainty can never be a criterion for a mental adventure. Kids know this instinctively. My eight-year-old grandson Andy figured out how to get on the Web but couldn't care less about doing a routine computer task for his mother. The first question is always, What's in it for me? Mother Teresa and Gandhi both had to answer this question. There is always a point of view from which *any* task can satisfy enlightened self-interest. But if a good reason can't be found, stay in bed. (Andy could have reframed the job for his mother as a finger exercise, a chance to polish his skills.) So I often told my students I hoped they would never work a day in their lives, "work" being something you have to do rather than something you get to do. Only slaves do things against their natures.

15

Fear as a Motivator
And No Birds Sing

Fear means destruction.
It makes the hand tremble and the mind waver.
—Frank Crane

I still remember a story I read years ago that explains what I think happens to well-intentioned teachers over time. In William Carlos Williams's "The Use of Force," a doctor watches himself change from a kindly healer to a brutal bully as he tries to get a tongue depressor into a little girl's mouth. She may well have diphtheria, and he has to get a look at that throat; it's for her own good. At first he is in control, but she puts up a fight and it soon becomes force against force. The horror is that the doctor forgets all about his original purpose and his whole being centers on prying open that mouth. He does prevail. Sure enough, she has been hiding her diphtheria; now he can save her. But at what cost? The fierce little girl has learned what it is to be dominated by another human being, and he has discovered something in his nature he will see in the mirror every morning from then on.

In our school systems the common view is that students have to be made to learn, as if growth and change were not in learners' own best interests. But if you want a bunch of students "spragging" their feet, try making them learn. If you use a whip, you can get 'em to tote that bale, but they will be awfully slow and awfully dumb, and they will of course hate you and will frustrate your intentions every chance they get. Call it the need for autonomy; call it the need to be free.

When I first started teaching I kept discipline. I gave assignments, I checked to be sure they were done, I gave pop quizzes, I watched for cheaters, and I corrected mistakes. I spent lots of time thinking up test items. In fact, teacher training was all about such things, an entire apparatus, all planned to make kids learn; in other words, The Use of Force. And as in any other correctional institution, rules and regulations *are* the *raison d'être*. Like all the other guards I had lost track of why we were there in the first place. Instilling fear of authority was certainly not it, not for me. But that is what every teaching device was: control, dominance. A letter grade on a paper is a club. Taking roll is a club. Even a necktie can be a club. Get it?

Out of frustration, I began to notice how pernicious these devices were. And since I loved classes when we forgot who was in charge—so much more learning, such unleashed intelligence—I began wondering how much of this rigmarole could be dumped. For example, what would happen if I didn't put grades on students' papers? I had noticed the first thing they looked at—and often the *only* thing—was the grade. I had diligently ferreted out every error and corrected it, and no one gave a damn. I went through all the teacher games of having them rewrite their papers, etc., etc., and still only the grade mattered. So I stopped that. No grades on papers. Wow, no complaints! Eventually, I stopped grading their work altogether. That was just fine with the students. The papers immediately got more readable, more alive, more authentic. I actually enjoyed reading them. Next I realized students think of corrections as criticism, not of their work but of them. If you are in authority you may think your markings are a service, but that is not how the kindness is received. So I stopped that. Precious little learning ever occurred from all that labor anyway. It was painfully inefficient. Instead, I simply responded to the writing as a genuine communication. My, my, what a change. Within a week or so I was getting the kind of written reflections every English teacher dreams of. They were telling me what they really thought, defending, arguing, exploring, explaining. I didn't even have to praise them. They simply wanted a witness. I treated their writing as authentic messages and responded to them as thoughtfully as I could. When they got their papers back, I watched them reading every single comment I had made. (How gratifying! It reminds me of the late Herb Caen when he observed someone on the bus reading his column. If that person read only partway and turned the page, it ruined his day.) Grading had served no useful purpose; it only interfered.

I remember my friend Sister Vincent down in El Paso feeling depressed about her students' writing. "I make them correct their mistakes," she said. "I show them how to rewrite. But it's so hard. They don't seem to care. And they don't make much progress."

"Vincent," I said. "When you can see something isn't working, stop doing that. Stop correcting. Stop helping."

"But what would I do instead?"

"Sometimes you don't have to do anything. Just read their papers. What your students want is a genuine witness. It's what we all want, someone to pay attention to us, what we do, what we say. When they realize you really mean it, you will be overwhelmed."

Whatever students do or say, whatever the subject, their behavior can be treated like a mandala. Witnessing *without express tendency* turns teacher training upside down. You see that all sorts of paraphernalia can be tossed out. But giving up the club is scary, and most teachers won't risk it. It's sort of like taking off the training wheels. Nonetheless, if a teacher values free and independent students, if self-determination is important, then artificial authority has to be relinquished. Even if teachers don't value autonomy, they will find abundant response when students are not being pushed around. Force in any guise—any attempt to threaten, wheedle, trick, beg, or bribe—contaminates the process. Teachers have only to consider their own experience to realize this. We *know* when someone has designs on us.

My interaction with students came down to one principle: Respond to desirable behavior; ignore the rest. Whatever is going on is what is being learned. Bit by bit I got rid of authoritative clutter till I couldn't see much more I could drop. There is always a little more to do, though, and there is backsliding on bad days. I noticed even the best classes were still "classes." No matter how great a session was, as soon as I said, "See you tomorrow," students became more their everyday selves and would behave in a freer and easier manner. It was as if we had been on stage performing. Now the lights came up and we could be ourselves again. So there was still something in those classes that was artificial. What could that be? Partly, it could simply be that reframing the idea of a classroom takes time. I have that trouble myself. You need someone who has never been conditioned to the mechanisms to see them clearly. (I remember my grandson Andy, who had been home-schooled, stopping by a high school class with his mother one day and whispering to his mom, "Let's get out of here. I'm getting classtrophobia.") So in our crazy mutual-aid classes we were attempting something new in an outmoded package. The old messages still influenced our behavior. For one thing, I realized that I was still seen as the person in authority. And that meant the element of fear was still there somewhere. I may have locked the baseball bat in the closet, but I still had the key. So in the most subtle way, they were still wary. That means my painting is still incomplete. There are still more touches, and there probably always will be.

Meanwhile, there is that little chat I had with Tony Calabrese, my colleague in the psychology department. I was always pumping my psychology pals for ways to make my teaching more effective. I don't care what school of thought they are from; I use what works. That involves a strong mix of humanistic psychology, behavior modification, and neurolinguistic programming (reframing). These viewpoints provide me with awareness of how people are and of what we need from our environment in order to get on with our lives—if we so choose. I just don't want to interfere in that. Anyway, I do know that you can reinforce behavior by responding to it, but a hot foot or an electric shock can get things done, too. The side effects are ugly, though. Force and fear are tools I want nothing to do with; I don't like living in a fear-filled environment.

So, as I mentioned earlier in this book, one day I said to Tony, "I'd like to get to the point where I never use fear as a motivator." I had gotten pretty far, but I still felt there were traces of it. "Well," said Tony, "if you want to do that, you're going to have to give up intention." As soon as I heard it, I knew he was right. And I also knew I would probably never get there. When you think about it, *intention* is an attempt to influence an interchange of minds. You have something in mind that you want to have happen. You have an agenda. It is damned hard to go through a day without trying to push it around some. In other words, the use of force! My God! That's taking things pretty far, isn't it? Yes, about as far as you can get. But what would teaching be like if we *could* get there? I think it would be wonderful. You have to imagine how you would be with students. "Teacher" and "student" would be inappropriate terms, wouldn't they? It means teachers would have to change the way they behave, not just in the classroom but all the time.

So for me *intention* is the barrier I would have to break through in order to enter a pure teaching environment, an atmosphere untainted by fear or coercion, however subliminal. It's tricky because trying not to try won't cut it. For example, when you're doodling, are you *trying* to do something, or are you just doing it? Or do you start out "trying" and then fall into a creative trance in which you are simply there, and you and the work are simply one thing going on? I think it's the latter. In other words, a teacher could come into a class with the *intention* of setting the stage for unselfconscious participation to take over. The intention would drop off, and then everything would be OK. That would be pretty good. Fear would have a tough time messing that up. I know our society isn't geared to such thinking, but if we want education to get off the dime, we are going to have to pay attention to the damage fear does to the minds that share this space with us. And my experience is that it isn't really such a far-fetched idea. In practice, the less the use of fear as a motivator, the more responsive the class and the more productive. Even tyrants ought to think this over. Pushing people around all day sends dictators home with a sick headache. If they get a kick out of browbeating, that's one thing. But if they want students to learn chemistry, then they will have to let them take over the learning for themselves. There is no way you are going to pry open their heads and cram it in.

16

Judging People
Turning Poetry into Prose

---

*Nor is the people's judgment always true:
The most may err as grossly as the few.*

—John Dryden

Recently I found out there are eighty one-room schoolhouses in Montana. Isn't that great? I hadn't guessed there were any public schools left in the United States on the cutting edge of learning theory. One teacher teaching all subjects and doing the janitor work to boot, K through fourth grade, kids helping each other, all sorts of stuff going on in one place at the same time. I'm a little jealous. When asked what he liked best about the school in Nye, a fourth-grade boy thought a while, looked out across the valley, and said, "Well, I'm not fenced in."

When I started teaching at Diablo Valley College in 1963, I discovered there was no entrance test. You didn't even have to have a high school diploma. No GPAs, no SATs. In fact, if you were able to stagger in off the street, you could enroll. You had to be eighteen, as I recall, and "educable," whatever that meant. In my department anyone could get into our best freshman English courses simply by enrolling, no screening whatsoever. It was called an open-door policy, another one of those California aberrations that keeps educators back East from ever venturing farther afield than the western border of Massachusetts. You didn't even have to have much money. Tuition, even parking, was free.

The hiring committee asked me what I thought of all this. I said I didn't know; I hadn't thought about it, but it would be fun to find out. By this time I was six years into teaching, and I did know figuring out how to be good at it was a consuming passion. A roomful of students was all I needed. I didn't care who they were, where they came from, what their values were. They all presented the same challenge. But they certainly were a ragtag bunch, and just looking at them would drive elitists nuts.

Even though I hadn't thought about how students get into a college or into college classes—bonehead English, remedial reading, precollege math—I had come head-on with tracking. In Stagg High in Stockton, California, we had the college-prep group, the general group, the misfit group, some kind of "gifted" group, and the Z students. Oh yes, and the special-ed group. Talk about being fenced in! There are no green valleys and mountain streams, nor is there breathing room in these ranked and filed environs. What there are are cumulative files and large staffs of civil servants keeping ever-growing folders on each specimen passing through the system. God knows how much of the education buck is devoured by the registrar's office.

The way it works is you come to kindergarten feeling kinda down. Mom has a series of Dads sleeping over. Your hair's never combed. You probably didn't have breakfast. And so on. You're sitting around not feeling very good about yourself. You don't interact with other students. You're unresponsive in class. You don't even know how to be read to. You're withdrawn. By the first evaluation you are classed as a slow learner. You need special attention. So they put you in with a bunch of other slow learners. Then your special-ed teacher takes over and works with you very slowly. Not much is expected of you, and lo and behold, not much is forthcoming. The cumulative folder grows with deadly predictability and by the time you get to Stagg High there is no question that you belong in the Z track. It is rare that anyone ever breaks loose from these institutional labels.

One student who did escape, Harry Stone, was in my nontracked freshman English class at DVC some years ago. One night I was reading his reflections about his junior high school experience. He had somehow screwed up on a placement test, and they decided he belonged in with the misfits. "They put me in with a bunch of assholes," he wrote. Thenceforward "They put me in with a bunch of assholes" became my aphorism for the whole sorry business of classifying human beings. Tracking, ranking, evaluating, testing, screening, placement, the entire mass of data in registrars' offices—it all comes down to the same thing: someone else deciding what anyone may or may not be. Someone else! Whenever I get in with a bunch of school people zealously figuring out some new way to sort out the human beings in our classes, I feel like Harry Stone. Where are you now, Harry? I do hope you're not in with a bunch of assholes.

At DVC the biggest space and largest staff were those of the registrar. Most Americans take it for granted that such meticulous recordkeeping on each student is reasonable. No one ever asks if we could get along without all this accounting. After all, who is served? Who wants these records? Who benefits? The learner? I don't think so. I remember a counselor telling of an Irish immigrant transferring to our school and our registrar sending to Ireland for his transcript. His school wrote back saying, "We regret we cannot send the records you requested. We are a very poor college, and we put all our money into education." When I taught a class at the University of Heidelberg a couple of years ago, I was delighted to learn that no records were kept on student performance. No artificial support system. Apparently, the university figured students had some good reason for enrolling and could determine for themselves their degree of involvement. It was their own business. How refreshing. So it is possible to knock off the surveillance. Teachers in this country probably spend more than half their time preparing and keeping records. What if that time were freed for learning their craft?

DVC did keep the typical records, but at least you could get *in*, and you could even take freshman English without a blood test. Conventional wisdom, of course, knew the college was doomed. Standards would go to hell; our kids would flunk out at Berkeley and San Francisco State. Good students all mixed up with the dregs. But throughout the years our students went on to the universities and maintained GPAs (for what they're worth) as good as or better than those of the four-year students or students from other colleges. We sent more students to these schools than any of the other ninety-some community colleges. So there. That should have settled it, but of course it didn't. It wasn't broke, but there was always a good-sized minority who wanted to fix it anyway. Don't bother me with the facts. It just ain't fittin'. In the mid-1980s, they mounted another attack. So I typed away on my Selectric and sent an article to our staff journal. Here is what I said.

> *Expert Judgment:*
> *(Who Died and Made Us Gods?)*
>
> Cut their heads off and they still won't die till after sunset. Back again, the urge to screen DVC students, to bunch them into kennels according to breed or whatnot. Placement tests! I'm amazed such a nutty idea can still find advocates, as if we've come no distance in all these years.
>
> The joke is it can't be done anyway. No two "abilities" or "intelligences" are the same. Isn't that obvious? We are all unique, each special. We all want to stay that way. We're designed through our DNA to grow more and more dissimilar as we actualize ourselves, like flowers or trees.

Teachers who think they are giving the same message to thirty-five listeners aren't paying attention. No matter what your basis for grouping, your problem remains the same: Thirty-five (seventy, a hundred) unique beings processing the group experience in as many different ways. There is no way out of it. Individualize your approach or fail. Thirty-five different results? That's no problem. That's the wonder and joy of it, that lush variety of response available in any group. It must be embraced and used.

An illusion that supports grouping is the idea that abilities are better or worse, that intelligence is higher or lower. People have different kinds of abilities—thank God. Intelligence is more like a slice of the pie than a location on the rungs of a ladder. When each mind represents a *viewpoint*, that invites sharing. The ladder idea sets minds against each other. Teachers who still think there really is such a thing as an intelligence quotient ought to stop whatever they're doing and read the literature. Surely everyone knows by now that those standardized tests are designed to *eliminate* deviant minds. Good grief! We're all uniquely wired. Isn't that splendid? Schools need to tap into that tremendous range of intellect and experience. If you can find two people who think alike, one is a clone.

There is no sound educational reason for segregating students on *any* pretext. I suppose all those strikingly different students in one classroom must seem terribly messy and inconvenient. "Gimme a bunch of properly prepared students and I'll show you some real teaching." S u r e. If such a group could be assembled, what would they need *us* for?

But suppose we really could find a way to separate students so that teaching would be more effective? Suppose students really did learn more and better in segregated classes? Suppose it were really logical to do that? I would say, "To hell with your logic; what have you done to the spirit of the student you branded stupid, ignorant, ill bred?" Those godlike decisions are fine—provided you don't know or don't like the victim. But suppose the victim is your kinda dumb but awfully compassionate older sister who works her ass off all day, raises her kids on a clerk's salary, and she comes out to DVC thinking that maybe there might be something here for her? Suppose it's your rebellious son who screwed off throughout the twelve years of program dullness of the American school system and he comes thinking maybe there could be *something* here to engage his mind? Or your brother's "retarded" or dyslexic or autistic daughter? Or your mother or your father? And, of course, sooner or later, yourself. Passing judgment has a way of coming home.

Astonishing, isn't it? Nothing fails like success. Our college has been getting along beautifully for a third of a century without screening its freshmen. They sign up for the damnedest courses, wash out, flunk out, withdraw, come back. Oh, it is indeed messy. And yet it works. We still look fine to transfer schools. Students do manage—without adequate guidance—to get what they need from us . . . sooner or later. Sure, we could do what we're doing better. But despite all the slippage, we've been a smashing success.

There must be something fishy about something so simple and reasonable. So what the hell, let's rip it all apart and get into the bureaucratic swing with all the other schools in the country. Let's hear it for SAT, CLEP, ACT, and the rest of the procrustean schemes now surfacing. How will the kids know how crappy they are if we don't rub their noses in it? They need our expertise. We're trained to show people what's wrong with them—and flunk them for it, too. We're doing it for their own good, and they should thank us.

From Ella Leffland's *Rumors of Peace:*

> But my homeroom teacher seemed nice, and I breathed more easily. Only for a moment—a dark fact was spreading through me: of my classmates here, each was a "poor worker" like myself, or worse, and the rest were from other sixth-grade classes, among them loud and messy Eudene who had a screw loose, and Dumb Donny Woodall. I had been demoted. These were the fools rounded up from each class and shut away together like cats with the mange. I took my seat with a hot, shaky feeling, knowing I must not look at my new clothes and remember how pleased Mama looked as I set off, or my throat would tighten and I would not be able to say, "Here."

Here's my point. Yes, let's put lots of our energy into helping students figure out which courses to take and when. But let's allow them the dignity of making their own choices. The right to ruin one's own life is sacred. Paradoxically, the exercise of choice is the one way to assure a society of actualized human beings. It would set my mind at ease if the staff and students of this college would adopt as their motto the sentiment at the end of Robert Frost's "Auspex":

> *Once in a California Sierra*
> *I was swooped down upon when I was small*
> *And measured, but not taken after all,*
> *By a great eagle bird in all its terror.*
>
> *Such auspices are very hard to read.*
> *My parents when I ran to them averred*
> *I was rejected by the royal bird*
> *As one who would not make a Ganymede.*

> *Not find a barkeep unto Jove in me?*
> *I have remained resentful to this day*
> *When any but myself presumed to say*
> *That there was anything I could not be.*

Postscript: The last time I looked the college had in place a nicely appointed testing center with a large, airy, newly carpeted classroom with forty-five new desks and a glass partition for monitoring (surveillance), a full-time faculty member on duty, and a staff of three or four record keepers. From time to time I would see a lone student in the big room hunched over a placement test, an achievement test, an aptitude test, an IQ test. Staff, facility, and materials cost the college at least $100,000 a year. The testing center has been there about nine or ten years now. So far, there is no change in our students' performance at transfer schools; there are no fewer dropouts, no measurable improvement in morale. Go figure.

Teaching Without Testing

Passing through American public schools I accepted without question the inevitability of testing. If it is taught it must be tested. It didn't cross my mind that test makers might not know what they were doing. But the day I constructed my first test, I knew for sure I didn't know what *I* was doing. And, yes, I had been through the methods classes. I had more preparation in psychometrics than most of my colleagues. I even had more math background than most people in the liberal arts. I knew a little about "standard deviation" (nice phrase, eh?). So here I was, applying my teacher training, thinking up brilliant questions to ask my students, phrasing them just right, thinking up three *wrong* answers for each right one. (They had to be close enough to "right" so as not to give away the wanted answer.) Then, I had to sort them out randomly and not make an obvious pattern of answers; I didn't want too many A, B, C, or D answers. Then I had to decide that my 50 or 100 items gave me enough of a spread that I could be certain the kids had indeed grasped what I wanted them to learn. (This was before computers, too.) Can you imagine the complications even this far into the process of making up a test? For example, what *did* I really want them to know or understand or use or be? How could I be sure these were valid aims for the kids? I hadn't consulted them, after all. If not the students then perhaps my colleagues would know. If not my colleagues at Stagg High, then maybe the National Council of Teachers of English? Maybe it was in a book somewhere? Not little old me surely! Gosh, I was fresh out of graduate school. Give me a break.

I knew standardized test items had to be examined for reliability, objectivity, and validity. The test had to do what it said it was doing. Could you count on it? There had to be some way to check. Even so, did it measure what it was supposed to? And were you careful to screen for bias? The test had to be fair to everyone. Ha! How could a high school English teacher in the middle of the San Joaquin Valley run the tests needed to make sure what I had dreamed up was OK? Good night! The Educational Testing Service spent years working on individual test items before it put together *one* test. And then, just the wording of a test item: How could you be sure you phrased it well? Could I affirm that every question was clear?* How do you find out about your test *before* you give it? If the question turns out to be ambiguous, do you have to strike it out or give credit for all sorts of responses? Or do you simply say what *you* meant by it is the way they should all take it? (I discovered over the years that any question is ambiguous. There is always more than one way to take *any* utterance.) And what about time limits? How do you decide how much time is reasonable? Should there even be time limits? And what about the setting; is there an educational reason for making it so scary and stressful? Ah, well, I was making up several quizzes a week and lots of tests each semester for each class. Think of the evenings and weekends put in on that.

Then comes the time spent preparing the class for the test and giving it. Then there is the scoring—now they have machines to do that—and then the recording of scores or grades. How did one decide the cut-off score between an A and a B? Did you use a bell-shaped curve and statistical formulas? Our classes were segregated, so how could that be appropriate? Shouldn't all the kids in the advance placement classes get As and all the slow kids get Ds? Then, too, what sense did it make to apply mathematical precision to a test riddled with flaws? Finally, conscientious teachers would feel obliged to spend another class period going over the test with the students once it was returned. A fine mess you've got us in, Ollie. What a bizarre activity. Here were vital, warm-blooded, thinking individuals, and here was the teacher spending scads of time working up a data profile. Keeping records was more important than working with human beings.

---

*Try it sometime: Write a test item, get ten people to answer it, then see why each chose the answer. See what each *thought* the question was asking. It is a humbling and revealing exercise in communication theory.

There is no way teacher-made tests can serve an educational end. They don't bear even the slightest scrutiny. They are such a mess we couldn't use them even if they were a good idea. To further complicate the picture I was only one of thirty-some English teachers, and we all had our own systems. All of them were arbitrary. There was no consistency. You could be a B student in Clark McKowen's class and a D student in Agnes Kaufmann's class down the hall. Over the years I heard of dozens of scoring and ranking systems. Some would end up with 1,000 or more points. Some would start with a score for the whole semester and then deduct from it as the course progressed. I thought that one was especially ingenious. Each day the student got in a worse jam. Agnes didn't really need test items. "I can tell a D student the minute I see him," she said.

The Myth of Objective Testing

Well, then, why not put it all in the hands of experts? Get a uniform testing system in place. How about a little accountability? How about standardized tests? It turns out they don't stand up under scrutiny any better than my teacher-made tests. They do give the illusion that someone is minding the store, but it just ain't so. First, the tests are created by private organizations or so-called nonprofit corporations whose staffs get hefty salaries, benefits, and perquisites. Second, *they police themselves*. Third, until the courts forced them to open some of their books, they operated in secrecy. There was no way to check the validity, objectivity, or reliability of the tests. You had to take their word for it. Or they would show you some fancy statistics their own people had made up along with little booklets explaining how their norms were established. Only recently have possible ethnic, social, and political bias in test items been challenged in the courts. Nor was there ever a review of assumptions about the testing processes. That is, what made anyone think short-answer tests or standardized essay tests served educational purposes in the first place? Where did that idea come from? Whose interests were being served?

What is the effect of a statewide or nationwide test on classroom practices? When I was a kid in western Pennsylvania, I remember in the eighth grade Miss Bergman taking a week to drill us on facts that were likely to be on state tests we were required to take. Teachers in New York geared their courses for the Regents' Tests. Nowadays, there is great enthusiasm for accountability exams, some way to promote uniform teaching throughout the country. And so it goes. You have to wonder how there could be so much consensus in favor of such a crazy idea. But everybody loves tests. We are a nation of test givers and test takers. Parents want them. Teachers, administrators, politicians, even the victims themselves—all love the beauty of a percentile, a letter grade, a finite number. It's a terrible disease.

Perhaps the whole mess can be traced to Alfred Binet, who figured out most kids at age ten, say, could do certain things pretty well. A typical child at age eight had a certain facility with numbers, words, space. So, if your child performs like a typical eight year old but is actually ten, then eight-tenths is 80 percent. The poor devil has an intelligence quotient of 80. Binet was benign enough. But forget him. When eugenicists like Lewis Terman decided to lump a whole human being into a finite number, wowzer! They started testing immigrants on Ellis Island, Army recruits, and, of course, American schoolchildren. A brave, new world was born with an ever-increasing appetite for statistics. Never mind that honest statisticians have urged extreme care in drawing conclusions from their data, schoolmen and -women were untroubled by their ignorance. Reading scores, math scores, and English scores were wonderful ammunition for getting school bonds passed. Of course, Scholastic Aptitude Tests, American College Entrance Tests, and Graduate Record Exams soon became the law of the land. No one ever asked if we should be doing this in the first place. Did we really need to? Could people learn calculus without being tested? Could you appreciate music, understand history, or read Shakespeare without being scored in some way or other?

Some people asked, of course; you can imagine what happened. Nothing. Banesh Hoffman's *The Tyranny of Testing* came out in 1962. Think of the title itself. If you ever took a test or invented one, surely those words would give you pause. They didn't. The book was ignored by teachers and vilified by test makers. I came to DVC in 1963 and in all the time since never heard any teacher other than Karl Staubach even mention it. On *my* trivia test that would be one of the items they would all miss. Hoffman was no wild-eyed radical. He was a mathematician who had worked with Veblen, Einstein, and Infeld. He was named Distinguished Teacher of 1963 by the Alumni Association of Queens College and received the 1973 Distinguished Writing Award. Jacques Barzun in his preface to Hoffman's book thought "it is the testers who are on the defensive . . . against the irresistible force of argument which shows that their questions are in practice as bad as in theory very dangerous." They *were* on the defensive, but they won.

There may someday be schools without tests, but don't hold your breath. There have been lots of books and articles since Hoffman's. I can't detect any impact whatsoever. For example, in 1977 *The Myth of Measurability*, edited by Paul Houts, brought together criticism by more than twenty-five writers.

The articles had been prepared not for a bunch of nut cases but for the National Association of School Principals and had made up two full 1975 issues of *Principal*. The general thrust of the articles is that short-answer tests are an abomination. That you can measure human beings is a MYTH, but who cares?

I discovered a lot of this literature after I had already realized there is something immoral in the whole business. Testing is a way of dominating others, a way to keep them in line, a way to dress subjective judgment in objective duds, a way of distancing teachers themselves from the deed. Because everyone likes it this way, no one has to answer for it. Not that people haven't tried. Ralph Nader took on ETS. Several test takers took them to court. Teeny tiny chinks have been made in the armor, but the basic assumption that it's a good thing to test people remains intact. There is plenty of information, though, for anyone who wants to look. For example, in his 1985 *None of the Above* David Owen takes on the whole concept of standardized testing and analyzes enough typically flawed SAT test items to satisfy any thoughtful reader that something is rotten in the state of New Jersey, where the ETS staff enjoys its luxurious nonprofit digs.

All sorts of evidence show that tests don't do what they are said to do. In fact, they do terrible things nobody talks about, like labeling people and ranking and sorting them, like playing hob with self-esteem. As Hoffmann observed, "Multiple-choice tests penalize the deep student, dampen creativity, foster intellectual dishonesty, and undermine the very foundations of education. Although test makers claim to be scientific, they drop their pose when cornered and resort instead to propaganda." But even if the tests were sensible, even if the questions were well made, there would still be the problem of what a student was thinking when that student put that mark beside an answer. To get any sense out of a score, William G. Perry points out in *Forms of Intellectual and Ethical Development in the College Years* (Holt, Rinehart and Winston, 1968) that "an item-by-item analysis for each student would have to be made. A simple raw score means nothing. Most tests prohibit thought *by setting precast alternatives and forbidding the respondent to say how he would form the question and qualify the answer*" [my italics]. In addition, human error, bias, and prejudice are involved in all test making and interpreting. Essay tests are subject to the same difficulties. There is no such thing as a scientific test.

Nonetheless, damning as the evidence is, the clickety-click-click of the testing machine goes merrily on. There is a marvelous certainty about this ritual, the assurance of unquestioned assumptions. It rids us of nagging doubt. I can't imagine school systems in which no guess-what-word-I'm-thinking-of games would be played. After all, if we didn't make up these tests, what on earth *would* we do? I like Hoffmann's little story he used to tell when people would ask him what we would do instead of testing:

> Suppose a man comes to a doctor and says, "I have these painful symptoms; my chest hurts . . ." and so on. And the doctor tries out everything, and he can't determine what the problem is. In the end the patient says, "Do you think I should perhaps give up taking strychnine after breakfast every day?" And the doctor says, "Well, for goodness' sake, yes, give it up." "Well," the patient asks, "then what will I take instead?"

When I gave up testing altogether, I had been teaching eight or nine years. I expected repercussions, but they never came. I might have been lucky. Maybe where I was teaching or the administration at the time or the times themselves made it possible. But from the mid-1960s to retirement, my classes were test-free, and I think to a great measure that is why they were, at least by my criteria, so successful.

Unobtrusive Measures

When you are working with whole human beings in real situations, abundant information is flowing back and forth. You see each person as a whole, not as a numerical abstraction. But if you did have to grade your fellow human beings, your holistic experience would provide a far more complete profile. You would know each other more intimately and intensely. Academic work would be in context. The grade you entered in your records would be much more accurate. As I became more and more disenchanted by the testing mystique, I began thinking of what to take instead of strychnine. Looking at the fine print I discovered that California did not require that I test people. What a surprise! I had to enter a final grade for each student and certify it with my signature. How it got there was between the student and me. I wonder how much of our daily routine goes on, not because we are obliged to go through these motions, but because we *think* we are.

Simplify, simplify. I discovered with all sorts of school busywork, not just with testing, the more I cast overboard, the more fruitful my work with students became. Almost from the beginning I wanted to get rid of anything in my teaching that was not essential. If it didn't contribute to our central purpose for being there together, then I would find a way to remove it. It wasn't just an urge for tidiness; it was clear to me that irrelevant claptrap muddled the process. Something as simple as taking roll, for example, sets a tone.

Needless instructions affect relationships with students and reveal what you think of them. If I had to get attendance data, as I did in certain courses, then I found ways to do it without interfering with our work. If your purpose is to cut out anything that doesn't look like a perfect educational environment, all sorts of ingenious options reveal themselves. Streamlining a course becomes a creative pleasure in itself.

When I gave tests I had noticed a certain wariness. Students didn't want me to know how they were doing. If they were unprepared or didn't understand, I was the last person they would tell. If they were shooting for an A, they would do anything to make me think they were terrific. Everyone was hiding out, and my job was to catch them up somehow. A sorry business, this hide and seek. Karl Staubach used to say, "If you want to know how a student is doing, ask, 'How are you doing?'" What a good idea. If students *want* to learn something or do something and want your advice or assistance, they will solicit it. Meanwhile, mind your own business. Healthy people will learn as much or as little as needed. Gradually, as I got better at teaching, I didn't need to ask. I already knew how things were going with a student, far more than I ever knew when I was in the test business. All that energy and time were spent directly in interaction with students and on getting better at teaching, not on abstract data. Over time, knowing how students were doing for grading purposes became less and less important. Although I cared deeply that the class was working optimally for each student—after all, that was the whole idea of my being there—providing information about that to other people seemed intrusive. I was interested in each student's self-actualization, not in slipping information to some employer or some other college. If they wanted to use screening devices, let them do it. I wasn't a placement service. I didn't have time for it, and neither I nor anyone else had valid instruments for such judgment anyway.

The Heisenberg Effect

But while I was working my way out of the judging syndrome, I became interested in the effect of the testing process itself on the educational environment. In physics Werner Heisenberg demonstrated the influence of an observer on what is being looked at. If you put too much force into your electron microscope, you actually affect the behavior of the electrons being observed. Too little, and you can't see anything. But it appears the Heisenberg effect applies in any area of scrutiny, not just physics. Or, you could say, all action, including teaching, is physical and in a real sense is subject to the same physical laws. We influence whatever we are part of. Was there, then, any unobtrusive way to see how the learning environment was working? It wasn't so much a question of how the students were doing as how *I* was doing. *That* was my business. Of course, we were all in this together, so how could I tell if what I thought ought to be happening was?

There were ways, and once the idea took hold, I began to watch for them. There are books on the subject, *Unobtrusive Researcher: Guide to Methods* by Allan Kellehear, for one. It's like this: You could plan where the walkways for our new campus should be, or you could wait a while and see where paths were formed. *Then*, put in your walkways. In other words, to find out what to do next, be guided by what's actually going on. Then take the next step. In San Diego, Leonard Newmark set up a linguistics program that took its pedagogy from what works. If something they were trying out was a bust, it was stopped immediately. In this way the program could stay abreast of the current mix of students and environment. Good stuff was kept as long as it remained useful.

In my own case I found that if I stopped taking grading so seriously, the students would. We could give our undivided attention to what we were doing—not to looking good. For example, I put no letter grades on *anything* students did, neither their work nor their behavior. Zilch. No grades. Any behavior that wasn't too disruptive of the matter at hand was absorbed into the mix. If someone did get out of line, usually it was another student who asked that person to cut it out. On rare occasions, the whole class might explore what to do about it. Students kept their stuff in folders, which I was allowed to review three times during the semester. I didn't grade those either. But if I had wanted to grade performance, those folders would have been an exceptionally informative portfolio. For the students, getting their things together three times a semester provided a chance to look over what all they had produced—out of their little old selves—and they were usually pleased to have someone else witness how far they had come.

I don't see why a portfolio wouldn't be sufficient in most courses, including the sciences. In fact, creative behavior (I would say *any* behavior) is known to flourish when nitpicky surveillance is minimized. That is, let students make all the mistakes they want. They will work out a suitable path for themselves. Constant correction makes us self-conscious and awkward. Students want to be successful in chemistry. They don't need to be graded minute by minute. Picture getting a score for each practice golf swing and then getting a grade at the end of each session. Wouldn't that be brilliant pedagogy? Where they are by the end of the semester or their golf game is what matters. (Of course, in a truly enlightened school, students could take as long as they liked, years if necessary. When you had mastered the subject, it would be so noted. Period. After all, what educational purpose is served by requiring mastery in a uniform time frame?) If not browbeaten by quizzes and tests, students will seek help when they need it. Wouldn't you? And would you really expose your shortcomings if you knew someone would pounce on them and make little notes in insidious record books?

During the semester we never talked about grades. We were absorbed in what was going on. We talked about that, about its implications and its connections with other things we had done or other events in the universe. We thought and wrote reflections, and someone would read and respond to our ideas in the same manner. Two or three times a semester, students would estimate how close they were coming to the course requirements. Not more than an hour and a half of students' time was spent on grades. Even in a judgmental institution, students flourished on the islands where intrusion was removed. Their enthusiasm and involvement were almost palpable. Over the years, thousands of satisfied customers passed through these classes and on to higher education or jobs—with no USDA stamp of approval or rejection. They did just fine. The abundant experiential evidence was positive. Most had indeed "got it"; their needs and mine were met. I wanted them to get the knack of something—like learning to drive—and they did. Usually not more than three or four out of a hundred didn't work out. I wanted them all to do well, so there was always more to learn about teaching.

17

Minimalist Teaching
Trying Without Trying

... there is only the traveling on paths that have a heart, on any path that may have a heart.... And there I travel—looking, looking, breathlessly.
—Don Juan*

On their way out the door at the end of our first session, students got my course requirements and a calendar of dates when things needed to be done so that we could have a good chat about them. These requirements fitted onto one page and were what I thought would provide a bountiful experience. But requirements could be modified in individual cases, if need be. I tried to provide circumstances that would allow anyone who felt like it to earn a top grade by putting in the time and without extraordinary effort: Do these things; get a C. Do those same things with obvious *enthusiasm* and *thoroughness*; get a B. Fulfill C and B requirements and *get results*—plenty of *growth* and *change*; get an A. One hour out of class for each hour in.

Since I wanted students thinking about our course work more or less constantly, I always chose to compress the work into a half-semester. Instead of three days a week, we met daily. That way we could keep the party going, so to speak. We were able to establish habits of behavior quickly so that attendance and outside work became routine and therefore effortless. It enabled

---
*From Carlos Castaneda, *The Teachings of Don Juan*.

them to think things through without interruption, intensively, a way of trying without trying. They were constantly working on getting their balance.

Here is the gist of the requirements handout:

Critical Thinking
Spring 199__

Office Hours: Daily, 1–2
Faculty Office 124, Ext. 436

This class compresses a semester's work into nine weeks, so everything is doubled up. You will need at least six hours a week to prepare for class. However, the work will be pleasant and stress-free. Evaluation will be painless and reasonable. Your own assessment of your work will be invited and seriously considered.

....

Minimum Requirements for a C

Attend regularly. Participate cheerfully and supportively. Work on the course at least an hour a day, five days a week.

1. **Attend regularly.** The success of the course depends on the full participation of all its members. Your cheerful support and attendance are essential.

    [I figured if that's what I wanted, then I might as well say so and reward it.]

2. **Prepare for class at least one hour for each hour in class, five days a week.**

    [They got weekends off, just like real people.]

Spend half an hour a day writing your reflections on assignments and class work.

[Same playing field for everyone.]

Spend the remainder of your study time on reading assignments and preparing for your group's presentations.

*[Groups of five or six read a supplemental book and presented its ideas to the class. The presentation was **not** to be boring.]*

Suggestions for writing daily reflections are attached.

[This was to be unedited reflective writing turned in daily and then kept in a folder.]

Synthesis:

A two-hour reflection written in the style of the daily reflections and then polished and edited. Due: _____ .
Suggestions attached.

> *[This took the place of regular reflections for a week so that no heroic efforts would be needed to produce it. I could never understand why students should be subjected to periodic crises simply because no one ever thought out a program from the learners' circumstances and perspective.]*

Text Response:

Please include your response to your reading in your daily reflections.

> *[I wanted all the work to be integrated, an ongoing process, everything connected to everything else and fitted together into a pattern by each student.]*

Texts:
> *[The three required texts were listed. Students were also to work with a group on a book from an attached list of six choices.]*

....

Minimum Requirements for a B

Fulfill the above requirements and demonstrate *enthusiasm* and *thoroughness* in all work in class and in daily reflections.

> *[I let them decide how to do this.]*

....

Minimum Requirements for an A

Fulfill the above requirements and get results. There must be plenty of *growth* and *change*.

> *[That's what I wanted, so that's what I asked for.]*

Your writings and class work are the main source of information for your grade. Save your reflections in a folder.

I was trying for minimum direction and structure. As much as possible within the institutional constraints, I wanted students to create their own "courses." I didn't want a bunch of Clark McKowen clones at the end of the semester. While he was at Penn State my friend Jim Doerter of Southern Oregon State College had done a study in which he discovered "painting students are influenced into a stylistic painting expression *similar to that of their instructors*" [my italics]. Students were rewarded for becoming more like their teachers. I didn't want that. I wanted *their own stuff*, not mine. It wasn't till I started teaching that I discovered how much autonomy we wrest from our students by our helpfulness. To complete my California credential requirement I enrolled in a guidance course at the University of the Pacific in Stockton and discovered how liberating minimal instruction can be. It was a Saturday morning class for teachers, and we were told the name of the course and reminded that the UOP library was available to us. Saturday mornings we would discuss our findings. That was pretty much it. It was the most powerful learning experience till then I ever had in a school setting. All my efforts were productive and completely determined by me! It was easy and rewarding. All schooling should feel like that. I took many other courses after that, and thenceforth I always took them in that spirit—regardless of the teachers' agendas. They had their purposes; I had mine. Gradually, I structured my own classes so that students would take charge of their own learning. I became a minimalist. The less I did for them, the more they filled the breach and the more potential for new insights. Of course, the better the classes got, the crummier I looked to the establishment. After all, where were the lesson plans, the attendance sheets, the detailed scores and grades, the corrected papers? But, my goodness, what a pleasure it was to be part of those classes! I "taught" these classes in the same spirit in which the students took them. As a consequence I was able throughout the years to refine my understanding of my field as an ongoing learning experience.

I wanted students to be cheerful and supportive. Those are traits of healthy human beings, so I made them part of the course requirements—and said so. No one seems to have been harmed by developing those behavioral changes. We had cheerful classes and we got results. Every class period a few valuable ideas were illuminated. Most of the time we all went home feeling we had put in a good day's work. The exceptions bugged me. My wife and daughters have reminded me they always hoped Friday classes were positive; otherwise, I would be preoccupied all weekend wondering how to set things right. I wanted my outside requirements to be reasonable and sensible, too, something I would be pleased to do myself. I hoped the texts and supplemental books would be fascinating and highly readable—Nobel-Prize-winning physicist Richard Feynman's autobiography *"Surely You're Joking, Mr. Feynman!"* and Benjamin Hoff's *The Tao of Pooh*, for example. (I remember a new philosophy teacher at our college being aghast that some teacher in the English Department was using a children's book to "teach" Taoism.)

I also tried to make the workload realistic. If I could get six *efficient* hours a week, that was a better deal than twelve of make-work. Puritans could never cotton to that idea. There is something decadent about it. But in academia there was no consistency anyway in the amount of work required from teacher to teacher, course to course. Some teachers thought requiring lots of outside work showed how tough they were or how important *their* course was. What sense did that make? Chemistry shouldn't require any more of a student's time than any other course. If it really did take more time for mastery, then more units of credit should be given. But no matter, students typically do one hour out for one hour in, regardless of what's required. It's a matter of survival. What's wrong with a forty-hour work week anyway? For that matter, why should students be put through hell at the end of every semester, completing projects, cramming for tests, and whatnot? If work is done steadily, why should the last day be more stressful than any other? Perhaps a culmination or a peak experience, but not torture.

With the calendar in place and the rules of the game established, class sessions became variations on a theme. No one, including the teacher, was ever quite sure what was going to happen. We might be scheduled to talk about *The Tao of Pooh*, for example, but how we would go about it was never predictable. In the midst of things, if we saw a productive tangent open up, off we went in that direction, but we never got lost. We were always working toward clarification, specific and general, and the daily reflections connected everything together and kept us on track. Everyone knew that toward the end a general synthesis would be sought.

I have rarely seen something like this tried in other fields, or in my own discipline for that matter, but there is nothing in electronics or economics or geology that would prevent it. It's a matter of putting students in charge of their own learning. That shouldn't be such a shocking idea; there are successful precedents. The one-room schoolhouse is an example. There are bits and pieces of the principle here and there—but seldom all at once in one place.

The trick is to put students into real situations. The ethnic mix in California colleges in the 1990s, for example, is an opportunity for comparative linguistics and a chance for native speakers to get a good look at their own language. And there is always a way for students of history, economics, math, myth, or music to do some firsthand work. I see nothing to prevent a student-centered accounting course being set up as an investigative and exploratory process, with lots of noisy mutual aid and each student being charged with piecing things together sooner or later into a meaningful whole. A daily reflective log would keep them focused. Some brave math teacher ought to try it sometime. The course could be called "Thinking About Trig."

As Twain noted, someone who takes a cat by the tail has a lot more information than someone who doesn't. That's just another way of putting John Dewey's principles of education. Wherever possible, concrete experience comes first, then synthesis, then theory. It's always better to use a real cat than a stuffed toy. It's all about what Whitehead called that second-handedness of the learned world. Anyone who has fallen asleep going through the tutorial for a computer application will know what I mean.

Assigning Grades

Much as I abhorred the idea of judging student performance, I was required by our college and by the Ed Code to get a letter grade recorded. So I had to find the least offensive way I could to do that. Most teachers don't mind evaluating and see no conflict between teaching and judging. After all, it's not the student being judged, some would say, it's just their work. Try convincing a student of that. Even if it were virtuous to judge performance (to what ends it is beyond reason to speculate), it didn't bother most teachers that there was no way to do a reliable, valid assessment anyway. There is no such thing as an objective grade. You have to put your head in the sand and discount nine-tenths of the variables to arrive at a number. The way you get the number is pathetically arbitrary anyway. I remember saying at a faculty meeting that a D or an F was punishment, pure and simple, and served no educational purpose. That went over big. But those grades do follow students wherever they go. Get some screening committee looking at a transcript riddled with D's, F's, and withdrawals, and it's big trouble—sort of like three strikes and forget you. The whole business does not advance growth and development one jot. It only interferes.

So how to minimize the negative influence of grading? What finally evolved for me was a variation of Karl Staubach's "How are you doing?" The students knew as well as I did what the deal was in my classes. I was sure they were better situated than I was to determine how close they were to meeting the course requirements. So I decided to come right out and ask—and see what happened. At first, three times a semester, but later only twice, I gave each student a grading sheet to complete.

The top half contained this instruction:

> Based on the course requirements, please enter the grade you have earned thus far: _____
>
> If you feel an explanation is necessary or if you want to cite extenuating circumstances, please use the space below.

The bottom half contained this instruction:

> In the space below, please evaluate any aspect of the course you wish, other than your own performance. Anything you like or don't like about the course that would help me make it work better will be welcomed.

That became my grading process. I asked them to turn in their folders along with the grading sheet in case I needed to refresh my memory of their work. Usually, it wasn't necessary. Most of the time the student's impression was the same as mine, and I would write, "I agree." If it seemed way out of line, I would write something like, "Maybe we ought to talk about this. I don't see how you came up with that grade." I meant what I said, and the students turned out to be reasonable. We had excised most of the stress in the grading process, and they really did have a lot to say about what got onto their transcripts. I felt the grades were far more accurate than those I had assigned in earlier days using traditional methods.

I never got entirely free of grading, but I was reasonably comfortable with paying attention to it only twice a semester and not taking that too seriously. Judging people had been one of my biggest pains in the neck. But for many years that was pretty much out the window. I had become a minimalist teacher *and* a minimalist grader. But there is more to be done. In my next incarnation I will work on it.

18

Getting Help
Relinquishing Control

There is no use for artificial discipline,
For, move as I will, I manifest the ancient Tao.
—Hsiang-yen

When I got my teaching schedule my first semester at Diablo Valley College, I discovered I was to be in class twelve hours a week. Twelve hours a week! At Stagg High I was in class twenty-five hours a week with another ten hours of study hall and lots of extra duties on top of that. Faculty meetings and the PTA were out of our hide along with all our preparation, all our own typing and duplicating, getting materials ready, chaperoning, reading papers, making up tests, record keeping, no real office, and so on. So when I looked at my schedule at DVC, I said, "Um, what am I supposed to do the rest of the time?" "You'll think of something," the dean of instruction said. I did. I was soon as busy as ever but with much more flexibility and freedom. I was still putting in sixty- and seventy-hour weeks, but on things I wanted to do.

The college did try to ease our work. Our department had a secretary who would type things, and the college production lab would duplicate class sets of handouts—if we provided the work far enough in advance. But in my classes, tomorrow's work depended on what happened in class today, so usually I couldn't take advantage of the services. That was all right with me. I was used to it anyway. Besides, I hated to torture a secretary with my lousy handwriting. So I typed my own stuff and ran off class sets in the back room of the English office, usually just in time for class. I was happy with the arrangement.

The thing about teaching, though, isn't so much having to do your own paperwork as being so isolated from dialogue about your craft. Most teachers have no one to consult on a regular basis. Administrators, more often than not, are seen as people to watch out for (just like teachers with their grade books). There is usually no one it is safe to come clean with about what's not going right, stupid mistakes, ways to set things straight. So teachers are reduced to figuring out the process all by themselves. Sure, they can chat in the teachers' lounge, but usually the talk is about how to maintain discipline or how to scare the kids into dropping your class or how to do pop quizzes, the sorts of things I wouldn't want to talk about or could never endorse in the first place. (The lounge was a good place to learn about tax shelters, though.) But in the early days we did have an unusual number of teachers actually interested in the process of teaching. There were all sorts of experiments going on, and I was right in the middle.

What's the optimum class size, for example? Five or six of us tried gathering our classes into one large room for some sort of demonstration: a film, a presentation, a multimedia experiment (no doubt on some McLuhan theory). We all worked together for that session and then would meet with our own groups later in the week. Or we would try a number of discussion groups scattered around throughout the week. There were all sorts of variations. We talked with each other about methods and materials, even about classroom furniture. I'm sure the teachers involved made lots of discoveries during those years. We were frequently in each other's classes, so we actually did see how classes on the same subject were conducted. That was tremendously helpful. For a number of years we did talk rather openly about teaching, and the administration was indulgent of our experiments.

Even so, most of the time I was the only teacher who ever witnessed my classes in action. I did get lots of student response, and that helped. But how would these sessions look from a teacher's point of view? The students were happy with whatever I did. They assumed every motion was calculated and that I knew what I was doing. In fact, most of the time I was never quite sure what might happen or that the approach couldn't be improved. I was always looking for ways to make things more streamlined or more effective, the deft touch, the elegant compression of detail. In my ideal college the whole staff would be working out such things all the time. Meanwhile, it would be lovely to have someone to talk with on a day-to-day basis about how things were going. As usual, one of the students provided the solution.

Carol Stout, a mother with three kids, had come back to school after being out twelve years or so. She had liked the atmosphere of my classes and had taken all of them. She planned to teach English, so she was especially interested in the nuts and bolts. What about being my teaching assistant? she asked. I had never thought about having an assistant. I had never delegated any of my teaching to others. What would I do with her? This could be a royal pain in the neck. But what the hell, the main thing Carol wanted was to absorb the teaching method, so I decided to give it a try and let her role evolve. I have found that is a pretty good approach, not only to teaching but to life in general. If you come to a new situation with too much structure, it keeps you from seeing alternatives. So I like to start with just a little bit of structure and then see what works as I go along. A lot of teachers think that's too risky, but that's probably because they've never tried it.

Like most people who are used to being in charge, I found it hard to give Carol anything to do. I didn't see much that I could delegate, but her role did work itself out rather quickly. I introduced her as the teaching assistant (TA) and told the class she was available to help any of them who might have questions or concerns. Meanwhile, she attended every class and kept reflections, just like all the others, except that her reflections were usually about the teaching method, its purposes and effect. Several times a week we chatted about how things were going, why things were done and the result, my own behavior, my interaction with students—all the things I would have enjoyed discussing with a fellow teacher. It wasn't long till we had defined this new dimension in my classes: The Teaching Assistant.

More accurately, the students defined the key elements. I still find it amazing how easily human beings, if not interfered with, absorb new events in their lives. Right off, they treated Carol as confidante. They told her things and asked her questions they never brought so openly to me. "What's Mr. McKowen like?" "Does he really mean what it says in the syllabus?" "Is this what he wants?" And they told her about their jobs, their fears, their love lives, their troubles in school, whatever is involved in turning a student into a human being. In their minds a TA wasn't a student exactly, nor was she a teacher. She was somewhere in between. Maybe *class counselor* is a more apt phrase.

So right away I got a bonus I hadn't anticipated. There is a gap in any class, however student-centered and human one might try to make it, and that gap was bridged by the TA, whom students defined as their friend. That pleased me no end. Not only was this new element a smash hit with the students, I was getting more accurate feedback about the effect of my actions, information I could put to use immediately. I knew right away if an assignment was too confusing or time-consuming, whether due dates were realistic, if a structure I had devised was workable. I got a clearer picture of what it was like to be a human being taking my classes. The next thing I knew, students were talking with Carol before and after class, having coffee with her, writing things for her eyes only. Because this particular TA was an older woman with teenagers of her own, young women, often even some of the men, consulted her about their personal lives, not so much for advice as for an older person who would listen nonjudgmentally.

Meanwhile, Carol kept an eye peeled for ways to smooth out the business of the class so that we could get on with things more quickly. I was getting help I hadn't realized I needed. And now I could get a critique about my teaching almost continuously. We all benefited. Carol was learning about teaching, too, and was getting tuned in to the way students think. So it was good for her, for the students, and for me. Thenceforth, there was always a TA in my classes.

The One-Room-Schoolhouse Concept

Of course, having a TA in my class was simply the idea of students helping each other. The classes were set up that way, anyway, so this addition fitted in nicely with the overall pattern. I already knew that students learn from each other easier than they do from someone labeled "teacher." For example, Les Hatch, a counselor at our college, and Karl Staubach had devised an experiment in which marginal college students were matched in a tutorial program with marginal high school students at College Park across the street from us. That is, a DVC student with bad grades in math, say, was asked to tutor a high school or junior high kid who also was doing poorly in math.

They would meet once or twice a week at DVC and work on the younger kid's math. Guess what? Both started doing better in school. Les and Karl collected data that showed our tutors were more likely to stay in college and got better grades than did students in a control group. The younger kids got better grades, too, and had more positive attitudes toward school.

But the anecdotal evidence was even more encouraging: The older students, sometimes for the first time, felt needed. Someone looked up to them and sought their guidance, not just about a school subject but about their lives in general. They had a new sense of worth; they were responsible for another person. The younger kids adored having a college student take an interest in them, and they felt special going over to the college where the big kids hung out. Of course, peer counseling was not a new idea, but pairing *rejects* was, and it was touching and beautiful to see.

Of necessity the one-room schoolhouse had to let kids learn from each other, but the benefits were that they had more self-reliance and self-worth than we see in most modern schools. Those eighty one-room schools in Montana have much to teach us. And it doesn't have to be the best students who do the teaching. I remember among my fellow practice teachers at the lab school in Indiana, Pennsylvania, Mary Fennel, who had had to struggle through our college math classes, turned out to be one of the better teachers. She knew what it was not to understand and was more thoughtful and compassionate in finding ways to make it all make sense. On the face of it you wouldn't think it would work, but in practice it almost always does. Teachers to whom a subject comes easily tend to be impatient with "dumb" students and wish for advanced placement classes. "I prefer to work with the gifted students."

Teacher's Pets

I don't hear it so much anymore, but it used to be conventional wisdom that it is not professional to get emotionally involved. I don't know who thought that up, but if an artist *isn't* emotionally involved, what's the point? The whole idea of work is involvement of the highest order. If students are merely placeholders, teaching is a drab enterprise. Almost from the first moment as a teacher, I could see that students didn't want to be treated objectively. One way or another, they insisted on being recognized as whole human beings, special. They all wanted to be teacher's pets. Amazing as it may seem, teachers want to be human, too, just as much as the students do. The trouble is things get messy with all those unique beings manifesting. A roomful of nonentities is manageable, but a roomful of complete human beings is crowded. However, it can't be helped. I had to work with that-which-is, not some imagined ideal world. Real human beings are a lot more fun than robots anyway, so I fiddled with ways to accommodate everyone, warts and all—with ways to see how special each one was. This decision certainly enriched my world, but it is the foundation of my teaching philosophy as well. That is, at the center of all teaching is one unique student who must be engaged. If there are seventy people in a class, then there are seventy different lessons—and seventy teacher's pets.

The other day I ran across some comments from Timo Wagner, a student in an intensive English-fluency course I taught at the University of Heidelberg in 1993. Timo was a music major who planned to be a high school teacher. In his last entry he decided to comment on the teaching method I had used with the class. I couldn't believe how much he had picked up of what I was trying to do and how succinctly he could express it. It is all about making each student special. Here is what he said.

Tuesday

Instead of reflecting on the subjects we talked about during the lessons, I would like to think about your teaching style. I could see the following principles and ideas:

- The most important thing in your lessons are the students. You give the lessons for them and not for you.
- Every student has his own way to learn, has a different level, different knowledge up to now. So all you can do is to arrange situations in which every student can profit the most and follow his own "learning track."
- You have things you want to talk about, sometimes also things "to get" and to understand, but not every single student has to get the same, "owning" the same knowledge at the end of the lesson, because every single person gets a lot of different things in every lesson anyway.
- You try to find topics that could interest people really, something that has to do with the real life of everybody, topics in connection to feelings, experience, or the general view of the world.
- You change often the topics and the methods, listening, reading, or feeling things or your body change, as well as materials (poems, stories, games, sentences . . .).
- You try to be yourself during the lesson (and not just then!). You show feelings as every "normal" person, say what you like, don't like, or don't care for.
- It also seems that you enjoy the lessons yourself (and you want to be a "professional teacher"), that you profit and learn from your lessons yourself.

Will Rogers never met a man he didn't like; I never met a student I didn't like, not once I got past the persona to the real person. There, I always found something remarkable. To be sure, there were a few students I didn't like and some who simply wanted to hide out. Even so, if I had broken through the barriers, I feel certain those spirits would have been as fine as any others. On reflection, how is it possible to teach and not be convinced that under the surface behavior is something positive, tender, and lovable? It would mean pettiness, cruelty—all the seven deadly sins—are genetic and immutable. But teaching requires the idea that growth and change are possible, that we can alter our behavior. That behavior may be disagreeable, but the soul behind it is not. I do here solemnly swear the fundamental force of life is positive and benign. Of course, lots of philosophies disagree, but it's practical to act as if everyone is potentially wonderful. It's simple behavior modification. A pragmatist could probably fake it, but it works better if you really mean it.

Selecting Teaching Assistants

After Carol Stout worked with me, students began asking how I selected my teaching assistants. Most teachers I knew who did have TAs chose the cream of the crop. But all my students were the cream of the crop—by definition and by experience. So if a student hinted around, I would ask, "Would you like to be a teaching assistant?" "Uh, well, yes, if you think I could do it." "Sure. Let's work out the details." *Any* student could be a TA. I decided almost immediately to let students self-select into the role. Surprising as it may seem, it worked out well. The TAs were getting the special attention they wanted from me and a look behind the scenes. They didn't have to have special talents. Just by taking on the title they reframed themselves, and their behavior changed. But the behavior was consistent with who they were. Sometimes I had four or five TAs in one class, all quite different, maybe a goof-off or a clown, a jock, a physics major, a musician, a hooligan, funny-looking people, religious people, atheists. Predictably, they brought different traits to the role and took different things from the experience. The job of each TA was tailored to fit. Without any suggestion from me, affinities emerged. There are all sorts of learning styles, and no teacher is an ideal match for every student. In fact most of the people who choose to teach have personality traits that match up with only about one-fourth of the students. About 75 percent of our students have to get on as best they can in an uncomfortable learning environment. But having four or five different kinds of people working with me greatly extended the likelihood of a connection. In a quite natural way students sorted themselves out, and soon each TA had a self-identified group.

Foreign Students as Teaching Assistants

I remember the first time I had a foreign student as a TA. I was getting more and more students from other countries; many barely spoke English. Mark Liu's English wasn't all that hot, either, but he wondered if he could be a TA.

Um . . . sure. The result was delightful. Not only the Asians but all the foreign students perked up. Their English difficulties were no longer a stigma. If Mark could be a TA, well, that put a different light on the acquisition of English. For me, a foreign TA wasn't that big a leap. Native speakers' command of the niceties of English varied all over the board. So assimilating nonnative speakers was a simple extension of the principle of individualized learning. I also knew that in about two years from setting foot in the United States most would be fluent enough to get along well in our culture. Some would always have heavy accents or never master the inflections; some would be speaking with barely an accent. Fortunately, we have become enough of a global village for most of us to realize that these aberrations don't really matter. In fact, the intercultural exchange is a banquet.

Now my chalkboard began to sprout aphorisms in Chinese characters, in Cyrillic, in katakana. Over time I had TAs from China, Korea, Taiwan, Iran, Afghanistan, Vietnam, and Japan. When nonnative speakers first appeared in my classes, they didn't want to reveal their limited command of English. But once they knew they would not be ridiculed, they began speaking out as much as native speakers. Of course, the American students loved it. However anyone used English, we welcomed it. It was *our* job to understand them, native or nonnative, not the other way around. For anyone interested in how language works, these classes were excellent labs. When I taught in Heidelberg I felt at home almost immediately. We accepted each other's linguistic medium as it was and worked toward interfacing as best we could. As a result we all developed our communication skills.

Reading Daily Reflections

My students wrote daily reflections about the course, and I would read and respond to them. These writings were a fundamental part of the process, and it was important to get them back to the students the next day while what they had written was still fresh in their minds. Since there were no grades on the papers, the students read every comment I made. I wanted to give them a thoughtful response; the whole idea of our courses, after all, was an exchange of real messages, genuine dialogue. But thoughtful reading was a time-consuming process. The reflections got more and more insightful and *longer* as we got deeper into our work; and although I did look forward to seeing how a session had been received and what sorts of connections and tangents the students would make, this regimen meant I had a set of papers to read for each class every day. Meanwhile, I was experimenting with larger classes, even mammoth ones, and papers were getting to be a bit much. But who else could do it? Who else could know the way I wanted the papers to be read?

It turned out the TAs could. One afternoon Valerie Turner, one of my older TAs, saw the stack of papers I had to read and knew I was going out that evening. "Clark, you're never going to have time to read all of those. I'll be glad to read some for you." So either I stayed up really late or I delegated some of the papers to her. Hmm.... She had had several of my courses, after all, and was familiar with how I read papers, so I decided to risk it. When the students got the papers with Valerie's responses, they thought it was fine. After that, Valerie would take some papers from time to time, and I began to see how TAs could indeed help with the reading.

After some experimenting it evolved that the TAs took over collecting daily papers, splitting up the stack among us, and returning them the next day. I got to read each student's paper two to three times a week, so I was never out of touch with each one's involvement in the class, and I of course had lots of direct contact with just about everyone every day. Now I had more free time for that. The TAs were told to read the papers the way I had read theirs: They were to write considered, compassionate, and thorough responses. They were not to "correct" the writing. Editing was inappropriate in this setting, anyway, and could easily shut down the openness of the dialogue. The TAs signed their names so that the students would know who the reader was. Anyone who wanted a specific reader could put that name at the top of the paper.

Reading all the reflections myself had been one of my last holdouts as a conventional teacher. Even with the additional readers, I was still reading as much as any other English teacher, so my conscience was clear, and the students were writing five times as much as the required department guidelines anyway. But the difference was that I trusted students and TAs to do their work without interference. I had to be willing to let them alone. Of course they were fine. I loved the involvement of students and TAs in this process. I would see them earnestly chatting before or after class about their reflections. And students began reading each other's papers on their own. There was a genuine interest in what was being said. So the whole thing worked out better than I could have anticipated. By letting go I was getting more of what I wished for. That seems to me to be a general rule of life, too. It's a rather Taoist posture, after all; just ask Pooh.

Simplify, Simplify

Over the years I saw elaborate teaching schemes, complicated grading systems, detailed units of study, and complex apparatus. One thing was sure: The fancier the scheme, the more certain it was to fail. The problem was always that it was the teacher's effort, not the students'. So I knew any artificial structure in a semester or two would have come apart. A teacher simply cannot do the thinking and planning for even two or three students, much less fifty or a hundred. But one teacher can conduct a full orchestra of self-sustaining, motivated students. The work gets done, there is no pushing and pulling, and it all flows quite naturally. I am always reading of attempts to reduce class size, but I think the money would be better used in showing teachers how to get large numbers of students doing their own learning, setting their own pace, and determining what style of learning works best for them. That would be a real revolution in American schooling. The result would be strangely familiar. It would feel a lot like a one-room schoolhouse.

19

Teaching Grammar
The Net of Enchantment

The early lilacs became part of this child.
—Walt Whitman

One of the hazards of my profession is being subjected to ubiquitous and incessant chats about proper English. In most people's minds, *proper English* is synonymous with *grammar*—and that's that. Frankly, I could care less if people have a fun time talking proper-English trivia, but *grammar* has scarcely anything to do with such small-minded nit-picking. To study how language works is to look into the very hearts and minds of human beings. A linguist is far less interested in what should be than in that which is.

When my students looked at linguistic structures, it was investigative and exploratory, never prescriptive. We wondered how things worked and what that might mean. If someone bitched about "I could care less," we would have a look. Maybe the opposite of what is said is what's meant. "Those are bad threads, man!" probably means the speaker admires the outfit. Or we will say "Great!" when we mean "Terrible!" What's interesting is the verbal irony involved, a rather poetic use of language. Or "I could care less" could be an elliptical expression. The whole thought might be, "I could care less, I suppose, but I don't see how." When we examined language in that manner, all sorts of vistas opened for us, and we became fascinated with how the mind expresses itself. It is remarkable that unschooled people can be champs at adapting language in all sorts of imaginative ways, generating new twists as they go along. All we have to do is pay attention, and there before our eyes are miracles unfolding. Our "grammar" sessions were always absorbing and revealing. We were discovering our own selves.

But that sort of "grammar" discussion seldom occurred at social gatherings or even at conferences of English teachers. Most people think students should be taught "correct" English and "proper" English. I often told my students all billionaires speak correct and proper English, whether they come from Texas oil fields or Boston's Back Bay or have arrived recently from Taiwan. Then we would see what that idea might mean. That, of course, would take us into the evolution of language and the history of a dialect or a variety of English. We would forget all about whether an expression was "right" and would concentrate instead on the amazing ways air can be shaped into meaning.

To our delight we discovered air can take on wonderfully diverse shapes. In fact, within the same household no two people speak in exactly the same way. Each person's language is as unique as hair color and shoe size. Paying attention to the differences is so engaging that there is no more desire to make everyone's English the same than to require that mandalas be identical. Everyone who teaches English ought to have that much sensitivity. Even a discussion of the word *grammar* itself could take up several class sessions.* Or "the King's English"† or "shibboleth." Can trying to use correct English cause cancer?

Once the style of my classes crystallized, we could examine the way people talk just as we looked into everything else. We did not correct each other's speech or writing, but we did take great interest in how each of us used language and in the differences. The study of language is a lifelong job for linguists, but it is an enduring passion for any self-actualizing human being.

Grammar: Where to start? A system of symbols through which creatures interact in terms of their total environment? A system of rules for speaking and writing a given language? Morphology and syntax? A term applied to the whole apparatus of literary study, critical, historical, and linguistic? Diction, usage, spelling, logic, pronunciation, punctuation? Or the Scotch variation of *gramarye*, which I like: *glamour;* to cast a spell or enchantment? Oh, and *that* connection: *enchant*, mutter a magic spell, to sing! Now we're getting to the heart of the matter. Why not take all of them and add on the roots of logic as well? After all, in the beginning was the Word.

†There's always someone at the PTA meeting who thinks it's high time we taught kids the King's English. One-time Texas governor Ma Ferguson took it to a higher level: "If English was good enough for Jesus Christ, it's good enough for the children of Texas!"

What often happened when we talked about "correctness" was that the dialogue would shift to a higher plane. Everybody knows very well what a speaker means by "I could care less" or "I couldn't care less." The question we wanted to explore is, Is that the sort of attitude one wants to have toward the world? Would Walt Whitman have been so indifferent to events of his life? How about Buddha or Malcolm X? That was always the problem with "correctness." What lay behind the words was the real issue. It was the same with logic: A man says he should have a job because he has a family to support and his kid needs an operation. Should he be given the job? No, it's not logical. Aha! But isn't that indifference to our fellow man the very problem in our society? There are indeed lots of stories in which the man is hired and becomes a wonderful support to the employer in all sorts of illogical ways. The reverse, too, of course: He ends up destroying the whole company. Ah, but does that mean the employer was wrong to hire him? What constitutes "wrong"? *What does it profit a man . . . ?* What's the point of our living? What's the real bottom line of running a business? And so on. The point is that "correctness" is the tip of the iceberg. Human beings have larger fish to fry. It is small-minded to become so caught up in superficiality. What sort of person thinks more of the logic than of the human beings involved?

That was always a problem for me. As far as I was concerned the language police had their sights on trivia, whereas there were worlds of wonder right under their noses. And in a practical sense, if "I could care less" appears in a student's paper, the real issue of the communication is that attitude of indifference. The message, the attitude, the feeling, of the writer is the real basis of the dialogue. How did that soul become so inured to life that events are shrugged off? What horrible abuse occurred to precipitate such a thick shield? You will never get to the basis of crummy writing by putting Band-Aids on surface blemishes. When the conversation becomes authentic, people care about their utterances; they select words and phrases more thoughtfully. It becomes important that words count. The conversants mean what they say. A teacher who wants authentic dialogue can't afford to dwell on trivia. But paradoxically, most infelicities of any import disappear when people really mean what they say. So in our classes we developed sensitivity to each other's words.

In fact, we soon realized that one's utterances constitute a verbal mandala. Each of us has a unique verbal envelope fully revealing of the spirit within it —if we allow the envelope to speak to us. We tune in by being quiet, paying attention, and making sure that our own expression is as true to our spirits as we can make it. Anyone who could care less about such matters would lose interest and drift away. But I never met such a person. Most of the time our dialogue was in choice American English. That is, the selection of language came closer and closer to matching the mind behind the words. *That* is correct English. A good way to teach correct English would be to read good poets.

But, out and about, I cannot recall ever being drawn into a conversation about that sort of correctness. It was always the trivia. People would tell about expressions they hated to hear and about how our language was falling apart. Amusingly, in the course of the diatribe, the speaker would use two or three expressions someone else considered lousy. Faultfinding has a way of boomeranging. What emptiness in our lives makes us want to correct others? Self-actualizing people don't have much time for living other people's lives. Usually, I would try to change the subject and segue into the etymology of ordinary words like *daisy* or *August*. I tried to get away from the faultfinding as quickly as possible.

Literacy

An officer of the National Council of Teachers of English told me recently that "we" (educators, I guess) do want our students to be literate. I think she meant that they should develop some sort of linguistic awareness. That is, she thought students ought to be well-read enough to recognize the limits of acceptance of their own discourse. I think she meant that a student ought to be conscious that "I was just laying around all day" is one way to say it but "I was just lying around all day" appears in print more commonly and lots of people elect to use the latter—even if "laying around" is the way people back home talk. I don't think the woman from NCTE would *prescribe* "lying around" or mark "laying around" wrong, but she did think educated people would have paid enough attention to know how people outside their neighborhoods handled such matters. I think so, too—sorta, but my students and I, I'm sure, would end up exploring the implications: Why would that matter? Why do people care about things like that? Do those reasons constitute an attitude we would want to buy into? Why would anyone need to alter his/her idiolect in order to participate in the broader dialogue?

There are legitimate reasons. If my variety of English really cannot be understood by someone I need to communicate with, then I or that person or both of us need to work out some sort of interface, some bridge. Certain movies imported from Great Britain, for example, really could benefit from subtitles. But if we really can understand each other, then why would either of us give up our version in favor of the other? The deep curiosity a language-based English curriculum generates leads to such questions, and my students invariably touched on usage, dialect, and "correctness" in the process of paying attention to each other. That's about as far as we need to go with literacy.*

But "literacy" does seem to be defined more broadly. It includes what I would call stylistics or the conventions of the print medium. That involves subject-verb agreement, punctuation, hyphenation, consistency in abbreviation and in the spelling-out of numbers and percent signs, and so on. None of that, of course, applies to speech, but it is certainly involved in written discourse. So, yes, a person who is going to mess around in the print medium needs to have some awareness in that area. How much? That is an individual matter. How the individual comes to such awareness, though, is critical. If you teach me your language and I become neurotic or learn to despise you, all is lost. Typically, as I noted earlier, punctuation becomes important to a writer who begins to care if the audience "gets it."

If writing becomes a part of that person's way of communicating, sooner or later he or she will have to develop consistency. A humanistic teacher has to trust that that will happen—or not. It is not the teacher's job to insist, only to open the possibilities, and then only when *consistency* surfaces as part of an ongoing dialogue. Writers working for a newspaper or magazine will have to conform to the house style manual—or have a paperweight hurled at them. We can't protect them from that. They will have to learn to duck.

As for conforming to other people's speech conventions, self-actualizing human beings do have to make choices. And these involve the reasons we spend time in other people's speech communities in the first place. Using or not using our own natal tongues involves character, chutzpah, self-esteem, generosity, and all sorts of philosophical considerations. My students discussed these matters animatedly, but what they ended up doing about it remained their own business.

---

*"Cultural literacy" is another matter, of course. Some people are horrified if college graduates cannot pass a trivia test on what's in commonly read books. That is just a form of snobbery, a way of screening who gets into the club. Walk into anyone else's linguistic neighborhood and you will find yourself just as ignorant as they would be in yours. The rest is simply comparing biceps. Or it could be a basis for dialogue, for sharing each other's worlds.

Appalachia and Times Square: Anyone's English as a Second Language

The matter of "correct" diction, usage, and so on puzzled me for a number of years. What bugged people who considered themselves purists really amounted to a couple of hundred items at the most. A lot (not *alot*) of it had to do with pronunciation: If you don't pronounce things the way people in my neighborhood do, you're wrong. And word choice: "fetch" versus "bring." But "That will fetch a good price" is OK—er, *all right* (but not *alright*). The composition handbooks keep getting published and keep on listing these. It's been going on for at least 100 years here in America—obviously to no avail.

What finally cleared up the "proper" English issue was Ed Sing from Taiwan. He sold me my first computer in 1985. I had a rough time understanding his English, but not only did we manage, we prevailed. He taught me how to use the damned thing. The man was a genius, not only in what made the machine tick but in programming as well. He had his doctorate not in computer science but in metallurgy. "So how come you got so good at computers?" "Interest." "Ah." The point of this anecdote is that Ed Sing did not speak my dialect. His spoken English was lousy, but *it was not a barrier to anything he and I needed to do together.* He was a well-educated man, both in his own culture and in the scientific part of mine—in fact, far more so than I was. Neither of us was on a higher plane because of the way we spoke English.

Of course, all over America, but especially in the San Francisco Bay Area, more and more people from other countries have begun mingling with people born here. Indeed, in the last few years more of my students were from other countries than from the United States, many of them with advanced degrees. Even the new president of the University of California had a heavy Asian accent. So English as foreign language was the norm for most of my students. It finally dawned on me: *My* English is a foreign language to *anyone* but me! The farther I travel from Derry, Pennsylvania, the more foreign it is. Even in the English-speaking world the differences can be so profound as to be almost impossible. Ah, but not impossible if I need to learn how to run my computer.

Why then should we not extend this courtesy to people who grew up in this country? Why not treat anyone else's English as a foreign language? And why not treat our communication with each other as simply a matter of finding a way to interface our two language programs? That takes judgment out of the mix altogether and gets down to business: sharing each other's minds. Interfacing is a much more profitable approach than using difference as shibboleth—and a lot more fun. I am sure my classes took a logarithmic leap when we learned how to explore each other's minds and the cultures embedded in the language of those minds.

School English

> Any fool can make a rule
> And every fool will mind it.
> —Henry David Thoreau

Like everyone else, when I started teaching I tried to get students to learn correct English. The trouble was that I soon found the rules were inconsistent and arbitrary. Someone had decided what ought to be and then made up some wild logic to justify it. Like most students, when I was in school I never doubted the textbooks. A "sentence" was whatever they said it was, and out of awareness I figured out how to identify "sentences" in the controlled schoolbook environment. We were never asked to examine English as she is spoken. Kids are brilliant at figuring out what's wanted even if it is not clearly expressed. So those of us who wanted to get along with schoolmarms learned to give the wanted response. But when I tried to teach from the schoolbooks on grammar, it was hopeless. Relying on my own assimilated "correctness" didn't help. I would immediately find my explanations fell short and ran into exceptions, niceties, and complications. Language was anything but the cut-and-dried drills designed to make our students sound like the Cabots and Lodges. Most of the people who wrote the grammar books and taught the courses had never met a real live Brahmin, but that never troubled them.

Anyway, I couldn't stand it. The whole business needed sorting out. It didn't take much thought to see how absurd school English was. Anyone who actually used it would have been carted off to the booby hatch. As someone said, "If you did learn 'correct' English, who would you talk it to?" I never found *How come? How about lunch? Gotta go,* or even *kid* in school grammar books. Off guard, English teachers said, "It's me," just like the rest of us. The truth is, as for how language really works, most English teachers didn't know what they were talking about. Few had had even one college course in the nature of language or in linguistics. I remember asking one purist what courses he had studied in college. "Young man, I knew grammar before I went to college; it wasn't necessary to *take* courses." Such certainty does cut down on the botheration.

I wasn't much better off than my colleagues. I had had only one elective course in philology, and that was simply a more detailed version of the Latin grammar overlay applied to our Germanic tongue. The map did not match the territory, of course, and I had to figure my own way out of the maze. (This was another time when the truism was brought home that the best way to learn a subject is to teach it.) I was soon reading books with titles like *Linguistics and English Grammar, Aspects of Language, English Syntax, Transformational Grammar, Structural Linguistics, Psycholinguistics, Language and Myth, Language and Thought, Leave Your Language Alone, American English in Its Cultural Setting, the Joys of Yiddish, Black English*, and so on—scores of books, anything I could get my hands on.

One book that helped me get my head on straight was Albert H. Marckwardt and Fred Walcott's *Facts About Current English Usage*, published by NTCE in 1938. They had the novel idea of checking acceptance of 230 usage items by linguists, the English Council, authors, editors, business-men and -women, the Modern Language Association, and speech teachers. The opinions of the specialists were at variance on 121 of the items, even within the specialties. English teachers were the least accepting. My guess is they never bothered to look at what was going on outside their classrooms. The most accepting were the linguists. Many items rejected by English teachers were used regularly by established writers. If it is still in print English teachers might profit from browsing this book a few hours and reflecting on its implications.*

Eventually, it all fell into place, and a major gap in my philosophy of teaching was filled in. For one thing there was no good reason for everyone to write or speak in the same way. There isn't any "same way." After all, there are well over 280 million people using English in the United States alone, never mind the billion or two speaking it all over the globe. Getting along in a broader, more generalized language community is a bicycle-riding kind of skill. It can't be taught, but it can be learned. Showing students *the right way* is impossible. But discovering that it is impossible and seeing all the variation on a theme is fascinating to any inquiring mind. In a deep sense investigation

---

*See also *Harper Dictionary of Contemporary Usage*, William and Mary Moms, eds.

of language and all its nuances and implications is, as I have emphasized throughout this book, what the study of the native tongue is all about. The nature of language is either the background or focus of the entire English curriculum. Vigorous involvement and thoughtful reflection lead to the very result most educators say they want: literacy. This kind of literacy means being comfortable with one's own variety of English and with the broader language community as well. Specific adaptations in the second-language environment depends on each person's way of interfacing with "foreigners."

These "foreigners" might include a student's history teacher. How to interface with this native speaker? Moving from San Francisco to New Orleans means adapting to that second language. Getting a job at the *New Yorker*, again, requires interfacing with a target environment. And so on. There is no way to teach for all eventualities or even the most common. Each contact with another language environment calls for unique adjustment. Such accommodations would be second nature for graduates of investigative and exploratory English programs.

The Structure of English

A writer can learn to do literary cartwheels, tightwire acts, wheelies, and *entrechats* without studying the structure of English sentences. Most accomplished writers developed their skills without formal study of their native language. On the other hand it would be hard to find an experienced writer who does not have an absorbing interest in how a sentence works. My students were no different. Under the right circumstances they thoroughly enjoyed seeing how their utterances ticked. Someone threatening to teach them how to write properly could count on resistance; it's only natural. But if you said, "Let's see which group can be first making a sentence out of these words: *beamish, reppix, ludder, sudally, up, conded, nectles, the, ronky, frangled, had, when, the, and, cerded, her, the,*" it was always a hit. Groups would rush to get their sentences on the chalkboard, and a great debate would ensue about the "correctness" of each other's structures. In the process, my students, when they tried this exercise, made up their own grammar terms, like *glue words*, and discovered form-class words on their own. They sounded a lot like linguists, even though they did not know conventional terminology. They realized they knew all about English sentence structure in a way that a Taiwanese would envy.

Then we might reverse it and substitute nonsense words for the structure words and provide familiar form-class words. Then we would see what insights might emerge. I never knew what aspect of language might be emphasized, and that kept it stimulating for all of us. It was an easy step to offer as a koan McLuhan's "The medium is the message." What is the meaning of a structure called a sentence? What does it mean to pour thoughts into these vessels? Is a sentence a meaning in itself? Would stuffing the products of one's mind into Chinese structures make a difference? And vice-versa: Does sentence structure massage the spirit? Is the medium the message, as McLuhan said? All sorts of questions would come up. The answers weren't the important thing. Asking the questions was. In fact, if a question was really settled I was disappointed, for all these games and discussions were a means of getting us all to see into the mirror of language in a vivid and conscious way. "So that's what's going on!" We were seeking a poetic experience of our own thought processes, cognition of our own selves. The real test of these investigations would be whether we were marveling about how language works twenty, thirty, forty years later. I run into some of these students from time to time, and it does seem they still do think about such things.

There were all sorts of ways to turn language upside down so that its secrets fell out into our hands like rubies. You could compare sentence lengths and use of clauses and phrases, examine vocabulary, and watch for the wildest variations of sentence patterns. Instead of what should be, we looked at what is. As a result we saw the amazing adaptability of language in a way students of schoolbook English never glimpsed. It was an entirely different emphasis, expansive instead of restrictive. Playing with nonsense sentences and the like made most students realize how accomplished they really were at English grammar. They were masters of English syntax and had been brilliant at it since they were five years old. They saw what a sentence can do for all those piles of words in an unabridged dictionary. A dictionary tells us little about how English speakers think. The English sentence tells us everything.

So we were always trying to get beyond the facts to the poetry embedded in them. That was the purpose of our experiments. Once they knew we weren't there to amass facts but to tease out their meaning, most students wanted to come to class—and even bring guests. What English teachers need to know is that right inside every student's head is all the raw material for a thorough study of language.

Why Not Take All of Them?

If we take *grammar* in its broadest sense, it turns out to be the foundation of all study, of all learning. Of course we must "teach" it, for it is the invisible structure in which our thought is cast. Teachers who realize the linguistic basis of their discipline will be more effective in helping students become "native speakers." In the sense my classes took it, prescription gives way to description, to discovery (dis . . . cover, un . . . cover). And the purpose is to get at the spirit that generates language, the magic, the glamour. That is why correcting students is so demeaning, so disruptive, so counterproductive. Emphasis on error results in awkwardness. A good English course does not make students ashamed of the way they talk. Look for the insights, the revealing turn of phrase, and the whole atmosphere changes. An inclusive study, one that welcomes diverse ways of manifesting is positive and supportive and makes full use of the universes gathered in a classroom. Everything a good English course needs is right there, right inside those "many masks of God." Something full of wonder, wonderful, is going on. That is certain, and examination of its grammar (including all those many meanings of the word) is a way to glimpse it. We can't leave anything out; syntax, metaphor, morphology, etymology—any aspect could be the key. Should we teach "grammar"? What else is there?

20

Eccentric
Islands and Causeways

---

*Without bigots, eccentrics, cranks, and
heretics the world would not progress.*

—Gelett Burgess

My colleague Bill Middleton hated the expression "the student." It is as if there is one such person cloned millions of times and each is the same and should be treated the same as every other one. It's a good way to depersonalize the infinite variety of people we work with. But my students would never let me get away with that. They insisted, or so it seemed to me, that the learning environment be tailored to fit each person. When I paid attention I could not find even two people with exactly the same learning style; there is no such thing as homogeneous grouping. So once I caught on to that, my classes were always one-room schoolhouses. The students figured out how to accommodate each other, and I learned to get out of the way.

The challenge is to provide an optimal learning environment for whomever is there. When a twelve-year-old kid appeared in my class, he was assimilated. Re-entry adults, cops, people who had served time, a woman in her seventies, even some nut cases—they were all instances of the same principle: No one is "normal," of the norm; we are all eccentric. My job was to recognize that eccentricity and work with it. A teacher interacts not with who "the student" should be but with who *this* student is. So the envelope of who an acceptable student could be kept expanding, 100 percent being the ideal.

So it was with "handicapped" people, too. At first I would think, "I'm not trained to work with paraplegics, the deaf, the blind." But then I wasn't trained to work with human beings of any sort! The education courses were about "the student," not eccentrics. I had had to learn on the job. It was the same with people in wheelchairs and those with seeing-eye dogs. Even if there had been a book on it somewhere, I would still have had to get down to specifics: *this* teacher getting to know *this* person who happens to be in a wheelchair, not that person over there who is also in a wheelchair.*

I would be a little nervous starting out, but, oh, the rewards. I was always being taught, always being welcomed into a new world. I learned lots about state-of-the-art wheelchairs, which turned out to be similar to quality bicycles. I had a student, one of whose aspects happened to be blindness. But I had a student who happened to be a brilliant drummer, one of *his* aspects. One student drove me nuts with his indifference; I couldn't get him fired up about anything. Then I realized, good heavens! this was the most authentic existentialist I have ever met! (We're still friends—I guess.) When these little universes would open up, the classes were like an art gallery. I was never bored; I can't imagine it. Those classes remind me of the blurb on the back of Oliver Sacks's marvelous *The Man Who Mistook His Wife for a Hat*: "The story of individuals afflicted with fantastic perceptual and intellectual aberrations."

Reviewing Sacks's *The Island of the Colorblind*, Patricia Holt wrote, "One of the reasons for the immense appeal of neurologist-turned-author Oliver Sacks is his *complete lack of judgment* [my italics] in exploring illness and disease. To Sacks there is almost no such thing as disability; there is only the body's awesome capacity to develop complex and fabulous new resources in the face of stunning adversity." That sounds like a description of all the students in all my classes, all fantastic worlds to be imagined with heart and mind. What a privileged life I have had. Tracking, indeed!

When Bea Worthen took my class the issue of who is actually "handicapped" was brought into my awareness more vividly than ever before. What is a *handicap*, after all? Wearing glasses? Singing off key? Color blindness? Greed? I wrote up my experience with Bea for *Family Circle*. The following is a version of that 1982 article.

---

*Read John Hockenberry's *Moving Violations* for *his* declaration of independence.

My Hearing Handicap

"If this works out, I'll be surprised," I thought as I copied the name and Social Security number from the notepad Bea handed me. She was deaf and wanted to enroll in my class. I had had a deaf student some years before. It had been a trying experience. We both had worked hard, but the results were slight. Imagine the difficulties. Any message had to be written in longhand with the response in the same form. Forget any class discussions. The interchange was nearly zero. Would this be a repeat of that dismal experience? Sure, I would like to help, but I had no training, and would it be helpful for anyone if the whole class had to slow down? And, really, was it worth it to Bea? How much could she possibly get from this?

As it turned out, there would be one difference: an interpreter. That would certainly improve chances of something getting through. I guessed there would be plenty of problems, but what the hell.

So we tried it out. When I arrived for the first meeting, there were thirty-five people, Bea with her notepad, and no interpreter.

"No interpreter," Bea wrote and shrugged.

"What happened?" I wrote.

"I don't know where she is."

Oh boy!

Then Bea handed me a lined pad with a carbon. Would I ask someone to take notes and give Bea a copy? OK.

So we started out: a discussion with responses from all over the room—voices Bea couldn't hear. She could read my lips some, but that was all and I knew not nearly enough. Surely this was even less meaningful than watching TV with the sound off. For Bea couldn't know what the responses were nor even what had sparked them. And I was sure whoever was taking notes couldn't be *that* good. As for Bea, she seemed to me like a person in a waiting room, tuned out. In her place, I would have begun to seethe.

Enter Marya, breathless. Bea's eyes click on, hands start. "Commuter traffic," Marya says and signs. The feeling is electric, as if a circuit has been activated. It's exciting, for me, for the whole class. Marya sits beside me, facing Bea. Whatever I say, she lip syncs and signs, corny jokes, puns and all. Whatever anyone says is passed on to Bea. All nuances. When Bea raises her hand and signs a question or comment, Marya is her voice. But it is so smoothly done there is no question that this is Bea speaking. By the end of the hour I am amazed. A virtuoso performance.

"Tell Bea I enjoyed this," I say to Marya.

"You try it," she says and waits quietly while I do. It takes a couple of repeats. Bea watches closely. But with gestures and animation, I get through. It feels good and Bea laughs.

After that Marya appeared every day, and I became more and more impressed with this team. Their fluency was striking. Their achievement must surely surpass that of a foreign-language interpreter. It had taken Marya six years in several universities to reach this proficiency, she told me, and she was still learning. New symbols were being invented constantly. As for Bea, you can be certain she used the skill with absolute enthusiasm.

And what of her achievement in the class? That is the point I have been coming to. She probably got more from the discussions than any hearing student. We hearing creatures can get away with inattention. We all lose track from time to time and would be exhausted from a full fifty minutes of concentrated participation. But for a deaf person and an interpreter, it is impossible to goof off. Imagine the consequences. There is an acuity and intensity I have never seen in even the best hearing student.

As for me, my performance was sharpened, too. It was natural to take care that I was getting through; I watched closely to see that I did. And I checked with Bea to confirm it. I say natural because I knew my audience. Bea had a special bias, her deafness, that I had to recognize. If I didn't, my message would not be received.

I think the other students got the message, too. They were an unusually nice bunch anyway, but I sensed that they were better students in that class than they usually were. And I was a better teacher. I spoke more carefully and tried to be more articulate. Well, hell, with Marya there, signing the entire transaction, who wants to look inept? The tone was elevated. And then, too, there was this bright, enthusiastic deaf person hearing more than anybody else!

The two of them taught us what it really was to hear. We hearing people have a long way to go to get that good. When I think of what Bea was absorbing, I suspect we are all metaphorically deaf. It takes a lot of caring on both sides to get through to each other, and intense attention and vigor. But when we achieve it, it feels so good!

The other day a young woman was outside my office studying my schedule. With signs and gestures she told me she wanted to enroll in a class I was about to begin. If she is willing to put up with my handicap, I think I can squeeze her in.

Postscript: Bea was thirty-something when she took that course back in 1981. She had two little boys and had not been in school for a long time. Now her boys are grown men, and their mommy has her master's. So that all worked out nicely for Bea. But I think every class she was in benefited. Getting to know the spirit of one deaf person heightens our awareness of deafness in general. So we read articles and books about signing with enthusiasm. Is sign language really a language? How we answer that affects how schools for the deaf are run. When Gallaudet, a college for deaf students in Washington, D.C., appointed a hearing president, it evoked such outrage among the students that a deaf president had to be selected. I'll bet every student who took my class with Bea had a heightened interest in that news story. When Oliver Sacks's *Seeing Voices, A Journey into the World of the Deaf* came out, guess who read it with fascination.

Bea's is a story about a deaf person, but Kabir Arghandiwal took a class with me, and now the Afghan culture is an abiding interest. And so it goes. All these students not of the center—eccentric—bring as much to a class as they take. The more we pay attention, the more eccentric everyone is revealed to be. As for myself, I know of no one but eccentrics. In such a setting everyone benefits. All the other students are more awake, not just during that class but for the rest of their lives, whenever they read a headline or a poem or eat in an Afghan restaurant. You could call it a liberal education—or simply *noticing what's there.*

21

Large, Compressed, and Combined Classes
Laboratory Schools

*First we shape our dwelling, and
afterward our dwelling shapes us.*
—Winston Churchill

Class Size

Conventional wisdom has it that smaller is better, one teacher and one student being the ideal. I remember telling Erich Pohl, the director of the modern language program at the University of Heidelberg, I was a little disappointed that there were only 19 students in my class. "You've got to be kidding!" he said. I wasn't. I told him if I came back sometime I wanted 50 or more. I don't like to shock my colleagues, but the truth is, for me, more is better. I don't know what the upper limits might be. I never found a room big enough to check it out.

This preference evolved gradually. Originally, I lobbied with just about every other English teacher for small classes. When I started teaching in 1957, the goal of the National Council of Teachers of English for composition classes was 25 students. Hardly any school system achieved that. It was just too costly. When a school did allow smaller English classes, classes in other departments were enlarged. Of course, that would outrage the other faculty. At DVC the English Department had been especially persuasive. Not only did we have composition classes averaging about 25, we taught only four classes a semester, instead of the typical five for other departments, and their class sizes were usually much larger. So there were continual wars over the years. They are still going on. Meanwhile, money for education in this country diminishes steadily. We have this philosophy that to be effective we need small classes. But there is no money. Impasse.

Beyond the common view that small is better, English teachers argued they needed time to help students with their compositions. Students ought to write at least one composition a week of 500 words or more, and that paper needed to be read and thoroughly corrected. Many teachers wanted time to work with each student separately. Then, if possible, the paper would be rewritten and read again by the English teacher. I don't know what was supposed to happen then. I can picture students reworking the damned thing all semester. Indeed, conscientious English teachers would schedule appointments and sweat with individuals over the latest *oeuvre*, spending countless hours on this endeavor. And that was only part of the job. There were, as I have said, lessons to plan, tests to create and correct, records to keep, background reading for the courses, and reading to stay abreast of current pedagogy. A good, traditional English teacher routinely put in 70-hour weeks.

To begin with, that had been my own experience. Every student meant at least one more paper a week to read, additional records to keep, and so on. And I didn't see enough of my family as it was. But a conflict developed. As the style of my classes evolved, I began to realize the value of having lots of viewpoints. A small group could get bogged down in a limited perspective; the bigger the group, however, the less that could happen. Someone was bound to introduce a divergent observation that would help illuminate whatever we were investigating. The larger the group the more possibilities to consider. The way the class was set up—general discussion, small groups, general discussion, small groups, and so on—we were able to get abundant response to almost anything we chose to observe. We had lively, interesting, and productive classes. Thirty-five was much more exciting than 25, and 70 was amazing. Students couldn't wait to get to class to see what would happen next. Neither could I. As a student I had never been challenged to investigate anything so minutely. It forced me to see my subject more thoroughly than I had ever imagined.

The same thing happened with the students. They loved hearing crazy takes on obvious "truth." In fact, one of the things they valued most about these classes was hearing what other students had to say. They liked what I had to say, too, but it was just one of 70 views. When you put all those ideas together and synthesize them, the emerging picture is much more vivid. No wonder they liked coming to class. Where else could these young minds get such a workout? It was better than aerobics. It was a lab for mind experiments. Once we had found a format for making use of all those brains, we were on a roll, pretty much the herd of horses my colleague Cynthia had described: thundering across the plains, all that energy and power flowing as one force.

I suspect such power is intimidating for most teachers. A lot of what I see in classes and institutions is designed to subdue the very thing I wanted to encourage. Tests, seating charts, taking roll, even the arrangement of furniture serve to keep the lid on. The power is vested in one person, who uses this energy to dominate 25 others. Obviously, when you are trying to control a bunch of wild horses, corralling them, breaking them, there isn't much time for anything else, is there? So, willy-nilly, teaching in most instances has little to do with ideas and lots to do with maintaining authority, hence that telltale word *instruction*. "Instruction" reveals how students are viewed, and it implies a hierarchy. You *need* small classes, to be sure, if you intend to instruct them.

"Instruction" also implies that the flow of energy is *from* the instructor *to* the students, passive recipients. In our classes they were the whole show. An idea was a starting point. What it became was *their* creation, a piece of art, something that had never existed in quite that form before. That's what brought them back with such enthusiasm. It was *their* class, and they knew it. I was never sure what would emerge, but that was the way it was supposed to be. It meant my classes could always be fresh for me no matter how often I taught the "same" concept. But when the instructor is the whole show, what is transmitted is minimal, and there is little opportunity to examine the message, all that brilliance bottled up. What a waste!

But "instructing" is self-defeating in the first place. I saw early that no one can learn for another person. Like it or not, a teacher has to trust that a student can learn and will learn, given an authority-free environment. All my evidence confirmed that people want to learn and love using their minds. We don't like being dominated; we insist on making our own observations and on taking from a class what our own needs identify, not what someone else thinks would be good for us. That seems fundamental, biological.

Intuitively at first but then deliberately, I began enlarging my classes. I liked the atmosphere. There was another advantage, too, having to do with authority. If I wanted an authority-free class, what to do if someone was unruly? The minute I settled someone, the "town meeting" for a while lost its spontaneity, and it took a while to get the atmosphere back to the warm and friendly setting I knew was necessary for optimal involvement. Lots of people thought I ought to assert my command, and I remember the reaction of Pat Underhill, a teaching assistant (TA) about my own age, when I lost my cool and told off a troublesome student.

"I was so pleased," she told me later. "That's just what the class needed. They need to know who's boss."

"Well, I'm not pleased, Pat," I told her. "That's just what I don't want them to learn. I want them to be the boss. I want them to work out their own relationships. I felt like I wasn't teaching well today. Do you really think I'm not aware that I could assert authority all along the way?"

I went on to point out that this "sloppy" teaching wasn't accidental. And it worked, too. Years of experience had shown me that trust was well placed. Almost always the students found ingenious ways to absorb people who wanted to take over the class. There was always someone who wanted to be the center of attention or who wanted to dominate or who talked too much—or too little. It was a lesson in group dynamics that would make a book in itself. So when I blew up at a student, it meant I was still learning my craft. But even these aberrations could have value. The next day I told the class about the little chat I had with Pat, and that gave them a chance to make explicit what had been implicit. They saw, if someone was getting bossy or garrulous, it was up to them, individually or together, to assert themselves. And my TA found out something about teaching in a democracy. So even a screwup had its value. When you really don't know where a class will end up, anything that occurs can be used. It's all *objets trouvés* that can be turned into *objets d'art*.

But class size itself influenced the need for discipline. Surprisingly, the larger the class, the fewer the disruptions. If a student had a tendency to bully, it took a lot of guts to try to pull that in a large group. If someone wanted to run at the mouth, someone else would intervene. So even though we were a noisy bunch, the critical mass was enough to keep us on track. Most people, I have learned, want to use their time well. They like to have fun, but they want it to be productive. Once they saw the value of their own minds, even disruptive students usually settled down, and the class would stay on track with scarcely a nudge from me. Once the structure was established I was more like George Szell than George Patton. In fact, sometimes it would seem to me we should reassemble from the small groups, but I couldn't break them up. They were too absorbed in some idea we had started. So I took my cue from them and watched for a lull before calling them back together. We became improvisational jazz. Those were the best classes.

There were several reasons, then, for preferring the larger classes. Of course, something else was happening, too, that made it workable. I have described elsewhere what transpires in student-centered classes: They become mutual-aid groups, and there is less and less "teaching" needed. I continued to jettison traditional apparatus, leaving heirlooms all along the trail that no longer had a place in the new territory. Tests were out, correcting was out, predigested "lessons" were out. Students were learning from each other. TAs, among other things, were serving as liaisons, and I had learned to read papers for the gold, not the dross. Now most of my time could be devoted to the heart of teaching, not the window dressing. Almost from the beginning I knew I wanted every move I made to count, no busywork, no extraneous routines. Gradually that had come to pass. It meant I could put all my energy into the class I entered each day; each class could be an art class. And that is what did happen.

Can large classes work in other disciplines? Why not? The largest barrier is the perception that the teacher is the center. If the emphasis is shifted to the students themselves, teachers are freed to set up environments that stimulate learning. In an information age, faculty are no longer the source of data, even ideas. There is far more stuff all around than any human being can attend to. Learning how to teach oneself calculus is a far more valuable use of time than being instructed in it. What does one do when there is no instructor around? We need self-sufficient math students who are used to figuring things out for themselves. How else can a democratic society manage?

We can't afford small classes anyway, so finding ways to be effective in large groups is, if nothing else, a survival skill. Besides, human-being-centered classes are more stimulating for all concerned. They are better pedagogy, they accomplish what we all say we want, and in the long run they are more efficient. Once students realize they direct their own learning, all of a sudden they become brilliant. But faking it doesn't work. I have seen teachers dip in a toe but then back off; they can't bring themselves to jump in. They set up rules for small groups, for example, appointing discussion leaders, someone to take notes, someone to report for the group—and they even grade the performance. Then they get stilted, artificial behavior and decide students aren't ready for so much uncontrolled freedom, and so on. Large class or small class isn't the issue. A class truly centered on people works, but students will never fall for an adulterated version.

Compressed Classes

Each semester I got four courses started and then tried to keep four balls in the air for 18 weeks. That always bothered me. Just as I was getting focused in one course, I would have to drop what I was doing and start thinking about another one. I found that disruptive. When I'm "into" any art project, I don't want to have to stop for dinner. When I got an idea going in my critical thinking class, I wanted to follow it through to the payoff. I thought this must be just as big a problem for students as for me. Having students and teachers trying to think about four or five courses at the same time doesn't recognize the value of uninterrupted periods of thought. We need time to sit still and stay with an idea until we get the feel of it or see where we need to be going with our thinking. Distractions are the bane of deeper thought.

I got a chance to experiment with that idea when I was chairman of our English Department. I wanted to provide more access to our program. We were on an 18-week semester, but suppose someone wanted to start college right in the middle? Or suppose someone had to drop out of an English class because of work or illness and didn't want to have to wait till the next semester to start in again? What if they suddenly needed one more course in order to complete requirements? Or the reverse: What if someone needed to complete a course the first part of the semester? With imaginative scheduling there were all sorts of needs a community college could address. So we set up some options: early- and late-hour classes, Friday-evening classes, Saturday classes or weekend seminar classes, and compressed classes.

I tried the compressed classes and never went back to semester-long teaching. Instead of teaching four classes all semester long, I compressed them into nine-week courses. I taught two classes the first half of the semester and two the second half. Instead of two or three times a week for 18 weeks, we met daily for nine weeks, getting in the required 54 hours in half the time. Initially, this was done to provide more options for the students; and a number of teachers, not just in our department, taught at least part of their load in the compressed mode. And it did help. We were able to offer a lifeline to lots of students. It was another way of making our college more accommodating and friendly.

But the surprise for me was how much better my classes went when they met every day. We all know about distributive learning, the role time plays in acquiring understanding, and that, no doubt, is one reason for semester-long courses. But I wanted students to *catch on* to something. The model was an intensive course in language or bike riding, not gradual accretion of knowledge but a sudden awakening of ability or understanding. One minute I can't balance; the next minute I can. After the first quarter I realized compressed classes were the missing element in the teaching approach described in this book.

The difference was that we would get an idea going and would keep on mulling it over the rest of the day, sleep on it even, and instead of letting it decline for a couple of days, we would be right back at it the next day. That way it stayed fresh and focused as long as we remained interested in it. Meanwhile, the more global overall concept of the course enveloped us throughout this period. So we were working on the course as a whole, even while we were tinkering with subprograms. We were doing English all the time for nine weeks, in and out of class. That's mainly all we thought about. Our significant others must have learned a lot about English during those weeks. I loved it.

One thing I insisted on, even when a course dragged on for 18 weeks, was that students got their papers back the next time I saw them. If you are all excited about an idea, you want feedback yesterday, not a couple of weeks later. If there is too much delay, we can barely remember what we were so worked up about. Even after a long weekend it takes a while to get going again, but with compressed classes that never happened. There was continual feedback, continual communication and reinforcement. We kept the fire stoked. It was the difference between a conventional French course in a typical American college and total language immersion in Paris. The compressed classes were total-immersion classes, continuous and intensive.

From the beginning the quality of these short-term classes was so striking I knew there was a learning principle here that hadn't been given attention in most academic programs. Students were more enthusiastic and more productive, but the work was of a higher quality, too. Within a few days we became a team, one multifaceted organism working on one thing. It's like running. It takes a while to warm up, but then runners hit their stride, get that second wind, and the process itself takes over. The runner is simply part of it. So what we stumbled on was a way to institutionalize the atmosphere artists and thinkers require for their best work.* The critical element is a medium that fosters such behavior. It is a simple but powerful solution. I am sure the difference I saw would be just as dramatic in other subjects. Concentrate on one or two subjects at a time instead of four or five and stay with them rather continuously. Just that one departure from convention would produce better learning, regardless of teaching philosophy.

Combined Classes

For a while, before the college got settled, we tried out all sorts of teaching arrangements. A classroom with rows of chairs all facing the teacher's desk seemed purely arbitrary, and some of us wondered about the nonverbal message. So we varied everything we could think of. If something useful emerged

---

*Hemingway in an interview said, "You write until you come to a place where you still have your juice and know what will happen next and you stop and try to live through until the next day when you hit it again."

we would try to make it part of our regular work. It is possible we don't even need classrooms, for example. There have been books on classrooms without walls, communities as classrooms, apprenticeships, work-study courses, and so on. We did workshops, seminars, marathon sessions, even weekend retreats for the whole college (when we were one-tenth the size the college is now). Some of us experimented with a college-within-a-college, four or five teachers from various disciplines working with perhaps 150 students.

One semester I tried a jumbo class: Thirty-five students took only one 12-unit course, with just one teacher—me. The registrar broke it into credit for psychology, freshman English, social science, and the nature of literature. During the course everything was combined. A psychology teacher and a social science teacher agreed to be consultants. During this semester the students and I had only one course to think about, not four or five. The college had inherited some portable tin buildings from the army, and we commandeered one for the semester. It was scheduled to be torn down anyway, so we could do whatever we wanted with it. One of our first projects was to paint it. We also brought in a refrigerator, a couple of rugs, and some audiovisual equipment. It became our workshop. Then we set about generating our course. (By this time, working together had made us a team.) Since there was no model, we worked out the logistics as we went along, the students playing as much a part in shaping the course as I did.

The idea was to blend our four "subjects" into one seamless investigation, incorporating elements of these disciplines organically into whatever we were examining. We were using language all the time anyway, and the disciplines came to the fore or remained in the background as we went about our work. From time to time our consultants would check over the course requirements for their regular classes and determine how close we were to meeting them—directly or indirectly.

There were all sorts of time and space advantages. The room was ours for the semester, so we could come and go as we pleased, and we could leave unfinished work lying around without having to set it up and take it apart each time we met. We weren't confined to 50-minute classes. We could stay on a project as long as it took. Though I didn't realize it then, we had transplanted the one-room-schoolhouse idea to a college setting, with all the implications and possibilities. It was the most challenging experiment I ever tried and also the most rewarding, a seminal experience. Much of my teaching philosophy and practice grew out of that semester with 35 college kids in a tin building.

A semester working without a net made anything I tried out later on seem conservative. That semester shaped me; I wasn't afraid to try anything that seemed like a good idea. Even then, though, I knew we were not likely to fail.

I had read the research: Almost any innovative project will be more educational than conventional practices. It's easy to see why. When you are trying something *for the first time*, you are at your best. Your mind is engaged, your spirit is there, you pay attention. Your involvement can't help but affect the atmosphere, and the students catch the disease, too. In the long run even activities that "failed" turned out to have a positive influence on my teaching, whereas activities taught by rote left me—and the students—feeling stale and dispirited. The element of chance, of never knowing for sure, is essential to any learning situation. It always has to be "for the first time." That's the key to happy teaching. Undo your belt and look for trouble, Zorba said. Then use what you learn. Someone said success and failure may be looked at not as reward and punishment but as information. That one-room-schoolhouse semester was loaded with information.

Laboratory Schools

I never did give up the idea that a college ought to be innovating continually. There was a laboratory school adjoining our teachers' college in Indiana, Pennsylvania, where we seniors could get a little experience teaching. Why not make all schools learning laboratories? We never know for sure what we ought to be doing next, anyway. Let's see what works and what doesn't. A faculty that isn't cocksure is more likely to learn and discover than one that is settled in its ways. One thing longevity is good for is that you can watch students come and go. I saw that practices that worked with students in 1970 didn't hold up in 1980. A closer look revealed that something that worked yesterday won't work today. Everything—this particular mix of students, the environment, technology, everything—changes all the time. The only constant is change. To me, a master teacher is someone who has been at it a long time and still doesn't know anything for sure. It isn't always comfortable, but it is a lot more fun than staid complacency, which is always simply a failure to see what's happening. A college with young practice teachers and a faculty charged with trying things out would benefit all concerned. The lifelong research project for teachers is teaching and learning. Why not say so and get on with it?

22

Objets Trouvés
The Poetic Mode

Why, who makes much of a miracle?
As for myself, I know of nothing but miracles.

—Walt Whitman

And then there are sail-toads. Squashed and run over enough times, they make good Frisbees. Once I looked out my office door and saw John Stevens,* a psychology teacher, poking along like *Night of the Living Dead.*

"What's going on, John?"

"I'm walking around at half-speed."

"Oh."

Thus, it came to pass that a slow walk became a feature of almost all my classes. Anyone who tries it for a half-hour will see some of the benefits immediately. In Goethe's words,

> People seek a central point. That is hard and not even right. I should think a rich, manifold life, brought close to the eyes, would be enough without express tendency; which, after all, is only for the intellect.

When one walks at about one pace per second, the world becomes a vast museum of infinite wonder. When we are "going somewhere" our focus is out

---

*John later published *Gestalt Therapy Verbatim*, a book of dialogues with Fritz Perls, and distributed it out of his garage. Real People Press went on to publish a number of significant books on therapy and is now located in Moab, Utah.

ahead a few feet. But when we slow down, when we are simply walking around, the focus recedes to where we are. There is time to see sail-toads, bits of paper, buds unfolding, cracks in the pavement. Instead of passing through the surroundings, we move in an envelope that travels with us. And there seems to be plenty of time to get everything done.

John Wheatcroft in his way had done a half-speed walk through Jonson's "On My First Daughter" back in Bucknell in 1956. The did-you-notice game with the Brueghel painting is another variation. We took the time to see what's there. Students would come back from our slow walks all aglow. To me, just their witnessing their own worlds was sufficient, but there were always many other implications. A half-speed walk, for example, is like a lyric—in fact, *is* a lyric. I have seen students scratch their heads at this haiku by Onitsura:

> *Look! Cherry blossoms*
> *all over! Birds have two legs!*
> *There: Horses with four!*

But after a slow walk, they understood it completely. If you want to teach poetry, a half-speed walk will get students in the right frame of mind immediately. In fact, reflections after our walk would blossom with unsolicited poems. It was just natural. A liberal education must surely involve taking a slow walk. And what could be a more practical study method? When one slow-walks algebra, learning seems effortless.

Words and Things

One way the slow walk figured into our English classes had to do with what words can and cannot do. Students talked of how vivid everything became simply from their having paid attention to it. This reminded me of a passage in John Fowles's *The Magus*. The narrator described sunlight in a glade, and

> the white roar of the little fall, the iciness, the solitude, the laughing, the nakedness; moments one knows only death can obliterate . . . but at first it was for me an intensely *literary* [my italics] moment. . . . I had forgotten that there are metaphors and metaphors, and the greatest lyrics are very rarely anything but direct and unmetaphysical.

It was this eidetic way of seeing I wanted the students to realize, seeing directly, without the intervention of words. Then, I wanted to see what words could add and also what they took away.

The first task, then, was to stroll around and after a while bring back to class something they would not notice ordinarily. That was all. We took a look at what each had brought back. Next, I asked them to go home and figure out a way to present the object in its "thisness" so that an observer would see *it*, not a meaning a human being assigned to it, not some use it could be put to. That is a lot harder than it may sound, for we are so used to putting our stamp on nature—as in the case of the "educational" soundtrack for *Hands of Maria*.

The next session our classroom became a gallery. We went around having a look at a leaf, air, a wad of chewing gum, a hair, a human being one student grabbed at random and persuaded to be his piece of art. One student had embedded a piece of gravel in a globe of resin on a pedestal of marble. It was beautiful, a pebble brought from anonymity into the jewel-like state of being it had always had, much like the perfectly preserved creatures caught in midaction millions of years ago in globes of amber. "The universe is illuminated by the beam of attention." There were mobiles, framed objects, jewel boxes, and so on. One piece of bark had become a pendant on a silver chain. There were funny displays and lots that missed the mark but were nonetheless remarkable in their new role. The assignment was for noninterventionist art, but we gladly accepted what we got. If you ask for ice cream and someone brings you a steak, I say, "Eat it." The artist, after all, was the real center of all our work, and the art revealed the artist as much as the artist unmasked the object. We saw each other more vividly: "So this is what's going on in Mavis Autry!" (I always participated in assignments, whatever they were. How else can one know what it's like to carry out these tasks? Besides, I wanted in on the fun.)

Next, I asked the students to do with words what they had tried to do physically. By framing the object one way or another, they had illuminated it. We hoped the unobtrusive artist had tricked us into seeing the object directly, without the filter of mind, not an object that was a "flower" but a nonverbal "whatsis" with its own unique characteristics that one simply witnessed—without intention. Now, could we use words to do that, to draw attention to this particular petaled instance of the universe? The next job was to give the art a title. That is a tough assignment. We didn't want to call attention to the cleverness of the artist. The art would be in the artist being invisible—like God!

One student had framed a paper clip, a toothpick, and a dust ball. He titled it "Things." Another had mounted a clear plastic cube with the lid off. It was titled "Air." The human being was titled "Michael." He stood on a little platform and the title was carefully fixed to the platform, as for a piece of sculpture in an art gallery.

Some titles worked and fulfilled the assignment brilliantly. Most no doubt didn't. But the failures revealed the role of language in human interaction with life probably more vividly than did the "successful" labels. But that led to what labeling can do in the hands of an artist. For example, what would happen to the sculpture if it was labeled "Dust" instead of "Michael"? What if you presented a frame only and titled it "Nothing" or "All"? There were all sorts of implications for students of language, metaphor, and poetry. One variation was to create a haiku for the object—like Onitsura's "Birds have two legs." What if you put *that* poem or one like it right next to the pebble in the globe of resin so that people would realize the poem was intended to go with the pebble?

There are all sorts of tangents. You can wake up the dead metaphors in words and phrases, like *daisy*, for example: day's eye, eye of the day, the sun. Or you can do like Sister Corita and make ordinary expressions metaphoric by reframing them. She made you pay attention to "Wonder Bread" by putting the wrapping on a mobile cube, or woke up a passage from Thoreau by printing it next to a simple abstract watercolor. One striking painting was a childlike orange sun with a rectangle of magenta and a black semicircle. Next to that Corita wrote an expression from Goethe: "It is the property of true genius to disturb all settled ideas."

A slow walk can yield all that. It could certainly be the beginning of a class in poetry. It can be part of a course in how language works—and doesn't. In my skills class it was sufficient simply as a means of quieting the sensorium and damping down the chatterbox tape recording most people have going all the time. But what it really is is a lesson in taking time, in allowing all the time it takes to fondle an idea, an object, a biology specimen. We are in the business not of covering a subject but of uncovering it. My own experience is that that is the fastest way to get good at something. I can remember hurrying through course after course in upper-division schooling and having only a sketchy outline at the end. But an hour with "On My First Daughter" has informed my behavior ever since and in all sorts of directions no one could ever have imagined. Such is the power of an intense moment or something clearly seen and deeply felt.

There's No Hurry

Maybe gathering up the bric-a-brac of the campus might seem hard to justify in, say, an economics class, but some sort of slow walk through commerce would surely serve to focus students' minds more immediately on what's involved in the subject. Taking time is what it's all about. When my students slowed down, they said it seemed everyone else was practically running hither and thither. There was one exception. One student walking at half-speed encountered an old woman at the duck pond who was going along at that speed anyway. They had a nice walk together. They interfaced! A group of human beings who force us to slow down are so-called retarded people. Many of the ones I have known talked slowly, and if I wanted to communicate with them, I had to slow down my speech patterns to get into a rhythm with them. I would find myself quieting down. Their families and friends had the same experience. Far from finding these "slower" human beings a burden, they shared a lovely world of the now that most of us miss in our hurry getting from A to B.

I have seen artisans, too, accomplish much without seeming in any hurry. I remember Willy Adams, a cement worker, with measured, steady, effortless-looking motion mixing the concrete, shoveling, smoothing, and in the end: a piece of art. Willy hadn't even broken a sweat. Or the basket weaver in Baja quietly intertwining the reeds in the morning and still there in late afternoon with several fine baskets now beside him. And Maria Martinez and her pottery, of course. There is no hurry. We are not going anywhere. No doubt that is part of Fred Rogers's genius; he has such a calming effect on little kids—and grown-ups. So a component of the slow walk that I added was getting everyone to talk at a Mr. Rogers speed. People listen to each other and explain things calmly but don't try to make points or bludgeon each other with evidence. In fact, I found I gave much better directions for an activity if we did a calming exercise first and if we all had our eyes shut while I did the explaining.

I Came To

In one sense education is all about waking up. I remember Andrew Wyeth commenting on what happened to his sensibilities after the death of his father, N. C. Wyeth. Andrew had been a remarkable painter prior to his father's accident, but afterward, when the implications of that death—of mortality—struck him, he said, "I came to." There is seeing and seeing, and education, somehow, must unleash that power of witnessing unmasked this-ness. A simple act like deliberately walking slowly can bring us closer to that way of seeing. It's always right under our noses. We just have to take a look.

From Prosaic to Poetic

> Poetry is whatever I say it is, damn it!
> —Jeff Briggs, Student

Schools of education would benefit from "coming to." If anything affects the overall tone of endeavor it is switching from the prosaic to the poetic. All that that means is going for "an intense vision of the facts," as William Carlos Williams phrased it. He was talking about poetry, but any other way of approaching schooling is indeed torture. Education never has to be prosaic. Lesson planning can always be, "How can I arrange this next session in German (calculus, electronics, accounting) so that it is experienced intensely?" Thinking of it as finding the poetic mode is the key.

It can be direct or indirect. I often started class with a poem or a pithy aphorism—often something culled from a student's reflection—and we would either talk about it or simply let it serve to set us up for using our minds poetically. We used stories and anecdotes, too; in other words, literature: language used deliberately to unmask the ordinary. There is nothing to prevent literature from affecting all the curriculum, not just the liberal arts. They flow in and out of each other, and no chemistry class is complete without its being part of the joy of the mind. There are plenty of chemists who write beautifully about their subject. Loren Eiseley makes us realize what biology can be. Richard Feynman can make a layperson or a physicist realize the blinding beauty of quantum mechanics. Or Lewis Thomas, A. S. Eddington, Annie Dillard, Oliver Sacks, Colin Wilson, Gary Zukav. But it can also be W. C. Williams, John Updike, Gerard Manley Hopkins, John Donne, Robert Frost, Sharon Olds. There is no reason but sheer ignorance for separating the arts and sciences. Any thoughtful person knows they are all doing the same work: taking a good look.

When Rumi said, "Take down a musical instrument," it meant, *Get into the poetic mode. Don't try to do your work mechanically; it will be halting and awkward.* Why not music—and this includes verbal music—in every class? Give me one good reason. Why not stories and poems in financial planning? After all, what is such planning about if not the good life? And how good a life can it be if it is not poetic? Why not the "rare square root of minus one" in a class of American literature. Why wall out or wall in?

Ah, but there isn't time, some will say. The answer is it doesn't take more time. The time it takes to call roll—there are lots of ways that don't take up class time—could easily be replaced with a poem, a bit of music, a moment or two for relaxation. In our English classes students have introduced nonmathematicians to the fascinating world of base 12 or 8. There is wonder there. We have had laser demonstrations and listened to Mozart in the planetarium. It works both directions. The point is that we all learn better when our spirits are engaged. Educators need to keep in mind the way little kids imbue everything with their enthusiasm (*en*, in + *theos*, god). When students realize they are supposed to be fully involved, indeed are invited to be, and when the setting is clearly so disposed toward their spirits, remarkable transformations occur.

We used to have in-service meetings at DVC about bridging the disciplines, writing across the curriculum, and so on. But it's more than giving each other an occasional nod or once a semester having a guest poet in Biology 122. Music, dance, drawing, stories, and poetic language were the very essence of a normal life in tribal societies and still are in many cultures. The human being was—and is—an integrated person. It is a sadness that an institution would need in-service meetings to discuss something so obvious. Many societies teach their cultural heritage, their values, and their science through the arts, although they don't call them that. "We have no art. We do everything as well as possible." It is perfectly possible to teach poetically in a technocracy, too. In fact, it is more crucial than ever. But it isn't really the poems or stories or music as much as a change in approach and attitude. It always comes back to the philosophy of the institution and of the teacher: What, fundamentally, are we trying to do? Of course, we are studying physics, romanticism, or statistics, but it is always human beings who are doing this studying. We can never forget that. That does not mean the topic will suffer. On the contrary, it will be seen more clearly and more intensely. You can bet on it.

Reflections

One other way to stimulate a poetic or artistic experience of one's studies is to go home and think about it. Once I realized that I never taught any subject without asking students to write their reflections after every session. The idea was to keep our minds engaged in what we were doing and on the effect of our investigations on our schematics of reality. These were not really logs or journals but rather records of the *feel* of the experience, the emotive aspect, the spirit of it. I wanted to make sure the "intense vision of the facts" was a regular part of our thinking. It seems most classes are all about facts—even theories of criticism become the "facts" of criticism—but that is wrong. Seeing those "facts" clearly and intensely is what education really is. So math is incomplete without reflections that work up the *implications* of relationships observed. And so it is in anatomy or electronics. That's where all the value lies: in what we make of it all.

It wouldn't hurt to experiment in the sciences and indeed in all the curriculum with daily reflections of what went on at school each day and of the connections of those discoveries with everything else in a student's life, including love life, work, and family life. After all, it is all one thing going on, realizing life "every, every minute." Why reserve it for only saints and poets?

It isn't an accumulation of experience and information that makes an educated person but what one can do with those bits and pieces. Every course in every discipline should be practice in resuscitating dead metaphors. There is no point in being able to find the hypotenuse if you can't have a good time doing it. School is about *enjoying* the life of the mind. Education is nothing more or less than experiencing life poetically.

**Helen Bids Farewell
to Her Daughter Hermione**

*There is time
before I go
to mention the lily flowering
by the door—
how, when divided,
it multiplies.
I'm speaking now
of love.*

*There is time
to tell you
the only story I know:
a youth sets out,
a man or a woman returns,
the rest is simply incident
or weather*

*and yet what storms
I could describe
swirling
in every thumbprint.*

—Linda Pastan

23

Teaching Poetry
The Sound of Water

Nature is not as natural as it looks.
—A. S. Eddington

In the realm of language only poetry teaches. Becoming educated is learning how to use language poetically. *Remembering* how is more accurate, since we were all pretty good at it to begin with and forgot as we regressed into the world of prose. Not everybody regresses, of course. For those who do not forget, schooling could be simply the continuing development of the poetic faculty. If classes are taught poetically the maturing mind just goes on with its work. As the word is described in this book, *poetry* is simply using language with awareness of its metaphoric nature. If a message appears to be prose, the job is to bring it alive and turn it into a *poem*, an intense experience of the words, sentences, and paragraphs. Teaching and learning poetically is nothing more or less than making words count.

To do its job properly, education has to be artistic, poetic. Since the entire curriculum is linguistic, schooling is wordplay, pure and simple. Wordplay is essentially a did-you-notice game, like noticing what's there in a Brueghel painting or a mandala or a leaf or in the word *poem*. The business of any classroom is to take what's on the table and fiddle with it until it comes alive in every student. Then the teacher can go home and have tea. There's no reason this vivacity can't be the *lingua franca* of any discipline. Don't tell me it's not there in chemistry, in physics, in economics. There is spirit, vitality, and life in every subject in a curriculum. It is criminal to present the objects we look upon as dead things. It is counterproductive; we are here to *lead forth*—from nonentity into being, not to embalm.

If we approach schooling poetically all the time in every discipline, an appreciation of poetry will be as natural as breathing, for indeed using language with regard for its metaphoric power *is* natural. It doesn't make sense *(make sense!)* to conduct classes without engaging the whole being. When we do, of course, we are in the province of poetry. So that should be going on all the time, simply because it is the only way to teach effectively. It is what we do when we set the stage for the spirit embedded in *cosine* to meld with the spirit in a student-witness. Only then has that student learned. Another way to put it is to say that person "gets it." One can explain the idea of the cosine, but that is vastly different from *experiencing* the idea of the cosine. Students who have lived a poetic life will understand that their homework is to release the poem in a concept of economics, for that is the only way it can be understood. That concept came into being as a metaphoric insight in the mind of some poetic economist.* It had to have been an exciting discovery. It has to be experienced in the same way by anyone else who wishes to grasp it. Well, maybe not "grasp" it, maybe just take it gently by the hand and walk with it for a while.

Something else that happens in artistically conducted classes is that poems that actually look like poems spring up all over the place. Teachers can't help jotting them on the chalkboard. Ideas come to us as metaphors, and if we are clued in, we recognize what's going on and transcribe the experience in its pure form. So we get aphorisms, turns of phrase, haiku, rhymed couplets—all sorts of illuminating language. It is natural to read to the class a poem you ran across somewhere that bears on what you happen to be doing together. Often the poem is hidden in the prose, and the writer didn't realize it. But *you* did, so you extract it and put it at the top of the math assignment. You begin to talk more metaphorically, you become more tuned in to the import of what just popped out of your mouth, and you see that *that's* the way to say it, that the poetic way will come across beautifully, whereas the prosaic way won't. You begin class with a few lines just to warm things up or set the tone or focus on what's up for the day. You end with a punch line.

Once they see what's going on and that it's all right not to squeeze the juice out of ideas, students will follow suit. Their daily reflections in physics

---

*Who probably came in the kitchen and told his spouse all about it, and she probably said, "So what good is it? What can you use it for?" "I dunno. It's just fun. See, isn't it neat?!" The spouse, of course, is the utilitarian school system.

or computer science will be studded with poetic turns of phrase. Many will actually set words on the page *as* poems. They will jot unsolicited poetic stuff on the chalkboard, too, either their own or things they ran across, because the natural way to think about and express ideas is metaphorically.

In an institution committed to artistic teaching, language used with awareness of its educational power is the milieu in which learning goes forward. It is the language of the laboratory and of the classroom. So when they run across Bashō's

> *Old pond—*
> *frog plops in—*
> *water sound*

they get it immediately. They will have been thoroughly used to right-brained processes and will not have to be "introduced" to poetry, for poetry is the ground of thought.

Of course, I am talking about how it could be, not how most schooling goes. Only a handful of our students have studied in such an environment. Most shy away from anything that even looks like a poem. They associate school with dreary discourse and effortful, sweaty memorization and test taking. But they do live poetic lives outside the classroom. Even though school is anything but poetic for most students, they do exercise their natural bent for metaphor all over the place: reggae, rap, ads, lyrics, slang, hairstyle, perfume, vanity license plates, headlines, slogans, logos, body language, puns, put-downs, the works. Wouldn't they be shocked to see it all labeled *poetry*, for that indeed is the world they live in (the world we all live in), a world of allusion, rhyme, rhythm, alliteration, far- and near-fetched associations, hyperbole, irony, paradox.

But kids have learned to leave these jewels outside the classroom door. They are so used to dusty institutional language that they become confused at the mention of poetry. Neither they nor the explainers see the connection with their own lives, and poetry is "taught" out of context as just one more subject to be memorized and tested. Isn't that bizarre? The general result of schooling for most kids in this country is that they haven't written a poem since elementary school, think poetry has no practical connection with their daily lives, and don't like it very much. I doubt that more than four or five of my new students each semester knew they were poets and lived poetic lives.

But education need not be prosaic, and restoring the right-brained aspect of thinking is easy—once one accepts the idea. Most of this book can be taken as a primer on how to get whole-brained thinking into the daily give and take of all classes. Essentially, it is a matter of *allowing* artistic thought into the class. As I have said, humans have that orientation already; we teachers just need to get out of the way.

In general, then, poetry is integral and basic to the whole curriculum of any institution and the vehicle through which we comprehend our world. As I was writing this I read that Nobel Poet Joseph Brodsky had died. He wrote, "Poetry is perhaps the only insurance we've got against the vulgarity of the human heart." But I would say the heart is OK and that poetry is a way to hack through the shell of ice that surrounds it, as another writer put it. Frost said a good poem is a wound from which one never recovers. Brodsky thought books of poetry should be sold in supermarkets and left in hotel rooms. Peets or Starbucks coffee shops ought to offer packets of short verses along with the other condiments. For poetry is no more sacred than our morning tea, witnessed. It is living our lives as we go along, just your run-of-the-mill miracle. We have to keep that in mind lest we remove it from daily life and treat it as something out of the reach of ordinary people.

How to teach poetry? Just do it. Allow it. Respond to it. Have fun with it. Enjoy it. Don't make a big deal out of it. Treat it as a normal dimension of the learning environment. For God's sake, don't make a religious rite out of it.* After all, it is not something to be added to the curriculum. It is *how* we learn. It is not so much books of verse as it is whole-brained thinking. If we are not thinking poetically, we are not thinking. Teachers who investigate their own thinking processes will know this and will teach accordingly—unless they *enjoy* drudgery.

Poetry as a Subject

Since language and its metaphoric component are inseparable, poetry is the province of all disciplines, and students will develop their poetic faculties as they go about their business, learning anatomy, geology, music theory. But poetry can be a subject in its own right, too, like any other. It is ordinary language, used in its fullness, but it is also an art form like music, dance, or sculpture. When someone takes linguistic elements like words, punctuation, and structure and fashions them deliberately, it is like a painter selecting pigments, arranging shapes, deciding what to leave out and what to include. This art can be explored directly. If poetry is taught poetically, immersion for a

---

*Orson Welles speaking to college students: "In any work of art," he begins—then immediately corrects himself. "What am I saying? In any movie..."

whole semester or two or three or four—what the hell, forever, for that matter—can be a ripe plum or wild strawberries for the soul. After all, it is the largess of what's there that we're talking about. If we treat life as mere existence, we are impoverished. A course in poetry can bring life close to the eye and heart. All education is for that purpose, of course, but exploring poetry is a way of going at it directly.

When I wanted to explore poetry as a subject, I sometimes started out by asking the kids if the note I had left for my wife on the refrigerator door was a poem. I wrote it out on the board:

> Dear Ruth,
> This is just to say I have eaten the plums that were in
> the refrigerator and which you were probably saving
> for breakfast. Forgive me. They were delicious,
> so sweet and so cold. Love, Clark

Ha! "No, no, no," most of the students would say, "Damned poor, Clark. Forget it."

"Well, gee. I thought maybe . . . How about if I set it up like this?" Then I would write it out this way:

> Dear Ruth,
>
> *THIS IS JUST TO SAY*
>
> *I have eaten*
> *the plums*
> *that were in*
> *the icebox*
>
> *and which*
> *you were probably*
> *saving*
> *for breakfast*
>
> *Forgive me*
> *they were delicious*
> *so sweet*
> *and so cold**
>
> Love, Clark

---

*English teachers will recognize this as a William Carlos Williams poem, but I didn't bring that up until later on.

"How come you changed it to 'icebox'"?

"Oh, I thought it might make it seem less technological. Don't you think it fits in better?"

Actually, the poem was written when boxes that cooled things were called iceboxes. That could come out later. But, see, almost the first thing out of the hat was attention to word choice and the effect a word can have in a message. Pretty good, eh, teaching without teaching, just having fun? The students would get right into it, debating whether it was a "nice" message or just a con to sucker Ruth into accepting my theft of her plums.

"'Forgive me'—give me a break!"

"Well, don't you think someone who appreciates the plums, 'so sweet and so cold,' *should* eat them? It didn't kill Ruth, did it? And I really liked those plums right then and there. If you were Ruth, wouldn't you be glad someone you loved got that pleasure?"

And so on, back and forth. They would try out different words, adding some, taking some away.

"Why did you put 'This is just to say' in there? Isn't that just extra stuff?" "Why capitalize 'Forgive' and nothing else?" "Why set up the sentences on the page the way you did?" And so it went, for a good while, half an hour or so. A good poem, painting, or melody is worth at least that much attention. (This particular poem has informed my own vision of the world for forty years.) The kids were enjoying straightening me out and inquiring into my relationship with Ruth. But underneath the playfulness, we were also paying close attention to those words, their nuances and impact. What I enjoyed most, I think, is that they were asking the questions, not me. Without any prompting they also began to generalize on the prior claim of the moment at the expense of propriety, of an "intense vision of plums."

By the time we finished we all had that poem on our nerve endings. And as we fiddled with it, it came into vivid relief. We were getting "an intense vision" of the poem itself. Lines from the poem would crop up from then on in reflections and discussions. A good number knew it by heart. All the while we were still on the original question: Was that "note" really a poem? Did layout on the page help make it one? Punctuation, word choice? Did you have to use special language? If so, what made a word special? I knew we were on target when a student commented on her way out the door, "the plum was delicious today."

Ulteriority

With all classroom activities, explorations, investigations, and experiments, the object is to release the spirit stored in the metaphor, be that metaphor a theory, a painting, a torque wrench, a poem. Delight in the fullness of what's there, the pleasure in finding things out, is a good day's work. These adventures may have useful by-products. One might get really good at adding, at walking a tightwire, at figuring out a computer program, at using carpentry tools. But these skills, though not irrelevant, are not the focus. We don't ask students to write so that they will punctuate and spell correctly; they write to get their spirits *intact* into a physical form. We punctuate "correctly" so that our spirits *do* make it into the physical. We do not examine poetry so that students will be knowledgeable and conversant *about* poetry. Each class is an experience *of* poetry, a Good Thing in itself. My experience is that information about prosody is best gathered incidentally along the way. Get at the heart and nose in a Rumi poem, and you will have a hard time stopping students from reading all about him in the introduction of the book. You don't have to assign it. That would only spoil things, just about kill them, in fact.*

But, if it mattered, such a workout every day does net a goodly body of information over time. What's more, this knowledge is not merely *about* the art but becomes part of the awareness with which one walks the tightwire of the next poem. It will be hard for some to accept, but there will be little uniformity. Students will have different slants on the shared journey, and the information gathered will be determined by their own needs. A teacher has no choice but to embrace this diversity. Indeed, it would be sad if everyone's private bookshelf contained the same volumes.

The Poem Itself

But teachers have to keep their eyes on the ball. It is so easy to forget the poem itself. A poem is not a lesson; it is an experience—*in each person interacting with it*. It is spirit in matter. The work of the class is to tease it out, one way or another. If a poetry course isn't spine-tingling, eye-popping, what's the point? But most classes I am aware of are evaluative, judgmental: "Here is

---

*An unobtrusive measure of how the class is doing is to observe how often students will say, "Oh, I'll bet that's Hopkins [or Olds, Sakaki, Frost, Auden, Jonson]," and be right. When that starts happening, you know *somebody's* heart's on fire.

what is good about this poem. Here are its shortcomings. Notice the sprung rhythms; notice this feminine rhyme. See the assonance here? This is what makes poem A better than poem B." If there is any one thing separating a poem from a reader or listener, it can probably be traced to such a left-brained approach. That is why theory must follow experience. Criticism or theory will mean little unless one is a practicing poet; that is, we have to recognize our own creative, poetic, artistic nature and know that only through our art can we really acquire or transmit the essence, the spirit, in any communiqué—or even examine the content of our own minds. It ain't in no book.

There is another reason for students of poetry making their own poems along the way. It is the same effect that making mandalas has on one's viewing of paintings in a gallery. In both cases the observer is much more inclined to let the work speak in its own terms rather than impose preconditions on it. If one has made a mandala, done a few watercolors, or attempted anything in the plastic arts, there is a natural curiosity to examine what someone else has done and notice how it was put together. While we are taking a closer look, the art catches us off guard and speaks directly to our minds and spirits. When students look at the variety and imagination of their mandalas mounted on a wall, I sometimes ask, "How shall we look at these? Shall we decide which ones are best, which one fulfilled the assignment best?" Universally they will say, "Oh, no! Each one is unique. Each one is special." "How shall we look at them, then?" "Don't mess with them. Just see what's there."

The same thing happens with poems. We might display seventy haiku encapsulating the essence of a session. Students go around the room reading them and chatting about them with each other. "Shall we evaluate these?" "No, no. Let's enjoy all the different ways people experienced what we did together." Once they see that each creation has its own gestalt, it's easy to segue to poems they find in books. The tendency to prejudge doesn't even come up. They recognize kindred spirits, doing the same things they do, according to their own experience and their own souls. They realize the game is to see it as the artist sees it.

Is This a Poem?

There are all sorts of ways to pay attention to a poem. Sometimes I would ask the students to take a slow walk and see if there might be any poems lying around out there. Is a poem necessarily verbal? What makes something a poem? Sometimes they would be asked to bring one back to class. Sometimes, after we had experienced a found object as best we could, I would ask them to take a crack at capturing the essence of their experience verbally. Just for a level playing field, occasionally I would ask them to confine their effort to three lines of five, seven, and five syllables. I didn't call these haiku, but usually someone would. Writing haiku wasn't the point, of course. Using the third eye was.

I remember leaving some blanks in Dylan Thomas's poem "The Force That Through the Green _____ Drives the Flower" and providing four choices for each blank. For example, what was the effect of *stem, plant, fuse,* or *sleeve* in the blank in the title line above? Groups worked through the blanks and read their versions of the poem to the class and commented on the various effects. They noticed that together the choices made a pattern and that the words had to mesh together for an overall effect. One couldn't toss things in haphazardly without getting a harebrained result. Sometimes a group would do that deliberately just to see how silly they could make it. Finally, we read Thomas's own version. This was all done playfully. I didn't insist that Thomas's version was the best. That would have killed the spirit of our investigation. What they did see was that his choices reflected his own nature and his own view of life. Only he knew if the poem matched his vision. If it did it was a success. Their interest was in getting the feel of what he did do, not what he should have done. What he "should have done" was their own poem, not his. That game worked out fairly well. They took a good look at Thomas's poem, but they also got a workout in prosody.

We turned poems upside down, moved verses around, changed words just to see the effect, tried reading them out loud with different emphasis. We were sacrilegious and disreputable, but we were never smug. We were just trying to see how things worked. And we always tried to read the poem the way we hoped the poet would have wanted us to. Sooner or later, there would be at least one serious reading out loud of the poem we were fiddling with. During these weeks more and more students were emboldened to read their own poems out loud. Gradually there emerged an outpouring of spirit that seemed to have been yearning to go public. All it took was total immersion. I knew the nonconscious mind would fit everything together, and students would get the hang of it effortlessly.

Sometimes, when we started a class with music and relaxation, I would read a short poem, without comment, while everyone's eyes were still closed. Or if something we were doing reminded me of a poem or some lines from one, I would put it on the board or just say it. Sometimes I would preface some activity with a poem that seemed to illuminate what we were doing. If someone's words seemed particularly vivid, I would repeat them out loud to highlight them. One-liners were always popping up, and we would acknowledge them. If someone out of awareness wrote something in a reflection I found arresting, I might pull it out, type it up as a poem, and staple the poem to the entry so that the student would realize the impact of those words. When a poem appeared in the middle of an entry, I would ask the student to read it out loud. Often I would ask everyone to dream up a punch line for the work we had done together, or give the experience a title, or capture it all in seventeen syllables.

Often by the time I got to class, the chalkboard would already be decorated with poems, either ones they themselves had created or ones they had discovered in their travels around the planet: from billboards, the lyrics of songs, newspaper items, milk cartons, from poets they had discovered on their own. The next thing I knew, they were passing poetry books back and forth. We were making poems or reading them all the time.

One reason I suspect so many people think they are not poetic and that poetry is not for them is that it seems like poets are not like the rest of us. Their work seems inaccessible, obscure, incomprehensible. Where does one start? But when they make their own poems, when poetry is seen to be everywhere, in all sorts of guises—playful, somber, silly, devastating—it ceases to be intimidating.

Foreground or Background

When poetry moves into the foreground, students who have had such ongoing experience as I have described will be well positioned to examine poems made on purpose. A good learning environment is poetic, metaphoric, anyway. That's the way the mind works. Whole-brained thinking is simply the way business is conducted. So poetic thinking is, or ought to be, involved in everything that goes on in schools, and the approach in a poetry class would be the same as for any other investigation. After all, we are all alchemists, attempting to turn base metal into gold. But that is a metaphor: We ourselves are that base metal—which the poem illuminates and reveals to be precious metal.

When we have such alchemists in our classes, it is easy to look at a poem with them. They want the same thing the teacher does, an experience that will change their lives. John Wheatcroft's approach in my class at Bucknell in 1956 is still the best: A clear reading of the poem out loud, an illuminating examination by the students of what's there, and at the end another reading out loud. I know of poetry classes in which students rarely *hear* a poem. In elementary schools a common denominator among kids who enjoy reading is that they were read to. That's all it takes. They don't have to be convinced. They know very well what's in it for them. It's the same with poetry. Students who hear lots of poetry need no persuasion. They are primed. Without even trying they find themselves able to interface with e. e. cummings, Ferlinghetti, Jeffers, Patchen, Neruda. No sweat. All a teacher has to do is keep the party going.

Messing Around

The process is the same as for any other subject: Mess around with it until you catch on. In my skills book I call this "The Mess-Around Theory of Education." To begin with, something comes to our attention, for whatever reason, and we decide to get to know it, understand it, master it, or skip it. Then follows a series of passes, and our own natures dictate what goes on, when, how long, and so forth. Sometimes we begin just by holding it to the light and turning it this way and that. We might set it down and never look at it again. Or we might come back later and look some more. We might zoom in and notice details. We might draw it or weigh it or unscrew it. We might make lists or focus on just one part. Throughout, we will be pulling back for an overview and zooming in from another angle. We have all sorts of tools for getting to know the world, and we choose the best ones for the job. Learning styles vary. Some people are essentially verbal, some visual, some tactile; some like to hear it. In a workshop, room has to be made for different approaches.

What is really going on is that the two hemispheres of the brain are making friends. The conscious part is gathering and sorting, preparing the setting. Meanwhile the nonconscious, metaphoric side is creating meaning, compressing, making a *poem*. At some point it downloads a printout to the conscious mind. That's why a learner has to be used to wordplay. Otherwise a perfectly wonderful "answer" might pop into the conscious mind, but it won't be recognized. When the message arrives, we don't want to miss it.

24

The Idea of a College
Out Looking for Trouble

We are all born searching for heaven. We can define it in many ways: outer space, human worthiness, enlightenment, and so on. The search for higher realms, the outer limits, as it were, is the strongest and most vital impulse of all.
—Henry Miller

In 1984 our college was looking for a new president. The editors of our staff journal asked us to send in qualities we would like to see in our next boss. I had a whole bunch of pet ideas I wanted to get off my chest, so I wrote the article that appears below. It focused on DVC, but I think it can be taken generally as well.

> ### The Idea of a College
>
> List the qualities of our next president? No thanks. Some capricious god might grant my wishes. It's happened before. An old lady once told me you never know a man till you shut doors with him. It cuts both ways. We'll be a learning experience for whoever gets stuck with us, won't we?
>
> Meanwhile, let's have some action. Let's give the new president a little present: Our Ten-Year Plan. By 1994,
>
> • Let's build dorms for a thousand students. Let's establish a hotel-management program to staff it. You'll love the effect a resident student group will have on our campus community. Besides, it's time we kick the county slumlords in the teeth. I know kids who pay $350 a month to live in a closet—

standing up. To make sure the dorms get built, we'll force Sue Nurock to chair the committee. [Sue was a family-life teacher who had almost single handedly caused a lovely child-care center to appear on our campus. Little kids could be cared for in this nurturing environment while their moms or dads took classes with us.]

• Let's finally have that staff clubhouse. Let's design and build it with our own hands. We've got staff here who are realtors, accountants, lawyers, craftsmen, architects. Sell shares. Call Milo Minderbinder.

• Yeah, and how about that tea garden we haven't put in yet at the base of the planetarium facing Mt. Diablo? Diablo ain't Fuji, but it will serve. Let's let students design, build, and staff it. Let's let our new president fend off the trade unions and contractors.

• More to the point, let's turn the whole college into a laboratory school. Let's make experimentation our *modus operandi*, try out stuff, mess around, get into hot water. *Let's question our assumptions.* Turn things upside down and get a new viewpoint. Get some young practice teachers in here. Let our journalism classes publish our findings.

• Let's get civilized. Start classes at 8:30. But let early birds start at 7:30, if they want. [The college actually did pick up on varying the hours. We got Friday afternoon and evening classes, Saturday classes, compressed classes, all sorts of accommodations.]

• How about a semester without books? Let's teach English composition in the fourth semester. Let's not teach it at all for a while and see what we discover.

• How about spreading the PE facilities all over campus—and have the nearest parking lot at Sun Valley [a shopping mall about a mile away]? While we're at it, let's have music, painting, and performing arts mixed in with everything else, too.

• Let's try out mastery education a couple of years. Everybody keeps plugging away until he/she makes it. What say we suspend short-answer tests and essay tests for a couple of semesters? Figure out some other way to measure progress.

Gee, this is fun. OK, some more:

• Let's call together our teachers of design, engineering, psychology, and so on and figure out how to redesign classrooms. How come desks are all the same color, shape, and size? How come they are so austere? What colors make people learn easier?

• How about our own radio and TV broadcasting stations? Let's make our own TV courses. Let's read *Cat's Cradle* on the radio.

- For God's sake, can't we do something human to our cafeteria? If we can't think up anything on our own, send someone over to Foothill [a nearby community college] and Stanford and *plagiarize*.
- While we're over there, let's pirate the best part of DeAnza's [another community college] hotsy totsy community service programs and conference series. Let's make Gerard Hurley stick around and run the whole program—and give him some decent funding for the film program while we're at it. [When I arrived at DVC in 1963, Gerard had in place the best film-appreciation program of just about any college in the country, long before film had become generally accepted as an art form.]
- We could lock every tenured teacher in solitary confinement until he or she comes up with an unassailable personally crafted philosophy of teaching—one worth dying for.
- Let's have no professional administrators: three-year terms for deans. Let them also teach. Try it out and see what happens. How about a president who also teaches?

That's starters. I admit maybe one or two of these ideas might not work. But you never know. Anyway, I'm sure of one thing: Even if every one of these ideas bombed, we would learn tons of things about teaching we're only guessing about now.

And it sure as hell beats gabbing about IRAs and the STRS [State Teachers retirement System]. Right?

Oh, well. 1994 came and went. That new president was at the college twelve years and is retired now, and the institution grinds on. I'm sure most of my readers thought I was kidding in that article, but bits and pieces of most of the ideas had been tried successfully here and there around the globe. I don't know of any school that put them all together in one package. But wouldn't it be something to treat an entire college as a learning laboratory? It wouldn't even be risky. There is plenty of research that confirms, by almost any measure one would care to use, the superiority of innovative programs—of almost any sort—over traditional curricula.*

---

*See the March 1977 *Phi Delta Kappan* article "Startling/Disturbing Research on School Program Effectiveness" by Wayne Jennings and Joe Nathan. It is startling and disturbing.

25

Earth Probe
Synthesis

Tell me, good Brutus, can you see your face?
No, Cassius; for the eye sees not itself
But by reflection, by some other things.
—William Shakespeare

Eno could see himself in no mirror, however brightly polished; no words could define him, however cunningly shaped and arranged. Though he knew that a reflection referred to something that was Eno, it was also *not* him at all. Whatever he said he was, he was, and yet he wasn't at all. *What, who, when* was he? Was it really he who asked these questions? Was there even a question to ask? Propelled forward as he was, was there time to ask a question? WHAT WAS GOING ON?

Suddenly he emerged on a strange, totally unfamiliar planet, an Energy and Atom Recycler through Temporal Holography ("Earth"), knowing neither who he was nor how he got there. Had some angry god banished him to this chaos? Had he been selected as a special intelligence agent to probe this alien soil light-years from home, to somehow master it and return with his cache to the data banks of a nonphysical world he could not at present even remember? Nothing made sense. Sense itself did not make sense. Sense had something to do with stimuli and his responses, and, out of awareness, he grasped that he was equipped with nerve endings that were nothing more than tools he was using to collect stimuli and figure out this puzzle. He knew that nerve endings themselves were *not* Eno. And yet, perhaps... If he *had* been sent to probe this world, to study and to understand it truly, then naturally he could not "know" it merely by observing. His intelligence was not specialized to observe in the first place. If there were beings in this planet, he would have to adapt his intelligence to something approximating the tools they presumably possessed. To understand them, he would have to be one of them—completely; he must not even know that he was a spy. Possibly those who sent him might monitor the process, perhaps tag him somehow so that they could retrieve him at the optimum moment. But tagging would not really be necessary because he would always be obvious to his own kind in their own structuring system.

Possibly, then, Eno's identity was out in the open, but neither the target race nor he himself were capable of sensing it, as though they were tuned to a radio frequency that couldn't pick him up even though his waves were all about them. He thus might penetrate the target race, taking on more and more of their characteristics until the crucial moment when he would be yanked home for analysis. But that was only one of the limitless possibilities of the riddle of his essence.

Eno was dimensionless. He did not belong to a place. He did not belong to a time. He had no length, no breadth, no thickness. Any form he achieved might seem to alter, but Eno himself always had been and always would be. He had entered this world through a crack in the time shield. One moment he was nowhere and the next he was physical, as though someone had twisted a kaleidoscope and Eno was the image produced. It was not so much a matter of travel as it was a matter of coming into focus or of being translated to another radio frequency. Suddenly, so it seemed, there was a new bias toward form and structure with a thrust toward definition, toward becoming finite. This urgency to define necessitated senses. He began specializing his nerve endings and developed a complete sensorium. Through its agency he became, or seemed to become, concrete. Senses were a means of differentiating, of separating, of setting up distinctions, billions of them, every particle separated from every other by a sensing structure whose nature it was to see isolates. This planet existed through differentiation ("this is different from that"), through the emergence of things, the separating of one thing from another—and putting them together as well! Eno was an emergencee, emerging from the galactic "mother" through the uterus of what his senses identified as the "human" form.

Earth Probe **297**

Immediately, he began his research. Because he did not even know he was a spy, he investigated automatically, to begin with. He sharpened his Early Yield External Sensors ("eyes"). Out of the gray blur, he forced entities to emerge, identifiable separations from the vast general jumble. From a few trifling particulars, he deduced general laws. Falling was dangerous. Eating was desirable. These were nerve-ending "concepts" felt but not intellectually known. He identified a nippled nutrient sack and grew himself flesh and bones, perfect camouflage for a dimensionless fellow. He became one with time and space. Every planet day new floods of data poured into his Master Integrator of Nervous Data ("mind"), where he automatically began to create a time-space first approximation of his surroundings, his own Boundary Of Dimensional Yin-yang ("body") being part of the structure. And each dis...covery hid him from himself more and more completely! Nonentity had merged with entity. The investigation had begun, and no one suspected a thing. Birth was so ordinary, just another emergencee.

For Eno the validity of the parts of the sensorium (nose, taste buds, fingertips) was unquestioned. That which worked was true. If one thing failed, he tried another and didn't think about how real or "true" it was. Only that which promoted his own toehold on the planet was important. Out of the sensorium grew a knowledge of the Synthesis of the Entire Life Force ("self"). He had to be totally "self"ish or become overwhelmed by the great wash of "things" pressing against the flimsy dikes of his new flesh. Eno was not conscious of the dangers. His flesh took charge, touched, and assimilated. He did not know this knowledge, this "nourishment," was his lifeline. His body did the work, and for him it was child's play! Literally. He laughed. He fondled, tasted, smelled, played constantly with sounds he could make with his tongue, air, oral cavities. He developed depth perception. He sensed warmth and burning, coolness and the pain of ice. Locomotion became vital. He grew himself "muscles" and forced himself to master Articulated Regulators of Manipulatory Skill ("arms") and Locomotor Extensions against Gravitational Supremacy ("legs"). He had become some thing, an entity, but his mind did not know it.

If there *were* watchers, they would have known the immensity of the experiment. The spy Eno was embarked on frighteningly dangerous reconnaissance *in complete ignorance*. He was hypnotized by the reality of appearance. Each planet day it appeared that he brushed aside another veil and disclosed more and more facets of this shimmering planet. It was all a matter of interstices, of course, intersections of electromagnetic force fields, but within the perception centers of this alien structure (his body) appearance was the only reality. Finally, in the third year of his new time sense, Eno made one of the most startling of his discoveries: his *own* identity. He had been busy dis...covering things out there; he now dis...covered his self. "I am!" he thought. This discovery launched him toward the next leg of his journey.

During the first stage of his planetary probe, when his senses automatically fondled the world so that he "knew" it on his nerve endings, Eno's experiments with sound had paid off in a magical assortment of talismans, Wave Ordinates Revealing Dharma Signs ("words") and "concepts" capable of giving him balance on this slippery sensate flow, a surfboard for riding out the waves. He could shape air and call nourishment to his lips for energy replenishment. He began to capture the world in this symbolic network. He mastered the linguistic code nearest at hand. The power it gave him over his perceived world was amazing. He spent most of his waking hours playing with and perfecting this new instrument. One network of intersecting concepts he identified as his *self*. That bundle of ideas had been given the code name *Robert*, but of course that referred only to the space-time mask Eno wore. *Robert* referred to the energy system of bones and kidneys, nose and fingernails. To *be* was to be *physical*. Was that the solution to his identity? Was Eno really physical? When he became *defined*, when he became *Robert*, did he cease to be Eno? Did nonentity cease when entity emerged? Were being and nonbeing one thing?

His parts were at once instruments for knowing reality and reality itself. For one could not *be* without the other. This new magical "language" was a probe for exploring, but it created that which was explored as well. The tool shaped the craftsman. Just as his new "eyes" had filtered the continuum of color and presented his mind a "reality" of only one sector of the spectrum, what he perceived through the language tool was limited *by* the tool. Language pinpointed the intersection of things, showed where the connections were, but it also determined what would be considered to intersect. It was a structure system that gave him a handhold on the planet, but was it *the* planet, or were there many planets superimposed on each other? If Eno had entered the planet as a tree, it would have been tree "reality" he would have experienced: different sensors, different filtering, different planet. What was *really* going on?

During his eighth planet year, Eno learned how to use *"What if . . . ?"* Till then he had seen directly; *he* was the center, and everything connected at that center. Now he discovered how to *imagine* himself seeing from locations other than the one on which he actually stood. That gave him tremendous leverage, for he could now play with the world mentally as he had been obliged to do physically in his earlier stage. First he had known the world physically; then, through language, he could say, "This *is* . . ." Now he could say, "What if . . . ?" He found that he did not have to touch things to experience them. He could look at the top of a cube and imagine its other faces, then determine how many sides there were without touching the cube. Certain misspent adventures with associates enabled him to see the five dots on top of a die and figure out that two dots would likely be on the bottom. Now he could *imagine* how something would be, how it would feel, by letting his mental fingers explore it. His major experiments now were mental. He could sit still and carry out the same work that his sensorium had had to do before. He began to use his body in a new way, to check, validate his imaginings. "If this happens, and this happens, then I'll bet this would be the result." He would then test it physically. Naturally, during this period, his autostructure (his body) sustained damage. One of his ARMs fractured at peak stress when he tested his balance theory on a unicycle. His digital manipulators sustained burns, cuts, bruises, and abrasions during his probes of wood, metal, clay, and stone. He sent repair cells to the affected areas, oxidized the raw surfaces, grew Superficial Coverings of Abrasions and Blemishes ("scabs") and went on developing his mental grasp of the physical world. He began to see that his own senses could limit and even mislead him. But he could get cross-references by imagining the world from other angles. How would it work if he experienced the situation not as human Robert but as, say, the structure system "tree"? How would the problem shape up if he looked at it as though he were a snail, a buttercup, or other human structure systems? He began to real . . . ize a many-centered planet and beheld its strange, deep center everywhere. And he extended his own senses, too, with microscopes and telescopes. A vast cross-referencing system developed.

This entire displacement stage, the "What if . . . ?" stage, exactly paralleled that in which his senses and muscles had identified and shaped a world for him. His mental "senses" now probed this world. He formed relationships and the relationships *were* his reality. For him, all that he noticed was all that there was. Though he used these processes well, they were as automatic as those of his earlier stages. The eye could not see itself. The planetary searcher had done his job perhaps too well, for he had entered into the life of the planet and assumed its characteristics completely. But was he air and water, emotions, sentiment, intersections of force fields? At this stage the questions did not occur. And without the question he could not discover his self, the Eno, and would continue imagining himself to be merely the surface being Robert. As long as he stayed within the psychophysical structure system he had defined, the combined mind-body package, the question *could not* occur to him. He felt he had completed his search. He was mistaken, of course, in fact about as far from the answer as he could get; and if he had stopped there the probe would have failed. But he did not know this. He felt he had finished, and he grew listless and depressed. Without something firing his mind and body, he felt pointless. Was he to sit out his remaining planet years working crossword puzzles and drinking beer? The planet, the lustrous jewel that had so fascinated him, now seemed more and more tarnished and drab. There was nothing to do, nothing to integrate. The fires burned low; the energy construct Eno began to decompose into nothingness. Still he lingered, pointlessly.

Finally, the probe almost burned out, reduced to reruns and insomnia, Eno found himself thrust toward a new genesis and discovered that the end was only a second approximation. Boredom and chance (mere accidents or part of a calculated design?) hurled him into a totally foreign region of the planet. He went on an adventure. Does it matter how it came about, where he went, with whom, or why? Such "accidents" do happen, and for some planetary explorers a new birth occurs. Throbbing through his body-mind came the old question: WHAT WAS GOING ON? His entire being responded. Nerve endings tingled with new data: His mind lurched into gear. In this far region of the globe he walked among beings of his own "human" class who appeared to experience a *different* reality!

Does it matter whether they were aborigines or university professors? They did not see as Eno saw or as the others of his party saw. The beings among whom they now found themselves selected *other* things to notice, and they summed them up strangely. One way for Eno to cope with this peculiar world was to translate it into terms of his old reality and force it to fit into his old construct. That was the common way out of the dilemma. Several of those in his party chose to do that. But as someone has said, translations are like the back side of a tapestry, and Eno preferred the front. If their reality was fixed up to fit his, it was no longer *their* reality. Later he would even have to question *this* preference: Why wasn't everyone sparked by the same drive to penetrate this new construct? Why did some cling to the old pictures?

At the moment, however, something more important occupied his thoughts: Everything he "understood" had been assimilated *outside of his conscious awareness.* That was a shock. He had had his "eyes" open, his "mind" open, but within a closed-off system!— his group's private, isolated world. How did he know that any of it was true? This brush with a *foreign* reality forced the likelihood that his reality was no more accurate than theirs. Wherever the truth might be, it would have to encompass *all* realities. That meant six billion human realities, tree realities, whale realities, rock realities, galaxy realities. Following the method he had used for his first two approximations of reality, he began with himself, with his own picture of reality. He began probing his own self-construct. He had constructed reality twice, through his sensors and symbolically; now he must go over the same ground again. What *was* going on? His picture, his awareness, was based on his sense perceptions, *sentience*, the capacity to sense. But these were specialized devices for filtering out very restricted kinds and amounts of information. Visions of infrared and ultraviolet, fourth and fifth dimensions, base 2 and base 12 in the numbering systems, came now to shake the basis of his world. Now the entire perception network, the senses, and the mind itself must be questioned. He set out without a map along an unknown road.

Down an unknown road, but perhaps *not* without a map. For Eno's investigation of his own sensors, of what had been called sentience, opened the possibility that his search was not so random after all. There now seemed to be some pattern to his behavior coming from deep within. He was not driftwood but a homing device. The gathering of data by the senses was not random but controlled, purposeful, intelligent. The body did not merely collect data as though it were a grain elevator or a museum. He saw that he put things together, that he integrated, organized them into a framework, a system, that information was mere raw material. Even the smallest Fixing And Cross-referencing Trace ("fact") could exist only by interrelating with all other "facts." The framework was already operating in his own mind. That particular framework functioned well in human entities but would not suit a cat or a tree. They experienced their own realities.

It appeared, then, that a deep structure directed his movements toward a physical fulfillment of its potential. Even the narrowest "fact" (2 + 2) was a *general* concept. The slightest bit of information was the result of a bunching process. There had to be within him already a blueprint for quantities before 2 + 2 could trigger his mind toward the general idea of 4. The process seemed to work like a hologram, the three-dimensional laser picture—any part of which could trigger the whole. Tape a laser picture, cut off any part of it, project it, and the whole image would appear. Likewise, the tiny fact of 2 + 2 was impossible to contemplate as an isolate, for it was embedded in a complete interrelated system. When Eno encountered such a "fact," he had to step back far enough and toy with it enough so that the system in which 2 + 2 was possible came into focus—very much the way *he* had come into focus at the beginning of his planet probe. And the numbering system itself was not isolated from the rest of the picture either, for by examining the situation in which 2 + 2 was possible, he could begin to grasp the entire sentient process, the whole process of differentiating and integrating, of noticing differences and of putting things together. Just as a point entered reality through the intersecting of lines, any bit of data gained its existence through the intersecting of concepts. Thus, an accumulation of bits resulted in the concept of 1, and that 1 could only exist as a *part* of a picture of reality, as part of a complete system.

So Eno began to turn his investigation away from the nerve endings inward toward the blueprint. Sensing was evidence that something inside was going on. It seemed that the instant the kaleidoscope turned and he entered into matter, became flesh, the impulse to generate a "human" nature was already there, and with adequate nourishment he would flesh out and fulfill that nature.

Now he began to guess an answer to one of his major questions. He had discovered that his senses were inaccurate and extremely weak. He could not see an atom; his temperature range was very narrow. How could his senses ever yield a true version of reality? When he apprehended (see *prehensile*) that the picture he was looking for was inside him, *already there*, sensing and perceiving took on new meaning. Sensors did not have to be absolutely accurate, for, if they triggered the right "nodes," Eno within himself would make up for any flaws and would activate his "nature" himself internally. He now saw nerve endings as catalysts. He knew that the operation did not take place out there. For this surgeon to know where to operate, crude indicators were sufficient; mere traces would suffice.

When Eno's research took this turn, he found himself in trouble with other "humans." That they were standing on a planet and that they were made up of atoms that were made up of space seemed irrelevant. "I'm sitting here on what I think is a chair, and that's enough. I don't have to go delving into the source of such ideas." To Eno, when one looked at himself so narrowly, he behaved narrowly and *felt* narrow. Because he did not see the world in its larger framework, such a person would always feel isolated and alone, would always be mis...taking his situation. For Eno, though the pain of experience was no less severe, indeed was even more intense, the large frame gave the struggle character. It was not wantonly absurd. As a Cosmos Held In Limited Dimension ("child") he had felt that the world he perceived did not exist for other people and had felt isolated and frustrated. It was only by following through till he could connect his perception to a total world, an inner world, that he could fulfill himself. The limited concept would likely have culminated in disaster, a grain wasting away in barren soil.

To say that he was sitting in a chair was the most incredible leap of faith that anyone could imagine. One was isolated within a limited and faulty sensing system; *every* thing was composed of fictional qualities. One *knew* nothing. Yet one "sat in a chair," a miracle of synthesis. That should have convinced the others. They had leaped to such conclusions countless times. But they seemed blind to their own sleight of hand.

In Eno's investigation there had been paintings, myths, mandalas, figures of speech, the whole structure of language—all pointing to what? He looked out and said, "That's a bush, and that's Eno, and that's God." It appeared that in this fashion he was classifying and organizing the *world*, but that was not the case at all. What he was doing was illuminating his own self. When Eno "became," there was a thrust within him; the pattern was already there. It was like the genetic code, but it was a nonphysical thing. It seemed to be saying to him, "Eno, you're a kind of creature composed of categories and patterns, and what you have to do is fill them in, to realize them." Thus, his fingers might crudely sense and report some shape. That signal, coupled with his mind, would yield "desk." It didn't matter that the signal was crude. All he needed was something to activate what was already there, to bring patterns into focus. For it was an internal world he was illuminating. It was the intuitive leaps his mind took that engaged and excited him; he would use anything he could get, however crude. He was a thrust toward lucidity, and that thrust could be triggered by dreams or... anything. Those leaps were not based on physical phenomena; it was the other way around. One did not have to experience every single particle of the physical world.

But that led to another question. If traces were sufficient, what need was there for sharpening or tuning his senses? He knew the answer: For triggering to occur, experience had to be sharp, intense. Though the catalyst could be rough, it had to penetrate. Even though the senses were not the answer in themselves, he did have to send out sharply in order to receive sharply. It had to be a vigorous thrust. If he was not intensely fooling around, the insights, the leaps of lucidity, would not happen.

And language was part of (or the same as) all the things he had been thinking of. Language (metaphor) could not be less vigorous or less honed than the physical network. Sharpening up metaphors was like sharpening up the senses. (Were not the senses metaphors themselves?)
Sharpening up one's use of language was like finding a way to trigger reality.

Synapsis.

Afterword

Teaching Human Beings
Serve Tea; Read the Leaves

If one is lost in the woods, what is the first thing one does? One stops, doesn't one? One stops and looks around.
—J. Krishnamurti

At the end of spring quarter in May 1988, my teaching assistant Richard Ferreira tried to capture the essence of our classes, what made them tick. He had been a student in three of my classes and a TA in two of them:

> It's funny how we have to think backwards in order to make sense of the present. To give meaning to the world around us, we must recall each moment that relates to the matter at hand. Looking back, I see a common thread in the impact of one single sentence or question posed. That's something I'm just now realizing: How crucial the form of a question is—and timing! It's amazing. *What* one says—and *how*—are critical aspects of communication, but to be effective, they must be taken as a whole. Subject and style. The art of teaching is to do it enough so that one doesn't have to think about it; it's second nature, as my mom would say.
>
> That's what a would-be teacher has to realize. When I look back now, I see teaching is all about making a statement have weight so that students will not take the superficial avenue but will realize these questions and observations are always intended to have broad and deep implications. In our classes we would get tuned up for the multiple possibilities. We got into the habit in our sessions

of playing with aspects. If I say, "Good bye," I mean it in the conventional sense, but I also mean, "God be with you," the original meaning as well as the current one, and other nuances as well. What if I become so centered that my "fare well" has its full poetic weight? Wouldn't that make my day?! And what if I begin to take my whole day that way, wouldn't *that* be something?!

I think that's what these classes are really all about, making the minutes count. They add up, don't they, to a life lived. I adore that idea. A semester of this sort of emphasis is quite literally enriching, fulfilling, exciting, something I never ran into in conventional classes, but something sorely missing. I look back at our classes with open eyes and a warm heart. I don't see how anyone could participate in such an environment without a love and deeper respect for humanity. I've seen the way my mind works; I've felt the way my spirit moves me. As a result, I move more fluently through my own time and space.

I have a couple of definitions for you:

1. **critical thinking**, n.—a process of achieving greater awareness of one's needs in order to fulfill one's potential as an individual.

2. **education**, n.—see **critical thinking** above.

They're the same thing!

There is something else I see that is a continuing aspect of these classes; I think every teacher needs to make it second nature: the art of paying attention. Students could say anything at all in our classes and you wouldn't blink an eye. You paid close attention. You really listened and tried to understand what was being said, and you did this uncritically. That's the key, to listen and see it from the student's point of view, not just the surface features but what they point to, the feeling under them. You were more attentive than my dog! That's what makes these classes work, a teacher paying attention.

So those two things stand out: (1) the habit of making a statement or question have weight, depth, and breadth, and (2) attentiveness.

Richard got it right. Using language poetically and paying attention are indeed the heart of teaching centered on human beings. It is simply a shift of emphasis, but it is a dramatic shift. In McLuhan's terms the medium certainly is the message *and* the massage. A judging, authoritative teacher cannot have responsive classes, classes in which students take charge of their own mental processes. No one can be authoritative and listen at the same time. If there is anything worth the trouble in a classroom give and take, it will emerge through attentive dialogue. If a teacher is attentive, statements and questions or rephrasing of students' assertions will clarify the dialogue, just as Richard Ferreira discovered. It is a way of going about things, a habit any teacher of any subject could make second nature. Form and function, substance and style.

The headline in this morning's *San Francisco Chronicle* is "Novel Plan for Teaching Reading." Oh me, oh my! The novel plan is to weave together the "phonics" method and the "whole-language" method. The plan has "grade-level" requirements: Kindergarten kids must know the alphabet, rhyming, upper- and lower-case; read some words. First graders must identify names, shapes; use conventional and "temporary" spelling. The next year kids have to understand syllables, consonants, and vowels and read independently; no more "temporary" spelling. Third graders have to read fiction and nonfiction and know common spelling patterns and punctuation. We're talking 1996 here, but this could well have been the big news story of 1957, the year I started teaching. After almost forty years, we're still in Plato's cave, gazing at shadows. It reminds me of Kathy's second-grade essay on flowers, in which she writes, "There so very pretty. don't you think so.?" and never gets an answer.

There are thirty different kinds of kids in every kindergarten class, each a unique bundle of wonder available for witnessing. But who's looking? All this money, all this apparatus, and no one saying, "Yes, flowers *are* pretty. I like violets. What are your favorites?" I'd like to write an essay:

Kids at Grade Level

There's Kathy with curly hair and freckles,
absorbed in the serration of one yellow leaf.

And Matthew, bruised and sad from Wednesday
night with Dad, needing a big hug and lots of love.

And here's Michelle, reading the paper upside down—
she doesn't know there's only one right way. I wish
she never had to find out. She's definitely not at grade level.

Mark can do wheelies; Steven can't keep his shoe laces tied.

Susan in her pretty dress, all scrubbed and combed. Mary in a
dress that's too big, all stained and drab. Gangly Bill
in his dude clothes. Scuffed sneakers, polished boots, Mary Janes,
K-mart plastic slippers—worn out, too big, too small.

Thirty vulnerable flowers in this garten. I attend each one.

We will never get to grade level.

A New Plan for Teaching Reading—
Or What Have You

There is a natural way of traversing the planet, and then there are schools. In 2036 there will be another headline about a new plan for teaching reading. It will be a revolutionary approach, combining phonics and the whole-language method. There will be much wringing of hands. No nirvana in sight. Is it possible that an entire school system could ever come to its senses—or come to? What would a math program be like in a human-centered institution?

Of course, there would not *be* a math program. There would be individuals developing—or not developing—mathematical fluency, awareness, sensitivity, yes, even facility, but for sure, "grade level" would be out the window. I have an idea for a New Plan for Teaching Reading (or What Have You). First, you have a retreat for all the reading teachers (that's *all* the teachers in the school, because reading is part of everything that goes on). Begin with everyone taking a musical instrument and playing until he/she becomes one with the music. (Remember, the mind is the ultimate musical instrument; so no one is left out.) The teachers will know they have achieved that state when they forget what time it is. Next, the group assembles on top of a hill and practices being dervishes. Once they have refreshed themselves singing and dancing, everyone will read a blade of grass, a pebble, twigs. These stories may be read right to left, upside down (whatever *that* is), or head between the legs (for perspective). Next come rubbings of their own souls, mandalas. Homework: Learn *by heart*, "In the midst of winter, I finally realized there was in me an invincible summer."* Take the rest of the day off. Ten demerits for each useful, practical, or necessary thing you do. Because we learn by doing, workshop leaders must participate in all activities.

Meanwhile, at the state level, the legislature will take a slow walk and read the corridor from their offices to the Senate chamber—or the grounds outside the capitol building. Koan for homework: *Behead yourself.*†

The afternoon of the fourth day, serve tea. Read the leaves. In the evening of the fifth day, read the stars. During the sixth night, have dreams. Read them to the workshop at breakfast. You get the idea. At some time or other everyone gets down to the basics: reading a human being, not *the* student, but Tony Archdeacon, in the flesh and soul. Let's see: hair color, texture, length,

---

*Albert Camus.
†Rumi.

kempt or un; eyes, number (visible third eye?), shape, size, color; lips, full, thin, sweet (trembling?); ears (open? wax?); chin; cheeks. Write a haiku capturing the essence of Tony. Draw his soul. Tell him how pleased you are to have him in your class. Mean it.

Is there a fire in Ginny's head?* Did you notice that golden aura around Michael?† Attend. Have good attendance.‡

On the seventh day, be quiet.§

Think it'll fly?

Be a Mirror

The heart of any curriculum is the *human* heart. Nothing much will change until everyone involved realizes that: legislators, educators, teachers, parents, and most important of all, the human beings themselves in those classes. I would like to read in the *Chronicle* one of these days the headline "Novel Plan for Teaching." The article would be all about retraining teachers, not about jimmying the curriculum. The stuff of classrooms is not the heart of the problem. Our indifference to the heart of each human is. We have to change the way we think of the people in our classes. They (we) are not commodities. We are not products. Our uniqueness should be more pronounced at the end of a session, not less. Forget accountability; people are not beans to be counted. Forget the bell curve; we cannot be averaged. Success can be measured in the growing number of out-of-work therapists.**

We have to give up expectation. We have to give up intention. It is not our business to have something in mind for Mira Gafuri over by the window. The question is, as the artist puts it, What would Mira Gafuri in relation to me like to become? In the Novel Plan for Teaching we learn to hold up a mirror for Mira so that she can get a look. Some part of Mira is interested in the

---

*Yeats.

†Buddha.

‡William Carlos Williams.

§You Know Who.

**Most Americans are neurotic. Far too many are in bad shape. Well, now, where do they spend most of their waking hours between ages six and eighteen? How about affirming the human spirit for twelve years? I would rather meet on a dark street a mentally healthy adult who never got good at math than a neurotic who did. (Sure, there may be Samaritans who are neurotics, but it's chancy.)

ideas of mathematics—but in her own way and in her own time, not ours. So the new plan is all about what a teacher is and what a teacher does. Better, what a teacher is *not* and what a teacher *must not* do. We will flog that poor dead horse until we absorb as our bedrock awareness Gibran's observation: "Your children are not your children. They are the sons and daughters of life's longing for itself." We have no idea what worlds they will inhabit. We can give them our loving attention but not our thoughts. They must have their own thoughts, not ours. We can't protect them; we have never seen the tigers they will meet.

Schooling has been a meddlesome business far too long. We need to mind our own business. Our business is learning how to interface with each mind in our class, to clear a path so that it can go forth unhindered. We must learn to respect the sanctity of these beings. We have to let them be so that they continue becoming.

Be a Window

In the Novel Plan for Teaching, teachers would learn to become invisible. We would become clear glass through which our students would view their worlds. At some point even that glass must dissolve. We become brilliant teachers when we reduce ourselves to zero.

Learning Theory

As a young boy, physicist Richard Feynman used to spend summers in the Catskills, and on weekends he and his father went walking in the woods and would take a good look at interesting things going on there. The mothers of the other kids thought that was wonderful, so it ended up that the other fathers had to take their children for walks on the weekends, too.

> So the next Monday when the fathers were all back to work, all the kids were playing in the field and one kid said to me, "See that bird; what kind of a bird is that?" And I said, "I haven't the slightest idea what kind of bird it is." He says, "It's a brown-throated thrush," or something. "Your father doesn't tell you anything." But it was just the opposite. My father had taught me, looking at a bird, "Do you know what that bird is? It's a brown-throated thrush. But in Portuguese it's a ___, in Italian, a ___." He says, "In Chinese it's a ___,

in Japanese, a ____." Et cetera. "Now," he says, "You know in all these languages what the name of the bird is and when you're finished with that, you'll know absolutely nothing about the bird. You only know about human beings in different places and what they call the bird." Then he says, "Now let's look at the bird and what it's doing."

—From the PBS interview with Feynman,
"The Pleasure of Finding Things Out"

The subject of teaching is always a specific, particular human being, like that one particular bird, that unique pattern of organic energy, not history, biology, or topology. Carl Jung said that all the million mandalas he had examined, all the clinical experience he had had, were a jumping-off place for his interaction with the client seated before him. No other mandala was this person's. No other configuration matched this unique information-processing organism. "Now let's look at this bird and what it's doing." Now let's look at this accounting student and what he or she is doing. Institutions simply cannot apply a set of rules, however effective in however many instances, to *this* accounting student. This set of circumstances has never existed before. That is why teaching is art and not mere technology.

The phonics method, the look-say method, phonemics, and roomfuls of learning materials will not teach anyone to read. Love might. If you want to sell a car, keep your eye on the ball. The ball is not the car, not your wonderful salesmanship. The ball is the customer. Forget the car; forget you. Fall in love with *this* customer, and you will sell more cars than anyone in your agency. Likewise, accounting is not the ball, your teaching knowledge isn't it. *This* student is. Become fascinated with *this* person and more students will do well in your accounting classes than in any other classes in your college. When we pay attention, we never swim in the same river. Everything is different everyday. Yesterday is a cliché. Today is alive and must be lived here and now. That is how it must be with teaching. Thirty years of moments bring us to a beginning. We have no choice but to plunge in.

This is not a new idea. My brave new plan for teaching, radical as it may sound, is nothing more than learning theory put into practice. Schools of education could make it their credo to teach all their classes as models. Prospective teachers could be their own learning labs and observe their own learning patterns. Student teachers could examine what makes them want to learn, *as they learn*, and notice as well what makes them passive. Participants could compare notes. "How do I actually learn? When am I at my best? What role does my conscious mind play, my nonconscious? Does a helpful teacher really help?" And so on. Every class in a school of education could easily be an example of the best teaching and a hands-on, practical, and immediate laboratory, as well. Why not? Am I missing something? Isn't it strange that teachers have to learn to teach all on their own, usually in isolation? Schools could at least encourage networking.

Most of the things I discovered about teaching were already known, but I never saw anyone take that whole body of knowledge and put it into practice. I never witnessed enlightened teaching; a bit here, a touch there, but never the whole package all at once. It is quite true we all must create own systems or be enslaved, as Blake said, by someone else's. But there is no reason the search cannot begin where I am leaving off. A new teacher could begin by chewing on the best findings and take off from there. As it is, before they can get down to the good stuff, the best and most dedicated must disentangle themselves from a century of hopelessly destructive practices. No wonder so many bright young people throw up their hands; schools are hotbeds of mediocrity.

If anyone really wants schools to be effective, such teacher-training programs would be a surge forward. Certainly, almost anything would be an improvement. By whatever criteria, innovative and experimental classes get better results than conventional ones. So there's not much danger of screwing up too badly. Besides, a bumpy road calls for more attention than a smooth one. Mistakes are great teachers; we always recount the journeys that went awry but rarely think about the ones that went as planned. Teachers need to get into jams.

Doing Nothing

Is there such a thing as teaching? The more I think about "teaching" the more my thoughts are directed to "learning." *Teaching* turns out to be all about *learning*, and the job is to understand how creatures learn. I remember my colleague Richard Rystrom, then a reading specialist with the University of Georgia, saying, "I'm paid for what I know, not for what I do." I puzzled over that for a long time, but applied to teaching it makes good sense. The teachers I admire the most don't do much, but much gets done. The touches that make such a difference are almost invisible. In such classes it may be hard to discover who's in charge.

Each learner, of course, is in charge. Learners are like musicians in an orchestra. All the instruments playing at once could be a mess, but a good conductor facilitates peak performance. Conductors don't play instruments, but they have to know lots and lots about making music, and they have to be good at orchestration. If everything clicks, the orchestra—including the conductor—becomes one instrument. A teacher can do that. The payoff for an artistic teacher is in those moments when a group of individuals becomes one melodic, philharmonic whole. The engaged mind turns schooling into education. The experience itself, as with any artistic endeavor, is the payoff.

Joy, *bliss*, then, is the only thing that can sustain an artist. Of course, being invisible doesn't invite Teacher-of-the-Year awards, because the whole idea is to become so good at setting up a learning environment that participants don't even realize the artistry that produced it. In such an environment learners go about their work the way little kids do, unselfconsciously, without sandbox guidance, yet with such confidence and assurance that the teacher fades into the setting, like a chair or a window. Autonomous students are hard on teachers' egos, of course, but there's no helping it. Art is not a career. Intrinsic rewards nourish artists, not tenure or accolades. Nor does gratification lie in virtuosity. Over time a cement worker or painter or violinist may develop remarkable technique and control, but those serve only as an entrée. Skill, erudition, information, experience, and knowledge may bring us to the threshold, but we still have to get in there and sculpt or paint or dance. Yesterday's achievement is a cliché. The performance cannot be mechanical; otherwise a technician could conduct the orchestra—or the class.

Koans for New and Renewing Teachers

In the 1970s, Sister Corita was a champ at breathing life into dead metaphors. It isn't the topic or subject that makes an educational experience but how classes go about their business. It is not all that far-fetched to treat classrooms as learning labs. The Zen koan is a good metaphor for the process. Novices learn but are not taught, proceed at their own pace, are rewarded only by the flash of insight, digest koan I before going on to koan II, and are free to penetrate the koan any old way at all. That is such a fine idea for students, maybe it will do for teachers, too.

Aerobics for the Mind / Mind Openers
(Recommended for Faculty Meetings and Legislative Sessions)

1. A poem must not mean but be. (Archibald Macleish)
2. An intense vision of the facts. (W. C. Williams)
3. Because a fire was in my head. (W. B. Yeats)

4. Silver apples golden apples. (Yeats)
5. The early lilacs became part of this child. (Walt Whitman)
6. Did you say *dance?!* Come on, my boy! (Zorba)
7. Unheard melodies are sweeter. (John Keats)
8. You have taught me your language. (Caliban)
9. To see or to perish. (Teilhard de Chardin)
10. there so very pretty. don't you think so.? (Kathy, age 7)

It Ain't in No Book

What a shame. The chapters of this book have led to the place where it began. How to teach ain't in no book. Ideas in print—for that matter, any ideas—are dead as dodos. Through our tinkering we mingle with matter and re-create the universe; it's our job. That's what reading, writing, listening, speaking, thinking, painting, and roller-blading are all about. It's the fundamental metaphor of this book. So this book is a koan, as are all things. The idea of teaching is to let human beings in on this big secret: turning chance encounters into koans. That's also the secret of happiness: *What would these moments in relation to me like to become?* Our worlds are illuminated and warmed by the koans we create. We do not get answers, but we weave magic circles around illusive miracles waving Hi! in $E = mc^2$, in Dryden or Truffaut, in *The Magic Flute*, in six-foot rabbits, and in dust mites. It ain't in no book, Satchmo, but what a wonderful world.

Suggested Reading

Barks, Coleman, and John Moyne, editors and translators. *Open Secret, Versions of Rumi*. Threshold Books, 1984.

Campbell, Joseph. *Myths to Live By*. Viking Press, 1972.

Campbell, Joseph, with Bill Moyers. *Joseph Campbell and the Power of Myth*. Doubleday, 1988.

Camus, Albert. *The Myth of Sisyphus and Other Essays*. Knopf, 1955.

Cassirer, Ernst. *Language and Myth*. Harper and Brothers, 1946.

Dewey, John. *How We Think*. Regnery, 1933.

Edwards, Betty. *Drawing on the Right Side of the Brain*. St. Martin's Press, 1979.

Feynman, Richard P. *"Surely You're Joking, Mr. Feynman!"* Norton, 1985.

Hoff, Benjamin. *The Tao of Pooh*. Dutton, 1982.

Hamilton, Edith. *Mythology*. Little, Brown, 1942.

Houts, Paul L. *The Myth of Measurability*. Hart, 1977.

Jung, Carl G. *Man and His Symbols*. Doubleday, 1964.

Jung, Carl G. *Memories, Dreams, Reflections*. Random House, 1961.

Koestler, Arthur. *The Act of Creation*. Dell, 1964.

Langer, Susanne Kathlenna Knauth. *Philosophy in a New Key*. Harvard University Press, 1957.

Lathem, Edward Connery, editor. *The Poetry of Robert Frost*. Henry Holt, 1969.

Marckwardt, Albert H., and Fred Walcott. *Facts About Current English Usage*. National Council of Teachers of English, 1938.

Miller, Henry. *Nothing but the Marvelous*. Capra Press, 1991.

Richards, I. A. *How to Read a Page*. Norton, 1942.

Rogers, Carl. *On Becoming a Person*. Houghton Mifflin, 1961.

Skinner, B. F. *Beyond Freedom and Dignity*. Knopf, 1971.

Williams, William Carlos. *Selected Poems*. New Directions Books, 1917–1949.

Index

"A Generative Unit," 106–109
"A Minor Bird," 85
affect, 30, 136
Agassiz, Louis, 66
alchemists, 288
alpha rhythms and learning, 92–94
American College, The, 3
American College Entrance Test (ACET), 219
Anderson, Maggie, 151
Armstrong, Louis, 94, 97
"Ars Poetica," 42, 147
art, teaching as, 13, 15, 20, 75, 89, 96, 112, 113, 121, 305, 311
art gallery, the, 12, 140, 155–157, 256, 273
arts, the, 9, 79, 138
Ashton-Warner, Sylvia, 52
attention, 121–125
"Auspex," 215
authentic, being, 30–32
author of ones life, 34

Barzun, Jacques, 219
Bashō, 281
beam of attention, the, 34, 93–94, 122, 139, 150, 273
Beatles, The, 97
"Before Names," 57
Belafonte, Harry, 86, 94–95
bell-shaped curve, the, 3, 217
Best American Short Stories, The, 12, 142–143
Binet, Alfred, 219

bliss, 13, 171, 313
"Brain, The," 126–127
Brain imagery, 202
Brautigan, Richard, 192
Break the Mirror, 68
breaths, counting, 91, 92
Brueghel, Pieter, 22, 49, 123, 151, 152, 272, 278–280

Carreras, José, 159
Carroll, Lewis, 149
Castaneda, Carlos, 52, 225
Chardin, Teilhard de, 34, 121, 177, 314
Cheever, John, 123, 141, 158, 198
Chesterton, G. K., 41, 202
Chief Crazy Horse, 8, 99
Children's Games, 122, 151
Chomsky, Noam, 58
Churchill, Winston, 261
Clark, Guy, 94, 96
class size, 234, 242, 261–264
classes,
    combined, 261, 267–269
    individualized, 214
    large, 265
"Classtrophobia," 207
Cline, Patsy, 159
competition, 101, 199–202
Conroy, Pat, 52, 54
correcting papers, 163, 165, 183, 207, 253, 264
correctness and precision, 43, 173, 180, 245, 246, 247, 249, 251
Crane, Frank, 205

create (source of the word), 32
"Creation, Creatures, and Creativity," 29–32, 34, 126, 220
creativity and language, 28
cumulative files, 212

Dancing Wu Li Masters, The, 1
deep grammar, 58
Demuth, Charles, 12, 200
Dewey, John, 9, 125, 166, 230
Dickenson, Emily, 39
did-you-notice game, 121–125, 140, 272, 279
discipline, 2, 4, 16, 87, 125, 206, 233, 234, 264
Donovan, 97
drawing, 39, 40, 66, 82, 138, 139, 151–158, 166, 199, 201, 219, 277
Dryden, John, 211
Durrell, Lawrence, 15

eccentric, 33, 255–259
Eddington, A. S., 276, 279
editing, 101, 159, 166, 167–170, 180, 192, 241
education, the purpose of, 4–13
Educational Testing Service, 216–218
Eisley, Loren, 190
Elgin, Suzette, 196
Eliot, T. S., 117–118
emotion,
    intelligent, 95
    role in learning, 19
    in the thinking process, 12, 19, 37, 77, 94, 95, 97, 112, 125–126, 136, 172, 237, 300
Emotional Intelligence, 95
English,
    the discipline of, 39–55
    school, 249–251
    the structure of, 251–252
English class, what really goes on in an, 43
"English for Everyone," 44–51

English Journal, 44, 105, 196
expert, influence in the classroom, 103, 119, 123
"Expert Judgment," 213–216
expertise, 103, 119, 123, 143–144, 157
    giving up, 103

Facts About Current English Usage, The, 250
Farber, Jerry, 64
Feynman, Richard, 12, 39, 65, 228, 276, 310, 311
500-word theme, the, 47, 106, 173, 197
"Flower on a Crannied Wall," 141
force, 19, 54, 93, 103, 124, 130, 131, 191, 197, 205, 208
Ford, Henry, 135
Forms of Intellectual and Ethical Development in the College Years, 220
Fowles, John, 163, 272
frames of reference, 29
French Lieutenant's Woman, The, 163
Frost, Robert, 3, 63, 71, 85, 107, 124, 144, 158, 159, 184, 215, 282

Gestalt Therapy Verbatim, 271
Go-Between, The, 62
Goethe, Johann Wolfgang von, 121, 271, 274
Goleman, Daniel, 95
grades, assigning, 90, 165, 171, 200, 223, 224, 230–231, 236
grading papers, 206, 223, 228, 240
grammar,
    deep, 58
    teaching, 243–254
"Guard Duty," 201

haiku, 48, 139, 272, 274, 280, 286, 287, 309
handicapped, the, 256
Hands of Maria, 96–98, 273
Harlequin romances, 159
Harris, Phil, 137

Heisenberg, Werner, 159, 222–224
Heisenberg effect, the, 159, 222–224
"Helen Bids Farewell to Her Daughter Hermione," 278
Herndon, James, 52, 54
Hockenberry, John, 256
Hoffman, Banesh, 219, 220, 221
hologram, 158, 302
holography, 126, 295
honing, 156, 173–175
Hopkins, Gerard Manley, 64
Houts, Paul, 219
"How Flowers Changed the World," 190
How to Read a Page, 141
"How to Write Swell," 196–197
Huang, Al, 1, 6, 20
Hughes, Robert, 138
humanistic classrooms, 20
hunches, 127, 200, 203

"I Am Not I," 111
I Saw the Figure 5 in Gold, 200
icon, 27, 29, 69, 71, 127, 150, 172
instruction, 65, 97, 135, 161, 178, 184, 222, 228, 263
instructor (meaning of), 4, 265
intelligence quotient (IQ), 93, 130, 214, 216, 219–221
intention, teaching without, 105, 133, 165, 208, 273, 309
International Reading Association, 131, 132
Island of the Colorblind, The, 256

Jonson, Ben 75, 76, 272
"Journey of the Magi," 117, 119
joy, 3, 13, 24, 25, 38, 41, 54, 84, 86, 126, 131, 142, 143, 172, 214, 276, 313
judgment, expert, 122, 145, 179, 180, 213–216, 230, 231, 306
Jung, Carl, 150, 153, 154, 155, 311

Keats, John, 44, 72, 90, 195, 314
Keillor, Garrison, 180

Kellehear, Allan, 223
Keller, Helen, 40–41
Kellogg, Rhoda, 150
koan, 84, 87, 102, 146, 252, 308, 313, 314
"Kool-Aid Wino, The," 192
Kunsthistorisches Museum, 123

language-centered education, 59
learning,
    effortless, 7, 24, 80, 225, 272, 275, 287
    natural, 124
LeCarre, John, 125
Leffland, Ella, 215
literary criticism, 141, 142–143, 157
"Lucy in the Sky with Diamonds," 97
Lueders, Edward, 73, 74

MacLean, Don, 97
MacLeish, Archibald, 42, 147
Magus, The, 163
mandalas, 149–160
mandalas, verbal, 157–158
Martinez, Maria 96, 275
Marvell, Andrew, 75
McLuhan, Marshall, 158, 234, 252, 306
meaning, 34, 42, 62, 68, 69, 70, 72, 114, 127, 129, 135, 194, 200, 202, 244, 252, 253, 273, 289, 305, 306
"Measures, Unobtrusive," 221–222
messing around, 18, 59, 64, 83, 94, 154, 247, 289, 292
metaphor, 27, 28, 33, 35, 36, 38, 41, 42, 59, 60, 62, 63, 82, 83, 85, 94, 98, 100, 115, 126, 127, 129, 139, 143, 150, 157, 179, 182, 183, 184, 187, 188, 189, 192, 194, 253, 272, 274, 278, 279, 280, 281, 282, 285, 288, 289, 304, 313, 314
    in the thinking process, 94
"Metaphor, Both Nose and Heart," 70–74
mind as a connecting organ, 22, 81
Mind Parasites, The, 93

"Minding Our Own Business," 41–43
"Minor Bird, A," 85
Mitchell, Joni, 94
"Momma, Look a Boo Boo," 86, 95, 96
monosigns, 81
Montage, 162, 190, 191, 192
"Morning Has Broken," 97, 98
motivation, 4, 16, 17, 18, 19, 20, 38, 90, 125
Moving Violations, 256
Mozart, Wolfgang Amadeus, 93, 277
Mr. Rogers, 91, 275
multitasking, 126
music,
    centrality in human life, 89–90
    natural, 98
    using in all classes, 90–92
mutual aid, 101, 199–204, 229
"My Hearing Handicap," 257–258
mystery beyond language, 40
Myth of Measurability, The, 219

Nader, Ralph, 220
"Name, The," 113
National Reading Conference, 132
Nature of Nature, The, 163
Newmark, Leonard, 223
None of the Above, 220

Objets d'art, 264
Objets trouvés, 264
Oedipus Rex, 31
"On My First Daughter," 75, 272, 274
one-room schoolhouses, 211, 255
Onitsura, 70, 272
open-door policy, 211
Ostrander, Sheila, 90
Our Totem Is the Raven, 10
Our Town, 121
Owen, David, 220

Pastan, Linda, 278
pastime, 31
Patton, 6, 264
paying attention, 91, 121–125, 306
Perls, Fritz, 271
Perry, William G., 220
Piglet, 7
plurisigns, 81
poetic mode in the process of learning, 271–278
"*Poiēma: The Poem of Creation*," 37–38
Pooh, 1, 7
Pope, Alexander, 142
Postman, Neil, 62–63
Practical Criticism, 144
Prado, Adélia, 57
prejudge, the tendency to, 145, 286
Primary Colors, 140
process *versus* curriculum, 31
Proust, Marcel, 41
Psycholinguistics and Reading, 134
Pythagoras, 83

reading, 129–147
    and the arts, 138–139
    a description of the process, 126–129
    developmental, 131
    and literature, 137–138
    as problem solving, 136
    programs, 130–134
    and self-esteem, 136–137
    speed, 130, 133
    as therapy, 135–137
    tests, 133–134
reason, 126
relaxation exercises, 92–94
remedial, 64, 130, 131, 135, 146, 212
ReQuest questioning procedure, 136
research, 3, 23, 38, 49, 59, 67, 108, 111, 130, 132, 133, 135, 150, 161, 164, 170, 171, 203, 223, 269, 293
research papers, 38, 195
"Reveille," 35–36
reward and punishment in composition, 165

Richards, I. A., 141, 144, 185
Rogers, Carl, 144
Rogers, Fred, 91, 275
Rogers, Will, 231
Rumi, Jelaluddin, 113, 276, 285, 308
Rumors of Peace, 215

Sacks, Oliver, 25, 256, 259
saints and poets, 33, 121, 278
Sakaki, Nanao, 67
Sanford, Nevitt, 3
SAT, CLEP, ACT, 215
schools, laboratory, 261, 269
Science Research Associates, 130
Schroder, Lynn, 90
Scudder, Samuel, 65
second language, English as a, 248, 251
self-love in the learning process, 21
self-image, 153
self-interest, enlightened, 204
sensorium, the, 16, 35, 72, 158, 274, 296, 299
Shakespeare, William, 46, 49, 64, 89, 219, 295
Shaw, George Bernard, 15
slow walk, 28, 85, 140, 271, 272, 274, 275, 286, 308
Smith, Frank, 134
"Someone's Singing," 97
spirit,
    and flesh, connecting, 74
    in matter, 36, 159
    in the printed word, 139–141
    role in learning, 23
Stern, Isaac, 3
Stevens, Cat, 97
Stewart, Jesse, 52
structure in educational processes, 99–109
student-centered (meaning of), 3–13
study, units of, 105, 242
Superlearning, 90
supralogical thinking, 27–38

syntheses, 194–195
Szell, George, 264

Tailor of Panama, The, 126
teacher's pets, 3, 237–239
teaching,
    the art of, 20
    centered, 5
    the meaning of, 1–13
    minimalist, 182, 197, 225–232
    a personal philosophy of, 5
    poetically, 33
teaching assistants, selecting, 235
"Teaching into the Future," 62
"Teaching Johnny to Walk," 64
"Ten Easy Ways to Make Learning to Write Difficult," 196–197
Tennyson, Alfred, 141
Terkel, Studs, 137
Terman, Lewis, 219
test day, 120
tests,
    entrance, 211
    placement, 131, 213
    standardized, 214, 218–221
thinking,
    hemispheric roles in, 27–28, 63, 149
    iconic, 127
    supralogical, 27–38
    symbolic, 28
Thinking About Thinking, 137
"This Is Just to Say," 283
Thomas, Michael Tilson, 8
Thoreau, Henry David, 36, 47, 99, 158, 177, 249, 274
"To Draw Pictures," 150
To Teach, To Love, 52
tone in the process of learning, 111–127
tracking, 212, 256
Tranströmer, Tomas, 201
Truffaut, François, 197
Tsvetaeva, Marina, 146
"Turning Poetry into Prose," 211–224

Twain, Mark, 8, 50, 54, 83, 140, 230
Tyranny of Testing, The, 219
T'ai Chi, 1

ulteriority, 177, 285
University of Tomorrowland, 64
"Unknown Feathers," 143
Unobtrusive Researcher: Guide to Methods, 223
Updike, John, 96, 143, 123
"Use of Force, The," 205

Velveteen Rabbit, The, 15, 17
viewpoints, 214
"Vincent," 97

Wasteland, The, 129
Water Is Wide, The, 52
Watts, Alan, 7
Way It Spozed to Be, The, 52
Weinphal, Paul, 35
Whitman, Walt, 64, 122, 125, 243, 245, 271, 314
"Why Do You Write Poems?" 68
Williams, Margery, 15, 17
Williams, William Carlos, 33, 81, 129, 133, 205, 276, 283, 309
Wilson, Colin, 93, 276
witnessing, 206
Word Power Made Easy, 131
Word, the, 59–60
Working, 137
writing,
    pleasure as the motivator in, 170–171
    reflective (in freshman English), 178–180
    teaching, 161–175
Wu li, 6

Yeats, William Butler, 7, 27, 143, 309, 313, 314
"YOUR POEM, MAN . . . ," 73–74

Zen Diary, 35
Zorba the Greek, 95–96
Zukov, Gary, 1, 6, 20